Teacher Education in Transition

Collaborative Programs to Prepare General and Special Educators

Edited by

Linda P. Blanton, James Madison University
Cynthia C. Griffin, University of Florida
Judith A. Winn, University of Wisconsin, Milwaukee
Marleen C. Pugach, University of Wisconsin, Milwaukee

LOVE PUBLISHING COMPANY®
Denver • London • Sydney

Published by Love Publishing Company
Denver, Colorado 80222

Library of Congress Catalog Card Number 96-78051

Copyright © 1997 Love Publishing Company
Printed in the U.S.A.
ISBN 0-89108-250-6

Contents

Foreword

David G. Imig, Chief Executive Officer
American Association of Colleges for Teacher Education

Teacher Education in Transition: Collaborative Programs to Prepare General and Special Educators is an important contribution to the efforts to better understand ways to transform Education Schools, and, with that transformation, to change practices in K–12 schools. It is a book about educational change. It recognizes fundamental reforms underway in American education and, building upon constructivist thinking and the appeal for integrated curriculums, suggests that the way we separately prepare general and special education teachers must end. The authors of this rich collection of case studies appeal for new integrated teacher education programs that draw upon the best models of both general and special teacher education.

That this is a timely text goes without saying. The debates occurring as part of the reauthorization of the Individuals with Disabilities Education Act (IDEA) in the 104th Congress attest to the urgency of considering new ways of educating all children. Efforts to waive existing special education rules and to constrain the costs of special education are part of a much wider debate about inclusion and "mainstreaming" and providing all children with free, appropriate education. This is part of a much larger debate to rethink the dual system of K–12 schooling that has emerged since the passage of PL 94–142 (Education for All Handicapped Children Act). These are challenges that go to the very core of special education and merit careful consideration by both general and special educators.

The book is also timely because it occurs while there is a fundamental rethinking of the nature of schooling in America. The opening chapter, by Winn and Blanton, offers a description of the separate system of schooling that presently exists in most American communities—one for youngsters with special needs and the other for "regular" children. Their contention is that just as youngsters in these schools are often divided and separated, categorized and isolated, as a result, so are teachers. Indeed, they suggest that two, often distinct, teaching professions have emerged and that this is potentially destructive to the interests of communities, parents, and children. It also thwarts efforts to transform schools and to assign whole school faculties greater instructional and curricular responsibilities. The Winn and Blanton chapter offers a comprehensive look at the current situation in the parallel preparation of special and general education teachers. It provides a clear and reasoned overview of the conditions that currently exist and the imperatives that necessitate change. For those seeking to understand why this dualism must end, this is important reading.

The editors of this important volume see the source of the problem as the historical separation of special and general teacher education. Their argument is that this separation has arisen because of essentially unconnected teacher preparation programs that engage simultaneously in preparing teachers for both general and special assignments in schools. They cite Goodlad and Field's point that, "this separation contributes to the separateness of general and special education in this nation's schools. Clearly, there is ample room for closer collaboration and a greater degree of integration."[1] They suggest that dual systems of preparation have emerged on most campuses over the past 25 years with few efforts to break down the barriers between the two systems. They insist that "collaboration in teacher education is absolutely necessary" and call upon faculty to join together to promote collaboration and to "reinvent" teacher preparation to end these conditions.

The editors suggest that only in this way can Education Schools contribute in significant ways to K–12 school reform. Such "reinvention" should lead to reconsideration of the characteristics and competencies of teachers needed in the public schools and the kind of teacher education needed to prepare these teachers. That is what this text is about. It documents the efforts of 10 Education Schools that have embarked upon a journey of "reinvention." The cases are about the efforts on a number of campuses to "unify," "merge," "integrate," and "fuse" the preparation of general and special education teachers. They are cases about "collaborative teacher education" which document the struggles of faculty to build scholarly bridges between special and general teacher education.

The ten cases build on the necessity of preparing beginning teachers who are capable of working across these divisions. The goal of many of the programs has been to prepare beginning teachers who are capable of working on interdisciplinary instructional teams, serving on curriculum committees which span grades, and teaching diverse youngsters with learning difficulties in both general and special settings. It anticipates schools in which instructional systems and school services have been integrated. It seeks to prepare general education teachers in ways to overcome the pervasive resistance to including children with special needs in their classrooms while, at the same time, educating special education teachers in ways that enable them to serve in multiple roles and to be more adaptable and flexible in their roles and assignments.

While the ostensible purpose of the book is about the process of collaboration between often discordant faculties over the preparation of teachers, the book is also about changing Education Schools. In the concluding chapter, Griffin and Pugach identify ten presuppositions, or conditions, or postulates for change and draw upon the case studies to illustrate their importance. While there is a significant body of literature on school change there is relatively little that has

[1] Goodlad, J. I., & Field, S. (1993). Teachers for Renewing Schools. In J. I. Goodlad & T. C. Lovitt (Eds.), *Integrating General and Special Education* (p. 243). New York: Macmillan.

been written on change as it occurs in Education Schools. The ten case studies are about the struggle of faculties and Education School leaders to simultaneously prepare teachers for both general and special education assignments of K–12 schools. These case studies, and the Griffin and Pugach chapter in particular, remedy the dearth of descriptive analyses about Education School change. The care with which these ten postulates are developed, along with the examples that are offered, make them important for deans and directors and faculty to consider as they attempt to fashion changes within their Education Schools.

These cases demonstrate that the move to create a more collaborative or unified model of teacher preparation is being realized. Designed to forge collaboration and integration within teacher preparation, these programs should contribute to the end of the division and separation of general and special education students and teachers in our schools. These are cases in which discourse and communication among colleagues has led to fundamental reforms in teacher education. They are cases in which a healthy consideration of externally imposed licensure standards has promoted change. There are cases in which faculties have joined to examine the overlap in the knowledge and skill of general and special educators and fashioned collaborative programs based on consensus and agreement. There are cases in which partnerships of Education Schools and K–12 schools enable all teacher candidates the opportunity to experience real school problems and to work across grade levels, teaching disciplines, and other barriers that too often divide and separate teacher in too many of our schools.

The book raises the following fundamental questions that all faculties of education should consider as they contemplate the need for change:

- What is common among all of the separate programs that prepare general educators, special educators, school administrators, school counselors, school psychologists, and other faculty? What is different? What common conceptions of teaching and learning are held by faculty in these separate programs? What is the knowledge base that undergirds these common conceptions?
- Given a commitment to educate all children based on a clear understanding of culture, class, and language, and how they intersect with a disability, what are the most appropriate ways to prepare prospective teachers? How does the Education School faculty convey this common belief across all preparation programs? How do faculty work together to achieve this end?
- What types and kinds of faculty professional development are needed to promote the transformation of Education Schools? How can the theme of "collaborative teacher education" be promoted through professional development?
- How will we know when we have succeeded? What forms of documentation should be used? How will we go about that documentation as we seek a common vision for school personnel preparation? How will we share our results?

These are questions to be considered by every Education School faculty. They should lead to a fundamental recommitment to strengthen the preparation of all teachers. This should lead to collaborative teacher education.

Preface

More than ever before, teacher education is being challenged to prepare graduates who will skillfully and eagerly teach *all* the students who enter the classroom. In trying to achieve this goal, faculty members who prepare early childhood, elementary, and secondary teachers and those who prepare special education teachers are engaging in unprecedented dialogue about the real and the ideal relationships between their respective programs of teacher preparation. In a growing number of institutions of higher education, this dialogue has led to the development of more integrated, collaborative programs of teacher education built upon a common framework for what teachers should know and be able to do. Ten of these programs are represented in this book.

This project grew from work begun by a group of individuals in the Teacher Education Division (TED) of the Council for Exceptional Children. In April 1990, at a meeting of its Executive Board in Toronto, the TED Forum was initiated. Its purpose was to explore and identify issues in teacher education and examine how they relate specifically to the preparation of special education teachers. As the Forum matured over time, its aim was more clearly articulated as follows.

> The purpose of the TED Forum is to stimulate discussion and promote continued knowledge growth regarding the most contemporary issues and problems in teacher education and their relationship to the study and practice of the preparation of special education teachers. The Forum is designed to foster TED's leadership role in addressing teacher education in special education by providing a healthy tension between issues that arise naturally from TED's ongoing professional activities and those upon which Forum activities focus.

To advance the Forum's agenda and ensure that it became an integral activity within the teacher education branch of the Council for Exceptional Children, the TED Executive Board established a Forum Task Force, chaired first by Marleen Pugach and then by Linda Blanton. This task force was charged with using multiple structures within TED to promote the Forum's scholarly and educative function. To this end, special Forum sessions have been featured at each annual conference of the Teacher Education Division. As part of this effort, highly respected scholars in teacher education have presented their work and supported the Forum's goal of building scholarly bridges between special and general teacher preparation. The division's journal, *Teacher Education and Special Education*, published a widely cited topical issue on how research on teaching and teacher education might inform the preparation of special education teachers. Now, through this book, the TED Forum seeks to advance the dialogue even further by bringing together program descriptions from colleges and universities where special and general teacher educators have successfully integrated, either entirely or partially, their teacher preparation programs.

We could have highlighted more programs. We selected these 10 because we wanted to portray a range of institutions, from the small liberal arts college to major research institutions. We also wished to represent institutions from various regions of the country. In addition, we sought out authors who were active TED members and whose work at their home institutions represented a substantial commitment toward integrating teacher education.

In Chapter 1, Judy Winn and Linda Blanton explore the need for collaboration in teacher preparation and the larger national context in which these efforts are occurring. These authors explore specific factors that require general and special education teacher educators to work more closely in designing and implementing programs. In addition, they consider factors that influence how working together might be accomplished.

In Chapters 2–11, practicing teacher educators describe their own work in integrating general and special education. In each case the chapters are authored by faculty from general and special education. In some cases special educators took the lead role in writing the chapter; in others general educators took the lead role. Although the teacher educators represented in these chapters draw on different experiences and traditions of practice, all are committed to enabling prospective teachers to work with a diverse school population. In all cases the authors discuss their local context, the teacher education research that informs their practice, their reconfigured curriculum, the human aspects of their work, and the institutionalization of the integrated program.

In the last chapter, Cynthia Griffin and Marleen Pugach examine what happens when teacher educators collaborate across general and special education. Looking across the 10 programs, they pose several postulates that represent the common experiences of teacher educators in these efforts. Then they identify several critical issues that will have to be addressed if the promise of collaborative teacher education is to be achieved.

Although, happily, the reform of teacher education continues to flourish, written accounts of how the reform actually comes about on a program-by-program basis are still rare. We are grateful that the Teacher Education Division enthusiastically endorsed this project as a means of documenting the difficult conceptual and practical work that goes into program reform. Specifically, we are indebted to three of TED's former presidents—James McLeskey, Larry Johnson, and Kathlene Shank—for their support from the initial conception of the book through its publication and to Stan Love for agreeing to publish this volume to support the goals of the TED Forum. James McLeskey also reviewed the full manuscript and provided valuable advice as we completed our work. Cathymae Nelson at the University of Wisconsin-Milwaukee deserves special recognition for her incomparable expertise in preparing the manuscript and for her keen eye and editorial sensibilities. Above all, the authors of the 10 contributed chapters are acknowledged for telling their stories, for telling them well, and for meeting editorial deadlines to enable us to keep our original timeframe for publication—almost unheard of! Their stories are worth hearing.

Meet the Editors

Linda P. Blanton, Director, School of Education, James Madison University

Cynthia C. Griffin, Department of Special Education, University of Florida

Marleen C. Pugach, Department of Curriculum and Instruction, University of Wisconsin, Milwaukee

Judith A. Winn, Department of Exceptional Eduation, University of Wisconsin, Milwaukee

Meet the Contributors

Syracuse University

George Hext-Contreras, Teaching and Curriculum

Gerald M. Mager, Coordinator of Doctoral Programs in Educational Leadership and Teaching and Curriculum

Luanna H. Meyer, Inclusive Elementary and Special Education Program; Programs in Teaching and Leadership

Marie Sarno, Teaching and Leadership Programs

Gwen Yarger-Kane, Director, Professional Development School; Professor, Teaching and Leadership

University of Connecticut

Pamela Campbell, Special Education, Department of Educational Psychology

Charles W. Case, Dean, Department of Educational Leadership

Kay A. Norlander, Special Education, Department of Educational Psychology

Timothy G. Reagan, Bilingual Education, Department of Curiculum and Instruction

James D. Strauch, Special Education, Department of Educational Psychology

Providence College

Jane Callahan, Education Department

Thomas Flaherty, Dean, Graduate School

Junean Krajewski, Education Department

Lynne Ryan, Chairperson, Education Department

University of Florida

Vivian I. Correa, Chair, Special Education

Lynn C. Hartle, Instruction and Curriculum

Hazel A. Jones, Special Education

Kristen M. Kemple, Instruction and Curriculum

Mary Jane K. Rapport, Special Education

Tina Smith-Bonahue, Foundations of Education

University of Alabama

Alexander Casareno, Elementary Education

Edwin Ellis, Multiple Abilities Program

Sr. Madeleine Gregg, fcJ, Elementary Education

Phyllis Mayfield, Special Education

Barbara Rountree, Elementary Education

Carol Schlichter, Chair of Gifted and Talented Education

University of Cincinnati

Anne M. Bauer, Head, Division of Teacher Education

Jerald F. Etienne, Division of Teacher Education: Special Education

Ann E. Fordon, Gabbard Research Assistant, Division of Education Studies

Martha Hendricks-Lee, Research Associate, Cincinnati Initiative for Teacher Education (CITE)

Lawrence J. Johnson, Associate Dean, Research and Development; Director, Arlitt Child and Family Research and Education Center

Regina H. Sapona, Division of Teacher Education: Special Education

Nelson C. Vincent, Research Associate, Office of Research and Development

California State University, San Marcos

Toni Hood, Distinguished Teacher in Residence

A. Sandra Parsons, Coordinator of Concurrent Credential Program

Lillian Vega-Castaneda, Coordinator of Bilingual Cross Cultural Program

University of Wisconsin, Milwaukee

Alison Ford, Department of Exceptional Education

Ann Higgins Hains, Department of Exceptional Education

Chris Burton Maxwell, Department of Curriculum and Instruction

Marleen C. Pugach, Department of Curriculum and Instruction

Mary Jett Simpson, Department of Curriculum and Instruction

Linda Tiezzi, Department of Curriculum and Instruction

Utah State University

Benjamin Lignugaris/Kraft, Department of Special Education and Rehabilitation

Jay A. Monson, Head, Department of Elementary Education

Charles L. Salzberg, Head, Department of Special Education and Rehabilitation

Saginaw Valley State University

Stephen P. Barbus, Teacher Education

Ellen Curtis-Pierce, Dean, College of Education

Susie Emond, Teacher Education

Kimberly Prime, Teacher, Bangor Central Elementary School; Adjunct Instructor, SVSU

Miriam Sweigart, former Principal, Bangor Central Elementary School

The Call for Collaboration in Teacher Education

Judith Winn and Linda Blanton

Neither general nor special education alone has either the capacity or the vision to challenge and change the deep-rooted assumptions that separate and track children and youths according to presumptions about ability, achievement, and eventual social contribution. Meaningful change will require nothing less than a joint effort to reinvent schools to be more accommodating to all dimensions of human diversity. (Ferguson, 1995, p. 285)

As the number of students who are struggling in schools grows, the need for general and special education to come together to create the vision and capacity to educate all students becomes more and more pronounced. Collaboration by teachers is called for in the schools; likewise, it is called for in teacher education. General and special education teachers' traditional isolation from each other can be, and has been, a barrier to working collaboratively to reconceptualize schooling for all learners. This isolation can be seen as beginning with and perpetuated by parallel, noncollaborative teacher education programs. Collaboration between general and special education in teacher education programs—the dialogues, the examination of what should be taught, the rethinking of practicum experiences for teachers, the sharing of knowledge and expertise, the faculty modeling—all have high potential to support teachers' ability to work together for meaningful change.

In this chapter, we first explore the call for collaboration in schools—challenges to practices traditionally associated with separate general and special education, and the major current response to these difficulties—inclusive schools and classrooms. Second, we explore the larger educational context in which these collaborations are situated. In the discussion of the context of collaboration in the schools and in higher education alike, we consider the role of reform, changes in standards and accountability, and expanded views of teaching and learning. Finally, we consider the challenges teacher educators face as they work together to develop and implement collaborative teacher education programs.

The Call for Collaboration in Schools

Teacher education programs must prepare teachers for their roles in schools while at the same time working with schools to understand and define these roles to best facilitate the success of diverse learners. In so doing, teacher education needs to be responsive to the challenges that teachers face in the increasingly complex context of schools as well as the ways in which these challenges are beginning to be addressed. At all grade levels, the range of student performance is widening. Teachers are challenged to provide appropriate instruction for students who are working at many different levels and who are often from many different cultural and linguistic backgrounds. Additionally, teachers are challenged by the large numbers of students who are failing and dropping out of schools before graduation. This challenge is exacerbated by the pressure from the community for instruction that results in higher standardized test scores.

Coupled with the complexities of a changing student population is the increasing numbers of students being labeled for special education (U.S. Department of Education, 1995). Overrepresentation of students of color in special education (Artiles & Trent, 1993; Grossman, 1995; Heller, Holtzman, & Messick, 1982; Pugach, 1995) is still another contributing factor to this complex school context.[1] Overrepresentation raises issues about the lack of attention given to developing appropriate learning experiences for a wide range of students within general education. Likewise, misclassification of students, a particular problem in urban schools (Gottlieb, Alter, Gottlieb, & Wishner, 1993), can result in students being unnecessarily stigmatized and perpetuates blaming students, rather than searching for, and supporting, instructional changes within general education programs.

Educators are called upon to question why more students are not experiencing success in general education classrooms and to work together to make changes in these classrooms so that they will. Both special and general educators are part of the school context and, thereby, contribute to how successful or unsuccessful school practices will be. Both special and general educators contribute to the current problems of misclassification and overrepresentation of students of color in special education, as both participate in the referral and assessment processes. Similarly, both special and general educators must address the challenges that these problems have begun to create. Many of these challenges are germane to collaboration and, very simply, general and special education teachers need to work together. To do this, all teachers need common frameworks for viewing and accommodating differences and this is where teacher preparation must play a central role.

Teachers need common frameworks for addressing the needs of students who are struggling—students who often are pulled out of the general education classroom for instruction in resource rooms. Concerns have been raised about pull-out programs, even for students who are labeled correctly as having special education needs. The concerns center on lack of connectedness with classroom instruction, emphasis on low-level skills, lack of focused instruction, and stigmatization of students (Allington & McGill-Franzen, 1989; Haynes & Jenkins, 1986; McGill-Franzen & Allington, 1991). Within a reliance on pull-out programs, students who most need continuity are those whose programs are highly fragmented. For example, students who are pulled out may be receiving instruction in the classroom based on one conception of reading, and instruction in the resource room based on a competing conception. Instruction in special education settings too often lacks attention to students' developing strategic approaches to their work, an area of particular concern for students who are experiencing difficulties (Paris & Oka, 1986).

These concerns about the character and quality of instruction also have been raised about instruction in general education, particularly the instruction provided for students who are low achievers. Classroom observation studies have shown that practices such as time spent in actual reading, the predominance of teacher questions rather than student discussion, and the lack of attention to instruction for strategic learning are issues in both fields (Blanton & Blanton, 1994; Goodlad, 1990; McGill-Franzen & Allington, 1991). Overall, there is concern that curriculum and instruction for students who are struggling, in both special and general education classes, are focused too heavily on basic skills and too little on providing opportunities for reasoning and critical thinking.

General education has begun to implement changes in curriculum and instruction that make classrooms more accommodating for students who historically have been unable to succeed. Approaches based in social constructivist theory such as whole language, instruction for strategic learning, and cooperative learning emphasize the development of learners who are self-directed, able to identify problems and approach them in goal-directed ways, and profit from collaborating with others. Some special educators have shown interest in, and success with, these approaches with students labeled as having special needs (e.g., Englert, Raphael, Anderson, Anthony, & Stevens, 1991; Lyons & Beaver, 1995; Palincsar & Klenk, 1992; Slavin, 1996; Stires, 1991). Students with identified special needs, as well as other students who are struggling, have been found to benefit, as seen in their achievement and interest in learning (e.g., Allington & Wamsley, 1995). Overall, many of the changes in curriculum and instruction, and the manner in which they are carried out (e.g., student choice, explicitness about how to learn, small-group work, assessment based in the curriculum), allow for success for a wider range of students than do practices associated with more traditional general education curriculum and instruction.

Students who are struggling may need more explicit and guided instruction than other students; however, this kind of adaptation can be linked directly to accommodating general education curriculum and instruction rather than being separate from them. Even within this context, however, some students with special learning needs require more intensive instruction (Pugach, 1995). These students may be those with low-incidence disabilities, and those with more prevalent disabilities. Increasingly, new intensive instructional approaches are being developed and implemented with success (e.g. Clay, 1993; Hiebert, 1994; Taylor, Strait, & Medo, 1994).

Similar to classroom-wide approaches such as cooperative learning, intensive approaches are found to be effective with students who are labeled as having special needs or who are being considered for referral, in some cases eliminating the need for special services (e.g., Hiebert, 1994; Lyons & Beaver, 1995; see review by Slavin, 1996). If intensive instruction is considered "not as a last resort, but as a naturally occurring component of a healthy classroom community" (Pugach & Seidl, 1996), more students can truly be a part of such communities rather than fragmented from their peers. Conceptualizing intensive instruction as a part of classroom communities, linking it to more general instruction, and implementing classroom-wide curriculum and instruction that is more accommodating to a wide range of students requires special and general education teachers to develop a common framework from which to view curriculum and instruction in the first place—a framework that must be set in teacher education programs.

Problems with current practices, and the successful efforts to address the problems, indicate that improving students' school experiences occur best through partnerships between special and general education at all levels, including teacher education. These partnerships are needed particularly as we work to improve school experiences of students through inclusion of students with special needs in general education classrooms and schools.

Inclusion

Inclusion of students with special needs in general education classes and schools is becoming more prevalent (e.g., *Educational Leadership*, Nov/Dec, 1994). In more and more schools, the entire school faculty is accepting responsibility for all students. Although there is disagreement about the proper extent of inclusion (e.g., see Fuchs & Fuchs, 1994; Roberts & Mather, 1995; Stainback, Stainback, & Ayres, 1996), especially regarding issues such as retention of a continuum of placement settings, greater numbers of students with special needs are in fact being served in general education classrooms (U.S. Department of Education, 1995).

Inclusion demands many changes in schools. One of these involves changes in teachers' roles. Although teachers' roles in inclusive schools and classrooms are still evolving (Gable, McLaughlin, Sindelar, & Kilgore, 1993) and will vary in terms of specific settings and student populations, job descriptions for special and general education teachers already look very different from those of 20 or even 10 years ago. For example, teachers are more often co-planning and co-teaching, working together to directly instruct students with and without disabilities, and assessing their learning in multiple ways. Working in inclusive classrooms does not necessarily mean all teachers will have the same roles; teams are enriched by members having different strengths and duties (Ford, personal communication, November 20, 1995). It does mean, however, that links must be closer than in the past, links that are forged in a common understanding of students, of teaching and learning, and of the work of all team members.

Along with changing roles, inclusive classrooms and schools require changes in curriculum and instruction. As has been noted (e.g., Keogh, 1988), "business as usual" in general education classes is not likely to benefit students with disabilities. Advocates of inclusion have been adamant that success demands changes in, rather than adaptation of, traditional curriculum and instruction (Ferguson, 1995; Pugach & Warger, 1996; National Association of State Boards of Education, Study Group of Special Education, 1992). Best practices have been defined as:

— being grounded in an understanding of child development, subject matter knowledge, and developmentally appropriate approaches
— fostering students' pursuing and demonstrating knowledge in a variety of ways and at a variety of levels
— attending to and building on the social nature of learning
— providing opportunities for more intensive instruction for students who need it—students both with and without disabilities (Pugach & Seidl, 1995; Zemelman, Daniels, & Hyde, 1993).

One of the major challenges regarding inclusion is the need for general and special education to work together to develop curriculum and instruction based on the characteristics of best practices and which, by their nature, are more accommodating to the needs of diverse learners, including those with special needs, than programs traditionally associated with either general and with special education.

While general education traditionally has focused on curriculum development and implementation with limited attention to instruction based on individual differences, special education, especially for students with mild disabilities, has focused on instructional adaptations without a rich understanding of curriculum (Pugach & Warger, 1995). To develop and implement curriculum and instruction based on best practices, along with appropriate instructional adaptations—adaptations that some students will still need—all teachers need grounding in curriculum and instruction for individual differences, as well as an understanding of the interconnectedness between the two. With this understanding, teachers will be able to develop supports for students who need them, rooted in, and clearly related to—rather than fragmented from—the classroom curriculum.

Critical to taking on new roles and jointly developing and implementing curriculum for inclusive schools and classrooms is the development of shared beliefs about students, teaching, and learning by general and special educators. Beliefs influence the goals of schooling, views of the teaching and learning process, curriculum and instructional choices, and ways in which teachers work together (e.g., Kagan, 1992). Effective collaboration that supports equitable opportunities for all students cannot occur if teachers have different beliefs about children and learning and about teachers' responsibilities in relation to students in both general and special education. Inclusion is supported when both general and special education teachers share the same perspective, when they view students from a diversity rather than a deficit perspective, hold high expectations for all students rather than lowered ones for some, and commit to shared rather than divided responsibility for students—all of which challenge assumptions associated with inequitable opportunities for some students. These shared beliefs form the foundation for schools in which "all teachers would be expected to teach children and to assist each other in meeting the individual students' needs" (Lilly, 1989, p. 147).

In the end, the movement toward inclusive schools and classrooms is really a response to concerns that have been raised by special and general educators alike about the value and effectiveness of practices associated with separate special education and traditional remedial programs, as well as a response to concerns about the ways in which students who are struggling are viewed. Increasingly, general and special education teachers are working collaboratively—assuming new roles, sharing and developing expertise in providing curriculum and instruction that offers equitable opportunities for a wide range of learners, and in doing so, challenging long-held assumptions. Concurrently, long-held assumptions underlying separate teacher education programs are being challenged, and faculty in both general and special education are being called on to assume new roles and share and develop new curriculum and instruction to support and facilitate what is occurring in schools.

Like collaboration in the schools, collaboration in teacher education is expanding. Twenty years ago, when Public Law 94–142 (The Education for All Handicapped Children Act) was implemented, the integration of general and special education garnered only marginal interest. In teacher education, the Dean's Grants projects were the one activity that addressed collaboration at the teacher education level. These projects achieved little success in integrating programs and, instead, attended mostly to appending special education content to existing general teacher education curricula (Pugach, 1992). In the 15 years since these projects ended, however, the context has changed as a result of reform movements, standards, and new views of teaching and learning. These changes have set the stage for a different kind of collaboration in the schools and in teacher education.

The Context for Collaboration in Teacher Education

The context is ripe for collaboration in teacher education. We first consider school reform movements that have brought forth new visions for schools, leading to changing roles for teachers and subsequent reform in teacher education. Second, we examine the setting of standards for curriculum and assessment systems. Third, we review the ways in which teaching and learning have expanded and changed the course of research and practice in both arenas.

School Reform and Teacher Education Reform

General education school reform has been characterized by a series of phases, often referred to as waves (Rowan, 1990). These waves in school improvement over the last two decades have been based on the most current knowledge and research about teaching. During this time the research literature has changed from a dominant view of teaching as routine and mechanistic, requiring reforms that control and monitor, to views of teaching as nonroutine and complex and requiring teacher judgment and expertise (Rowan, 1990). This latter view led to reforms that heightened teachers' involvement in decision making and placed more emphasis on decentralized school structures. Currently, in what some refer to as a third wave of reform, the "restructuring" movement calls for changing the fundamental core of schooling (Prestine & Bowen, 1993).

At the heart of this restructuring movement lie themes and innovations such as (a) local autonomy, discretion, control, (b) collaborative communities, (c) site-based management, and (d) teaming (Newmann, 1993). According to Newmann, however, these innovations may not be sufficient to improve education. Consequently, he calls for an agenda that seeks a higher level of commitment and competence from teachers and school administrators. For teachers, as an example, "the most important new forms of commitment and competence" (p. 6) are clustered in the following themes: (a) depth of understanding and authentic learning, (b) success for all students, (c) new roles for teachers, and (d) schools as caring communities. Similarly, other writers speak strongly to the need to look beyond what might be called "superficial reforms" (e.g., simply engaging in the act of moving from tracking to heterogeneous grouping) and address basic tenets, principles, and contexts that underlie reform and actually may lead to real school improvement (e.g., Goodman, 1995; Tyack & Tobin, 1994).

Clearly, the restructuring discourse highlights key elements needing consideration in the transformation of schools. Many of these same key elements have been the focus of reports and dialogue on teacher education improvement (Sikula, 1990). Calls for changes in teacher education programs have been stimulated by a growing knowledge base about learning, teaching, and teacher education. In addition, the authority of accrediting and licensing bodies, and of state legislatures and state boards of education, has been a force to which teacher education has responded. The resulting changes in teacher education programs have included:

— incorporating the new knowledge of teaching and learning in curricula for preservice teachers
— providing opportunities for preservice teachers to work in diverse settings
— working in partnerships with schools to establish professional development schools (Darling-Hammond & Cobb, 1996).

In *Tomorrow's Schools of Education,* the most recent report of the Holmes Group (1995), the authors place professional development schools at the very center of teacher education reform. According to this group, only through these partnerships will reform take place simultaneously in teacher education and in the nation's schools. Other reform models also support the importance of professional development schools in teacher education reform (Darling-Hammond & Cobb, 1996).

In the 1980s, when much of the major reform effort was under way in general education, special education was experiencing its own reform movement. Because special education had evolved into a separate, parallel system in schools, reform in special education also evolved as a separate activity, with issues and concerns that differed from those in general education reform (Miller, 1990; Sailor, 1991). In recent years, however, the emphasis of general education reform on how to better serve a diverse, changing school population has brought the concerns of the two groups closer together. In the words of Sailor (1991), "This shift in emphasis in general education reform presents a window of opportunity for the emergence of a shared educational agenda" (p. 8).

Standard Setting and Accountability

Following on the heels of school and teacher education reform reports in the 1980s (e.g., *A Nation at Risk*, The National Commission on Excellence in Education, 1983) came a greater emphasis on standards and accountability. As summarized by Shriner, Ysseldyke, and Thurlow (1994), standards come in several forms and can be grouped in three frequently used categories: (a) content standards, (b) performance standards, and (c) delivery standards.

Content Standards

Content standards establish a core of knowledge within a discipline (e.g., math) that is incorporated in and set up as the standard for curricula and programs. These standards, developed by experts and professional groups in specialty fields, then serve as the basis for state, and potentially national, curricula. In reference to identified students with disabilities in schools, the instructional needs of these students are more commonly being linked to a system's curriculum goals or outcomes (McLaughlin, 1995). This link places more emphasis on what students with disabilities are being taught and, by inference, increases the need for collaboration between special and general education teachers.

In teacher education, content standards most often are referred to as the body of knowledge and skills (knowledge base) expected of those who plan to practice in the teaching profession. Although many colleges and schools of education have a history of articulating their knowledge bases, the stakes became greater when the national accreditation body, the National Council for Accreditation of Teacher Education (NCATE), redesigned its standards to require a written document (Wise, 1994). In addition, NCATE has specified some elements of a knowledge base that are expected to be present in all teacher preparation programs seeking its accreditation. One requirement is that novice teachers will acquire knowledge and skills to enable them to work with diverse populations (including exceptionality). This expectation set the stage and, especially, the need for collaboration between general and special educators.

Performance Standards

Performance standards, as defined by Shriner et al. (1994), refer to the performance expected of students as a result of the application of content standards. One prime example of performance standards is statewide public school student assessment. A few states have begun to include students with disabilities in these outcome-based assessment systems (McLaughlin, 1995), which, again, suggests the need for general and special education collaboration. In teacher education, changes are occurring in teacher assessments in which the aim is to go beyond the traditional format of multiple-choice questions and include essay components, portfolios, and classroom observations. An example of such a change is the Educational Testing Service's new testing series for teachers, the Praxis (Darling-Hammond & Cobb, 1996).

Delivery Standards

Delivery standards are standards that assure that the conditions are set for teaching and learning to occur. Two examples are state licensure for teachers and advanced certification for accomplished teachers. State licensure, which is often orchestrated by local and state politicians, is influenced currently by a consortium created by the Council of Chief State School Officers. This consortium of 28 states, the Interstate New Teacher Assessment and Support Consortium (INTASC), is working together with teachers and teacher educators to make licensing standards a reality. These licensing standards were developed from, and are compatible with, those of the National Board for Professional Teaching Standards, a group that has taken the lead in developing advanced certification for highly accomplished teachers (Darling-Hammond & Cobb, 1996).

Both of these—licensing and advanced certification—are mechanisms for assuring quality control in the profession. The changes and trends in each of them also influence teacher preparation. As one example, the standards developed by INTASC were incorporated recently by NCATE as one way of strengthening the expectation that teacher education programs rely on a defined knowledge base and specific student outcomes (Darling-Hammond & Cobb, 1996; Wise, 1994). These new NCATE accreditation standards require teacher education students to actually demonstrate specific skills such as "adapt instruction for culturally diverse and exceptional populations" (Wise, 1994, p. 9).

Another example of the influence of licensing and advanced certification bodies on teacher education is that these groups are drawing on the most current research on teaching and learning and are using this research to drive changes in both areas. For example, these groups have adopted the conception of "teachers as thinkers" (Darling-Hammond & Cobb, 1996). Certainly, standard setting, through accreditation, licensure, and advanced certification, is a potent force in the changes currently under way in teacher education. These major forms of quality control have established a context that strongly supports the need for general and special teacher educators to communicate about implementation of these standards.

Expanded Views of Teaching and Learning

Teaching and learning research has expanded greatly and, in some cases, taken significant turns in the last two decades. Cognitive psychology took the lead and influenced a large and growing body of research providing strong support for constructivist conceptions of learning (Prawat & Floden, 1994; Shuell, 1986), which in turn drives many of the recent curricular and instructional changes in general education. Inquiry has shifted from a research tradition strongly influenced by behaviorism (e.g., process-product research) to research that focuses on the complexities of teaching (e.g., classroom ecology) (Shulman, 1986). Much of this recent inquiry in teaching and learning relies heavily on qualitative research methodology, with lines of inquiry directed toward classroom contexts and teacher thinking (Barnes, 1989; Erickson, 1986; Shulman, 1986). Interestingly, these more recent forms of inquiry, used in both teaching and learning research, have been a significant departure from traditional thinking and re-search in special education.

Research and practice in special education have been dominated by behaviorist orientations, leading to mechanistic and procedural learner applications such as diagnostic-prescriptive teaching and token economies (Colarusso, 1987). In like manner, the findings of process-product teaching research have remained dominant in special education literature (Blanton, 1992). Although we see evidence in this literature of the influence of more recent conceptions of teaching and learning, these changing paradigms seem to be slow to take hold in special education. General teacher preparation programs throughout the country have begun to consider and incorporate the newer lines of research on teaching and learning into the delivery of their curricula (e.g., Feiman-Nemser & Featherstone, 1992; Tabachnick & Zeichner, 1991). Similar changes may not be occurring as frequently in special education. Many programs are still dominated by a competency-based approach to teacher education (Blanton, 1992; Sindelar, Pugach, Griffin, & Seidl, 1995). Competency-based teacher education has remained a mainstay of special education teacher education long after the approach peaked in the 1970s and long after it took a back seat to other movements in teacher education (Carter & Anders, 1996). The emphasis on teachers' thinking and decision making in general education teacher education presents a significant challenge for many in special education teacher education. If special education is to engage in any type of collaborative activity with general teacher educators, the two fields will have to communicate about and understand the different conceptions each area holds about teaching and learning. Further, both fields must communicate about the influence of these conceptions on teacher education.

Collaboration in Higher Education

The growth of inclusive schools and classrooms has the potential to increase the opportunities for success for a wider range of students within general education classrooms, to increase the opportunities for all students to engage in authentic and meaningful work, and to decrease unnecessary referrals to special education. General and special education teachers alike need to be prepared to work together to meet the needs of diverse learners, especially those who are struggling. To do this, teachers need to share beliefs about students, teaching and learning; to have a rich knowledge base about curriculum and instruction; and to know how to collaborate. To support teachers who can facilitate students' success in inclusive schools and classrooms, collaboration between general and special education in teacher preparation is necessary. This collaboration involves faculties in higher education sharing expertise, modeling collaboration and at the same time deepening their understanding of it and openly discussing beliefs and values. Collaboration in higher education, though it is becoming more prevalent, often faces barriers within the university and college culture.

Barriers to Collaboration in Teacher Education

The culture in universities and colleges may work against the very activity (i.e., collaboration) needed most to deliver quality programs to students with disabilities and other students whose needs are not being met. Settings develop a culture that dictates thinking and actions of those in it, and colleges and schools of education reveal artifacts of a culture that are similar from one university or college to another. We often see the same names for departments and programs, the same governance structures, and many of the same activities performed by faculty (teaching, research, and service) across institutions. These similarities are an outgrowth of the structures put into place in institutions of higher education (IHE). Like other organizations, IHEs develop structures to accomplish the work of the organization (Heller, 1996). In considering these structures (e.g., departments), a number of factors emerge as barriers to integration of teacher education programs in general and special education.

Earlier we noted the basic differences between general and special teacher educators in their perspectives about teaching and learning. If we consider this in relation to the departmentalized structure of most colleges and schools of education, we can see how this segregated structure supports the professional isolation and identities of different groups. In these separate departments, the faculty works in small program groups to develop and deliver curricula for its students. In most cases, decision making about program development and other issues relating to the preparation of students is not terribly difficult because the faculty speaks a common language based on similar backgrounds and experiences of faculty members. Only occasionally do many of these individuals venture beyond these boundaries for program development purposes. When they do, they might meet more conflict because the philosophical orientations of faculty from various disciplines may differ and create communication barriers. In addition, as Lilly (1989) pointed out, professional inertia can play a role and is often manifested in common clichés such as "we've always done it this way" (p. 154).

Reward structures for faculty on university campuses usually are not set up to provide incentives for the kind of program development required for collaboration. In many institutions, particularly in research institutions, research may weigh far greater than the teaching and service areas for tenure and promotion (Goodlad, 1990). Even in institutions where teaching is the primary focus, rewards seem based primarily on one's individual accomplishments. Added to the emphasis on individual accomplishments is the control that faculty members have over their professional lives. Faculty in IHEs often exercise a great deal of control over schedule, course content, and grading (Heller, 1996). With this control, the faculty is in a position to refuse to follow an agenda set forth by colleagues, a department head, or a dean.

The leadership in Colleges and Schools of Education (e.g., deans, department heads) may attempt to initiate change in the organization only to face opposition from faculty. As noted, the faculty exercises a great deal of control in IHEs, in which faculty governance is often the rule. In contrast, individuals in leadership roles may not always understand and support the need for faculty collaboration in developing alternative curricula for preservice teachers. This is an important consideration if we heed the research on effective schools, which shows how important leadership is to achieving instructional goals (Lezotte, 1989).

The issue of resource allocation also can be a barrier to the integration of general and special education teacher education programs. Resources (e.g., faculty positions) usually are based on how many student credit hours a program or a department generates. Recruitment of students and accompanying resources allocated to programs often are divided along department lines. This sort of division leads naturally to competition for students and resources. In addition, people in the bureaucratic structures on many campuses are reluctant to respond to different models for allocating resources.

Despite these barriers, collaboration in teacher education *is* taking place, challenging norms and practices created by the structures and cultures of IHEs. As efforts such as those described in this book become known, we can learn about changes that are needed to support the time, commitment, and risks that collaboration in higher education entails. This knowledge, in turn, can challenge the barriers to collaboration.

Learning to Collaborate

One of the greatest benefits of collaboration in teacher education is that it can provide much needed professional development by teacher education faculty. Alone, faculty in separate departments rarely have the breadth of knowledge about curriculum and instruction on the one hand, and about individual differences on the other, needed to prepare teachers for inclusive classrooms. In addition, faculty members are likely to have limited experience with collaboration themselves, and thus limited understanding of the challenges involved. Finally, their existence within separate programs may perpetuate a lack of examination of their own assumptions and beliefs. Collaboration in teacher education, by its nature, challenges faculty members to address and enrich their own grounding. Articulation and examination of beliefs and assumptions—both those of individual faculty and those that will anchor programs—is required.

Faculty members are also challenged to assume new roles and responsibilities—joint planning of programs and courses, team teaching, sharing responsibility for a wider group of students—that in many ways parallel the roles of teachers in K–12 schools. Through collaboration, faculty members can model and at the same time come to understand the realities, benefits, and challenges of the kinds of collaboration for which they are preparing teachers. Working together at the teacher education level also can help faculty members expand their own knowledge about curriculum and individual differences and, in turn, understand and model how those with differing levels of knowledge in these areas can collaborate.

The need for collaboration in teacher education between special and general education clearly is driven by what is—and is not—occurring in the schools. The challenge to rethink practices often associated with separate teacher education programs, and to work together in inclusive settings where diversity is valued and accommodated, requires that teachers' knowledge base be expanded and, most important, that they come to share beliefs that ground their work. If we are to make changes in teacher education, we must ask ourselves if we are prepared to go beyond one perspective to guide teaching and learning, a history of traditional teacher preparation, and a history of unchanging departmental and college structures. As the chapters that follow illustrate, this can happen and is happening in programs nationwide.

Rethinking traditional practices will continue as we increase our collaboration. As new teacher education programs develop, second generation issues inevitably will surface, and the expanding knowledge about collaborative teacher education programs will uncover yet other factors that will affect future collaborations. We will continue to learn from each other, as well as from our partners in schools, as we take on the critical task of developing teacher education programs that prepare teachers to provide equitable learning experiences for today's and tomorrow's diverse learners.

References

Allington, R. L., & McGill-Franzen, A. (1989). Different programs, indifferent instruction. In A. Gartner & D. Lipsky (Eds.), *Beyond separate education: Quality education for all* (pp. 75–98). Baltimore: Paul Brookes.

Allington, R. L., & Wamsley, S. A. (Eds.). (1995). *No quick fix.* New York: Teachers College Press.

Artiles, A. J., & Trent, S. C. (1993). Overrepresentation of minorities in special education: A continuing debate. *Journal of Special Education, 27,* 410–537.

Barnes, H. (1989). Structuring knowledge for beginning teaching. In M. C. Reynolds (Ed.), *Knowledge base for the beginning teacher* (pp. 13–22). New York: Pergamon Press.

Blanton, L. P. (1992). Preservice education: Essential knowledge for the effective special education teacher. *Teacher Education and Special Education, 15,* 87–96.

Blanton. L. P., & Blanton, W. E. (1994). Providing reading instruction to mildly disabled students: Research into practice. In K. D. Wood & B. Algozzine (Eds.), *Teaching reading to high-risk learners* (pp. 9–48). Needham Heights, MA: Allyn & Bacon.

Carter, K., & Anders, D. (1996). Program pedagogy. In F. B. Murray (Ed.), *The teacher educator's handbook: Building a knowledge base for the preparation of teachers* (pp. 557–592). San Francisco: Jossey-Bass Publishers.

Clay, M. M. (1993). *Reading recovery: A guidebook for teachers in training.* Portsmouth, NH: Heinemann.

Colarusso, R. P. (1987). Diagnostic-prescriptive teaching. In M. C. Wang, M. C. Reynolds, & H. J. Walberg (Eds.), *Handbook of special education research and practice: Vol. 1. Learner characteristics and adaptive education* (pp. 155–166). New York: Pergamon Press.

Darling-Hammond, L., & Cobb, V. L. (1996). The changing context of teacher education. In F. B. Murray (Ed.), *The teacher educator's handbook: Building a knowledge base for the preparation of teachers* (pp. 14–62). San Francisco: Jossey-Bass Publishers.

Educational Leadership, Nov./Dec. 1994.

Englert, C. S., Raphael, T. E., Anderson, H. M., Anthony, H., & Stevens, D. D. (1991). Making strategies and self-talk visible: Writing instruction in regular and special education classrooms. *American Educational Research Journal, 28,* 337–372.

Erickson, F. (1986). Qualitative methods in research on teaching. In M. C. Wittrock (Ed.), *Handbook of research on teaching* (pp. 119–161). New York: Macmillan.

Feiman-Nemser, S., & Featherstone, H. (Eds.) (1992). *Exploring teaching: Reinventing an introductory course.* New York: Teachers College Press.

Ferguson, D. L. (1995). The real challenge of inclusion: Confessions of a "Rabid inclusionist." *Phi Delta Kappan, 77,* 281–287.

Fuchs, D., & Fuchs, L. (1994). Inclusive schools movement and the radicalization of special education reform. *Exceptional Children, 60,* 294–309.

Gable, R. A., McLaughlin, V. L., & Sindelar, P., & Kilgore, K. (1993). Unifying general and special education: Some cautions along the road to educational reform. *Preventing School Failure, 37*(2), 5–10.

Goodlad, J. I. (1990). *Teachers for our nation's schools.* San Francisco: Jossey-Bass Publishers.

Goodman, J. (1995, April). Change without difference: School restructuring in historical perspective. *Harvard Educational Review, 65*(1), 1–29.

Gottlieb, J., Alter, M., Gottlieb, B. W., & Wishner, J. (1993). Special education in urban America: It's not justifiable for many. *Journal of Special Education, 27,* 453–465.

Grossman, H. (1995). *Special education in a diverse society.* Boston: Allyn & Bacon.

Haynes, M. C., & Jenkins, J. R. (1986) Reading instruction in special education resource rooms. *American Educational Research Journal, 23,* 161–190.

Heller, H. W. (1996). A rationale for departmentalization of special education. In W. Stainback & S. Stainback (Eds.), *Controversial issues confronting special education: Divergent perspectives* (2d ed., pp. 253–263). Boston: Allyn & Bacon.

Heller, K. A., Holtzman, W. H., & Messick S. (Eds.). (1982). *Placing children in special education: A strategy for equity.* Washington, DC: National Academy Press.

Hiebert, E. H. (1994). A small group literacy intervention with Chapter 1 students. In E. H. Hiebert. & B. M. Taylor (Eds.), *Getting reading right from the start: Effective early literacy interventions* (pp. 85–106). Boston: Allyn & Bacon.

Holmes Group. *Tomorrow's schools of education: A report of the Holmes Group.* (1995). East Lansing, MI: Holmes Group.

Kagan, D. M. (1992). Implications of research on teacher beliefs. *Educational Psychologist, 27*(1), 65–90.

Keogh, B. (1988). Extending services for problem learners: Rethinking and restructuring. *Journal of Learning Disabilities, 21,* 19–22.

Lezotte, L. W. (1989). School improvement based on the effective schools research. In D. K. Lipsky & A. Gartner (Eds.), *Beyond separate education: Quality education for all* (pp. 25–37). Baltimore: Paul H. Brookes Publishing.

Lilly, M. S. (1989). Teacher preparation. In D. K. Lipsky & A. Gartner (Eds.), *Beyond separate education: Quality education for all* (pp. 143–157). Baltimore: Paul H. Brookes Publishing.

Lyons, C. A., & Beaver, J. (1995). Reducing retention and learning disability placement through Reading Recovery: An educationally sound, cost-effective choice. In R. A. Allington & S. A. Wamsley (Eds.), *No quick fix: Rethinking literacy in America's elementary schools* (pp. 116–136). New York: Teachers College Press.

McGill-Franzen, A., & Allington, R. L. (1991). The gridlock of low reading achievement: Perspectives on practice and policy. *Remedial and Special Education, 12*(3), 20–30.

McLaughlin, M. J. (1995). Defining special education: A response to Zigmond and Baker. *Journal of Special Education, 29,* 200–208.

Miller, L. (1990). The regular education initiative and school reform: Lessons from the mainstream. *Remedial and Special Education, 11*(3), 17–22, 28.

National Association of State Boards of Education Study Group on Special Education (1992). *Winners all.* Alexandria, VA: NASBE.

National Commission on Excellence in Education. (1983). *A nation at risk.* Washington, DC: National Commission on Excellence in Education.

Newmann, F. M. (1993). Beyond common sense in educational restructuring: The issues of content and linkage. *Educational Researcher, 22*(2), 4–13, 22.

Palincsar, A. S., & Klenk, L. (1992). Fostering literacy learning in supportive contexts. *Journal of Learning Disabilities, 25,* 211–225.

Paris, S., & Oka, E. (1986). Self-regulated learning among exceptional children. *Exceptional Children, 53,* 103–108.

Prawat, R. S., & Floden, R. E. (1994). Philosophical perspectives on constructivist views of learning. *Educational Psychology, 29*(1), 37–48.

Prestine, N. A., & Bowen, C. (1993). Benchmarks of change: Assessing essential school restructuring efforts. *Educational evaluation and policy analysis, 15,* 298–319.

Pugach, M. C. (1992). Unifying the preservice preparation of teachers. In W. Stainback & S. Stainback (Eds.), *Controversial issues confronting special education: Divergent perspectives* (pp. 255–269). Boston: Allyn and Bacon.

Pugach, M. C. (1995). Twice victims: The struggle to educate children in urban schools and the reform of special education and Chapter 1. In M. C. Wang & M. C. Reynolds (Eds.), *Making a difference for students at risk: Trends and alternatives* (pp. 27–60). Thousand Oaks, CA: Corwin Press.

Pugach, M., & Seidl, B. (1995). From exclusion to inclusion in urban schools: A new case for teacher education reform. *Education and Urban Society, 27,* 379–395.

Pugach, M., & Seidl, B. (1996). Deconstructing the diversity-disability connection. *Contemporary Education, 68*(1).

Pugach, M. C., & Warger, C. L. (1995). Curriculum considerations. In J. I. Goodland & T. C. Lovitt (Eds.), *Integrating general and special education* (pp. 125–148). New York: Macmillan.

Pugach, M. C., & Warger, C. L. (1996). *Curriculum trends, special education, and reform: Refocusing the conversation.* New York: Teachers College Press.

Roberts, R., & Mather, N. (1995). The return of students with learning disabilities to regular classrooms: A sellout? *Learning Disabilities Research and Practice, 10*(1), 46–58.

Rowan, B. (1990). Commitment and control: Alternative strategies for the organizational design of schools. In C. B. Cazden (Ed.), *Review of research in education* (pp. 353–389). Washington, DC: American Educational Research Association.

Sailor, W. (1991). Special education in the restructured school. *Remedial and Special Education, 12*(6), 8–22.

Shriner, J. G., Ysseldyke, J. E., & Thurlow, M. L. (1994). Standards for all American students. *Focus on Exceptional Children, 26*(5), 1–19.

Shuell, T. J. (1986). Cognitive conceptions of learning. *Review of Educational Research, 56,* 411–436.

Shulman, L. S. (1986). Paradigms and research programs in the study of teaching: A contemporary perspective. In M. C. Wittrock (Ed.), *Handbook of research on teaching* (pp. 3–36). New York: Macmillan.

Sikula, J. (1990). National commission reports of the 1980s. In W. R. Houston (Ed.), *Handbook of Research on Teacher Education* (pp. 72–82). New York: Macmillan Publishing.

Sindelar, P. T., Pugach, M. C., Griffin, C. C., & Seidl, B. L. (1995). Reforming teacher education: Challenging the philosophy and practices of educating regular and special educators. In J. L. Paul, H. Rosselli, & D. Evans (Eds.), *Integrating school restructuring and special education reform* (pp. 140–166). New York: Harcourt Brace.

Slavin, R. (1996). Neverstreaming: Preventing learning disabilities. *Educational Leadership, 53*(5), 4–7.

Stainback, S., Stainback, W., & Ayres, B. (1996). Schools as inclusive communities. In W. Stainback & S. Stainback (Eds.), *Controversial issues confronting special education: Divergent perspectives* (pp. 31–43). Boston: Allyn & Bacon.

Stires, S. S. (Ed.). (1991). *With promise.* Portsmouth, NH: Heinemann.

Tabachnick, B. R., & Zeichner, K. M. (Eds.). (1991). *Issues and practices in inquiry-oriented teacher education.* New York: Falmer Press.

Taylor, B. M., Strait, J., & Medo, M. A. (1994). Early intervention in reading: Supplemental instruction for groups of low-achieving students provided by first-grade teachers. In E. H. Hiebert & B. M. Taylor (Eds.), *Getting reading ready right from the start: Effective early literacy interventions* (pp. 107–121). Needham Heights, MA: Allyn & Bacon.

Tyack, D., & Tobin, W. (1994). The "grammar" of schooling: Why has it been so hard to change? *American Educational Research Journal, 31,* 453–479.

U.S. Department of Education. (1995). *Seventeenth annual report to Congress on the implementation of the Individuals with Disabilities Education Act.* Washington, DC: Government Printing Office.

Wise, A. (1994). The coming revolution in teacher licensure: Redefining teacher preparation. *Action in Teacher Education, 16*(2), 1–13.

Zemmelman, S., Daniels, H., & Hyde, A. (1993). *Best practice: New standards for teaching and learning in America's schools.* Portsmouth, NH: Heinemann.

Note

1. Although the proportion of minority students in special education differs from state to state, Hispanic and Native American students generally tend to be overrepresented in learning disability programs, Asian American students tend to be overrepresented in programs for speech impairments, and African American students are overrepresented in several disability areas—especially mild developmental disabilities (Grossman, 1995).

Syracuse University's Inclusive Elementary and Special Education Program

*Luanna H. Meyer, Gerald M. Mager, Gwen Yarger-Kane,
Marie Sarno, and George Hext-Contreras*

Teacher educators in the School of Education at Syracuse University are not unlike faculties elsewhere in espousing values of both excellence and equity in schooling. We assumed, for example, that our commitment to preparing teachers for educating the broad range of students with diverse learning needs was evident in the content of programs and coursework. Further, students enrolled in our programs benefited from our positive relationships with area school districts that supported a variety of urban and suburban field experiences in multicultural schools that were also known for their own commitment to the inclusion of students with disabilities in the mainstream.

Through the efforts of key nationally known faculty members in special education, advocacy for the full participation of students with disabilities in school and community is part of the history of our educational community. In recent years, Syracuse and Syracuse University have been seen as a community of educators supporting quality inclusive schooling for students with disabilities—in principle as well as in practice. In support of this practice in schools, we offered degree and certification program options leading to dual qualifications in both general and special education. At the same time, however, the continuance of single-certificate programs in both areas seemed to reinforce a message sometimes heard in the schools: Inclusion is optional, and most teachers may choose to be either "general" or "special" educators rather than accept the responsibility and challenge to teach all children.

If we as a faculty were committed to quality inclusive schooling, why then did we represent inclusion in our own teacher education programs as an option—allowing the majority of our students to choose single-certificate programs and declare their intent to teach some and not all children? If we as a faculty believe that our schools have the obligation to teach all children and that children with disabilities have a right to be full participants in their school community, how then could we not "walk the talk" in our own educational programs? And indeed, should not staff development for quality inclusive education begin at our colleges and universities to ensure that new generations of teachers enter the profession committed to teaching all children? What happened next was a combination of perseverative planning by a small core of faculty from both general and special education, facilitated by external forces that created a structure for the changes and also set definite timelines for accomplishing them.

The Program

In New York State, as in many states, preservice teachers may enter the profession with either a bachelor's degree or a master's degree from a university or college with an approved program leading to certification. Prior to implementing the Inclusive Elementary and Special Education Program, our initial teacher education programs at the baccalaureate level included five separate possibilities, with single-certificate and dual-certificate programs in both elementary and special education, as well as the option of completing a six-credit course sequence for eligibility to teach at middle-school level. Our Inclusive Program replaced these separate programs with one degree and teacher certification program. No other elementary education or special education teacher education program is available at the undergraduate level at Syracuse University; this reflects our commitment that, upon entering the teaching profession, elementary education teachers must be committed to teaching all children.

Our Inclusive Program meets the academic requirements for:

— New York State Provisional Certification in Elementary Education (Pre-kindergarten through grade 6)
— New York State Provisional Certification in Special Education (at present, N-12)
— appropriate teacher certification in states with reciprocal agreements or similar requirements
— graduate study leading to the master's degree in education and eligibility for permanent New York State certification in elementary and special education
— graduate study leading to the master's degree in the student's specialization field in the liberal arts and sciences. If the academic subject is one

taught in elementary schools or special education classes, this graduate degree also may meet New York State permanent certification requirements.

Many of our graduates leave New York upon completing their degrees (approximately half come to us from out of state), and we designed the program following various state and federal guidelines to ensure that, to our knowledge, our graduates would be eligible for certification in other states across the country. This was done through careful checking that critical content, competencies, and course requirements that often appeared in state and accreditation requirements could be identified in our program review of the student's transcript. This process is facilitated by reciprocity with states in our region and, in addition, our graduates have become certified successfully in various states following graduation.

In New York State, teachers with provisional certification may teach for up to 5 years, at which point they must return to complete their master's degree and submit evidence of at least 2 years of successful teaching to become certified permanently. Thus, our Inclusive Program is an entry-level teacher preparation program, and it was our intent to prepare teachers to enter the teaching profession committed to teaching all children. We continue to acknowledge the need for specialization teachers at the graduate preparation level and offer various program options at the graduate level to prepare teachers for permanent certification as either specialist personnel or master classroom teachers. Graduate programs include elementary education, subject-area education majors (e.g., English education, mathematics education, art education) and special education (including a generic program, a program in learning disabilities, and a program in early childhood special education).

The Change Process

Systems change is as difficult and complex a process in higher education as it is in any institution. Change in general is a challenge, and the slowness of universities to implement change can easily be illustrated by comparing course and program descriptions across any given time period. Indeed, change in higher education may meet with particularly strong obstacles. On the one hand, a major purpose of higher education is knowledge production, and faculty and students often measure their contributions by innovation and refinement of most promising practices. At the same time, though, a major contextual value of universities is academic freedom and the promotion of diverse perspectives and ideas. A new program proposal—particularly one that will affect all students in a program—can be seen as an attempt to impose uniformity and compliance. Even when everyone agrees that something has to change, the necessary consensus for institutional change can be difficult to achieve in teacher education. Next, we describe the processes and strategies evident in our own change process as the Inclusive Program took shape and was finally implemented.

Context, History, and Shared Values

Syracuse University is an urban university offering a comprehensive range of program options to approximately 14,000 students enrolled in undergraduate and graduate programs. Eleven diverse schools and colleges include the College of Arts and Sciences and the School of Education, as well as a variety of strong professional schools such as Social Work and Human Development. Other well known schools are the Newhouse School of Public Communications, the Maxwell School of Citizenship and Public Affairs, and the College of Visual and Performing Arts, providing the context for the rich exchange of ideas and experiences across disciplines and interests.

School of Education programs have been small historically (our Inclusive Program admits approximately 60 students each year), affording students the opportunity to be part of a community where everyone knows one another within a relatively large university offering a wider social context and academic choice. Historically, we have been an "All-University School of Education," which means that many of our faculty hold joint appointments in both the School of Education and a major department in Arts and Sciences, such as the Mathematics and Biology Departments. This blending of professional and academic colleges reflects the belief that education and the academic disciplines should share expertise in content and process with one another.

Within the School of Education, both teaching and research traditionally have been valued rather than focusing primarily upon one or the other. Teacher education programs have served the important purpose of grounding theory and practice through the preparation of reflective practitioners for today's schools; these programs are part of the School's mission in combination with research and development rather than being a primary function. The Syracuse University faculty in special education is well known for both its scholarship and its advocacy, and includes names such as Cruickshank, Blatt, and Wolfensberger. Burton Blatt was Dean of the School of Education until his death shortly before inception of the Inclusive Program, and he was one of many promoting full inclusion and participation of individuals with disabilities in all aspects of school and community life.

Moving from Informal to Formal Planning

The idea for what is now the Inclusive Elementary and Special Education Program began as an informal discussion at our annual faculty retreat in August 1987 and continued among a small group of faculty within the School of Education throughout the 1987–88 academic year. This core of five to six key faculty members from what were then two separate divisions—the Division for the Study of Teaching and the Division for Special Education and Rehabilitation—became a self-appointed committee that met regularly with the goal of drafting a formal proposal. These faculty members were in various formal and informal leadership roles within the School of Education, lending credibility to their planning activities, and each person shared planning activities with other faculty members in their respective units. Some of these individual faculty members also began team teaching core coursework on an experimental basis to modify course content and model collaboration between special and general education faculty for our students.

Throughout this period, the faculty drafted formative versions of a unified statement of purpose. This was an ongoing activity that we found helpful in articulating shared values, principles, and practices that were a guiding force later as the program was implemented. The process identified a number of shared values reflected throughout our programs in the School of Education:

1. *Inclusion and equity,* asserting that schools are for everyone, everyone can learn, and schools are accountable for student learning.
2. *Teacher as decision-maker,* viewing the teacher's role as a reflective process supported by technical skills and knowledge of student needs guided by values.
3. *Multiculturalism in education,* recognizing the demographic realities of today's school population and viewing diversity as an enriching opportunity.
4. *Innovations in education,* promoting the development and validation of most promising practices in curriculum and instruction.
5. *Field-based emphasis,* valuing ongoing experiences in school and community coordinated with university coursework as critical to the development of capable and committed teachers.

Each of these is a widely held belief within the school, supported through specific components in the various separate programs.

Drafting the formal proposal for the planned inclusive program also was ongoing. The draft had to include the essential program elements and at the same time address the most relevant logistical issues. Having such a draft—being updated and revised based upon input from relevant constituent groups—also grounded us in the practical realities of teacher education. We attempted to develop a program-ready draft in a timely way and thus did not require consensus on a goal statement. The two activities of (a) consensus review on values, principles, and practices and (b) review of program proposals can (and did for us) occur simultaneously.

Moving ahead with draft versions of a formal proposal had several advantages.

1. The concrete problem-solving activities of the proposal activity maintained a sense of purpose and accomplishment for both the planning group and the School of Education.
2. The ongoing evolution of the draft communicated clearly to everyone that we were firmly committed to developing a serious program proposal—that something was happening.
3. Rather than bogging down on philosophical statements, the planning group was able to make practical progress toward solving the very real implementation issues that would confront the faculty and the school if everyone were to agree to adopt the proposal; because practical problems were being addressed during the talk, this process added credibility to the planning activities.
4. Potential obstacles and general fears about unforeseen problems were limited rather than looming large, given concrete plans to address those obstacles and concerns.

Some problems were solved philosophically in the context of open discussions. For example, at one point early in the planning, concerns were raised at a faculty meeting that our enrollment in elementary education would be affected; if a student did not want to teach special education and wanted only elementary education, would not that student go elsewhere? Because Syracuse University is private and student tuition is a major source of funding, this was a serious issue. A faculty member in elementary education said, "Well, if a student feels that way, perhaps he or she should not be a teacher, as there is no longer any such thing as teaching elementary education without students with disabilities in the classroom. Perhaps the student does need to go elsewhere." There was consensus on that statement. (Interestingly enough, now that we are nearly six years into the program, we know that the opposite has occurred: The Inclusive Program enrollment continues to increase beyond our projections.)

Concerns about other problems such as staffing and resources were addressed through concrete projections 4 years ahead, detailing course offerings, instructors, student enrollment, and field placements and supervision. These projections reassured us that our planning was realistic. The process also made clear that we did not have the staff or resources to continue to run parallel single-certificate, dual-certificate, and the inclusive program. We had to make a decision. We reached a point the year prior to final approval, when the faculty agreed that this would be our only undergraduate program in elementary and special education.

As formal drafts of the program design were completed, these were shared for review and revisions with the larger group of all faculty members responsible at the time for advising, instruction, and program development in both elementary and special education. This responsiveness also was critical in ensuring that all constituents involved in the program—whose willing participation would be critical later—were represented in the planning process and would perceive that their needs and concerns had been addressed prior to formal approval. This stage in the review process can be, and was, lengthy and sometimes painful. Unexpected agenda items suddenly appeared, and any lack of consensus in valuing the program direction of inclusion surfaced during the review process.

In our view, though, ignoring or bypassing this resistance was not an option. By showing a firm commitment to program development, along with a sincere response to concerns, movement continued to occur and later resistance diminished. Rather than viewing these discussions as *obstacles* to program approval, we considered them constructive in building a consensus of values, principles, and practices that will be needed many times throughout implementation of the new program.

Accreditation Reviews and State Certification Requirements

During the planning period from 1987 through 1989, two accreditation reviews supported the planning. Our NCATE review familiarized all teacher education faculty with required program components, giving us a common knowledge base that facilitated later discussions. Without that base, discussions of possible changes otherwise might have been hindered by uncertainties and misinformation regarding certification and accreditation requirements. During that same year, Syracuse University underwent its accreditation review by Middle States; the administration chose the School of Education as one of five schools to be included in this review, and our dean chose our planning for a new, inclusive teacher education program as a major focus of our review.

At this point, our informal planning group became official as the dean designated us as a Task Force charged to develop a formal proposal for inclusive teacher education. As we planned informally, our NCATE context reassured us that required content could be included. In addition, the external review team for the Middle States accreditation review was impressed positively by the idea of quality inclusive teacher education and also chastised us for not moving more quickly to implementation.

Changes in state certification requirements in Elementary and Secondary Education gave us added motivation and a concrete timetable for implementation. The State Education Department mandated program revisions in all teacher education programs that affected all graduates after August 1993, including course content changes reflecting increased emphasis on multicultural issues, adaptations for students with disabilities, and new requirements in the liberal arts and sciences. The new requirement, for example, that students must complete sufficient coursework to qualify for graduate admission in a field of study in the liberal arts and sciences involved negotiations with other units across our university to develop those specializations for our students. Finally, as one of the original Holmes Group Institutions, we wrote and received a Ford Foundation grant to establish a Professional Development School model in collaboration with area urban-suburban school districts. By 1989, our proposal was ready for formal review by the New York State Education Department and within Syracuse University.

Review within the university was a fairly straightforward process, but the ongoing discussions throughout planning helped to ensure that unexpected obstacles would not take us by surprise as the proposal moved through the various governing committee reviews at the school and university levels. Almost simultaneously, review and approval of our plans were sought from the two relevant offices in New York State's Education Department (one focusing on elementary and the other on special education, which were separate units at the time). Once we had a draft proposal that had undergone substantial review by our faculty, we shared that draft with relevant personnel in the state department even before formal submission. This was done to assure that we would be addressing any concerns that our certifying state agency might have that otherwise could preclude program approval with the state.

Personnel in our state agency responded favorably to our proposal, and we believe this response was supported also by our positive working relationships with key professionals in the agency in recent years. We were given full approval by the state; subsequently, the state has featured our program at three separate Higher Education Leadership Institutes held annually on innovations in special education teacher preparation.

Program Implementation

What had emerged was an entirely new program, with virtually all new coursework and program requirements. Following approvals, our first class was admitted in fall 1990 to begin the program; no new students were admitted to the five single- and dual-certificate programs it replaced unless they could graduate prior to September 1993 (though we had to continue supporting students already in those programs through to graduation).

The transition phase did not change teaching loads for faculty; during the first year of the new program, for example, faculty would be involved in teaching first-year coursework in that program plus sophomore through senior year coursework in the "old" programs, and so on until the last class graduated. The transition process did mean that the faculty was involved in teaching in both the new and old programs at the same time. It also meant that students in those programs overlapped. Student overlap created some difficulties early on as the older programs were more flexible and offered students more choices (leading to complaints from Inclusive majors about few choices), and the newer program clearly was more consistent with the overall approach of our school (leading to complaints from some students majoring in one of those programs about not being able to finish the Inclusive Program).

Major Program Components

Table 2.1 provides an overview of the major program components: (a) the liberal arts cluster, (b) the specialization area, and (c) professional education. The liberal arts core divisional requirements include writing skill courses and 36 credits evenly divided among the humanities, mathematics and natural sciences, and the social sciences. The three 12-credit clusters were modeled after the College of Arts and Sciences divisional (breadth) requirements for any undergraduate but included specific course-area requirements that we thought would enhance our students' foundational core.

Students also select one of sixteen 24–30+ credit specializations selected from the many academic major areas in the liberal arts and sciences. This requirement reflects both Syracuse University's longstanding requirement that elementary education teacher preparation programs have depth in a liberal arts area and a new elementary education certification requirement in New York State. This specified that teachers must complete sufficient study in an academic major in the liberal arts and sciences to qualify for graduate study in that field. The 60+ credit professional education major includes preparation for both elementary and special education certification.

Liberal Arts and Sciences Coursework

Diversity was a guiding theme not only for the professional core but for arts and sciences preparation as well. In identifying options for the liberal arts cluster, students were required to complete at least one course in the social sciences and another in the humanities with a multicultural focus (and this was defined as non-European/European American). We required another of the social sciences courses to be focused upon the family, and students are advised into one of several options available in other schools across campus. We negotiated specialization areas that were parallel to traditional majors (e.g., English, Mathematics, History) as well as interdisciplinary (e.g., African American Studies, Non-Violent Conflict and Change, Social Sciences Perspectives on Childhood).

In each instance, the concentration was validated by an academic unit at Syracuse University as one that would make a student eligible for graduate study in a relevant field, thus meeting the state requirement. We selected specializations most likely to represent subject areas relevant to the education of children, and we have allowed individual students to petition additional areas, provided

Table 2.1

Major Inclusive Program Components at Syracuse University

Component	Specific Content for Diversity	Rationale for Component
Liberal Arts Cluster (36 cr.)		
▪ 12 credits math and natural sciences ▪ 12 credits humanities ▪ 12 credits social sciences	Two courses from the humanities and social sciences cluster must be multicultural (non-European/European American). One course from social sciences CORE must be on the family. A third course from social sciences CORE is EDU 310, The American School, which emphasizes diversity.	▪ Broad base consistent with CORE arts and sciences requirement for all undergraduates. ▪ Addition of diversity requirements (9 cr.) and family course (3 cr.) to build multicultural knowledge background.
Specialization Area (24–30+ cr.)		
Selected from among 16 disciplinary or interdisciplinary undergraduate concentrations sufficient to enable application for graduate study in that major (e.g., history, psychology, sociology, math, African American studies)	Courses and course content are responsibility of field of study faculty from Arts & Sciences; all but one area have specialization advisors, and declaration of a major or minor is often possible.	▪ Today's teachers need concentrated background in a nonprofessional field of study to be more educated as teachers. ▪ Specific areas chosen for relevance to role of teacher.
Professional Education (60 cr.)		
Courses and field work in inclusive schooling, including many general and special education integrated courses. Courses have either general/elementary or special education prefixes (at least 24 cr. in each certificate area).	Diversity issues of gender, language, disability, ethnicity, and culture are major focuses of introductory coursework; multilevel adaptations, multiple intelligences, individualized planning, and teaming/collaboration are major focus of methods coursework.	▪ Diverse teaching and learning styles are broad base for program content. ▪ Multicultural and disability issues are represented within CORE courses as well as in coursework on those topics to ensure intensive coverage. ▪ Field work components (6–7) semesters ensures hands-on practice throughout (see Table 2.3).

they meet the dual criteria of preparation for graduate study in an academic area and relevance to elementary education.

One of our specialization areas, the Social Sciences Perspectives on Childhood, was established as an interdisciplinary liberal arts foundation for focusing upon early childhood education in particular. Students in this specialization area soon may have the option of certification in early childhood special education and be able to complete their six credit-intensive special needs coursework at this level rather than at the secondary level. New York State certification in special education has extended the full range through secondary level, but an expected change would allow individual annotations for either early childhood or secondary level in special education that would fit nicely within our program design.

The Professional Core

Professional education coursework emphasizes the role of the teacher as decision-maker and begins in the first year. Table 2.2 provides a listing of the 14 major goal areas and component knowledge and skills for the areas guiding the design of coursework, field experiences, and program activities; this is a dynamic draft document undergoing continuous revision based upon input from the inclusive faculty, our student teachers, and the cadres of teachers supervising students in the field.

These goal areas form the core of our teacher education expectations, and our students begin to organize their professional portfolios around activities and accomplishments for selected elements in each area. The goal areas both reflect and guide university instruction in our professional core as well; for example, the faculty in the First Professional Block teaches collaboratively and models thematic instruction rather than teaching as separate and discrete coursework in the different disciplinary areas.

At the end of the student teaching semester, students share their final form "exit portfolio," having created a display of their professional qualifications often used during the job interview process as well as providing an initial guide during the first year of teaching. A more detailed scope and sequence also has been developed by all faculty teaching coursework in the Inclusive Program, detailing the specific content knowledge and practical skill components covered by each course and other program components.

By no later than the first semester of the sophomore year, students begin a series of supervised field experiences working in schools and with children and their families. Table 2.3 provides a listing of these, including the sequence of experiences, rationale for each, and the requirements associated with various placements. Highlights of our field experiences include the unique year-long placement with a child and family. We wanted our students to see the world through the eyes of the child and family rather than always through the eyes of the professional school community, afforded by the more traditional school-based

Table 2.2

Program Goal Areas

Program Goal Area	Knowledge and Skills
Learner Characteristics	Multiple intelligences Diverse learning styles Disability learner characteristics Speech and language characteristics Health needs Physical characteristics (motor, etc.)
Diversity	Global Multicultural Socioeconomic Language Gender Alternative and augmentative communication
Theories of Teaching and Learning	Social context Cognitive Behavioral Constructivism Developmentally appropriate practices Systematic and direct instruction
Assessment	Diagnostic-prescriptive approach Multiple intelligences/modalities Performance assessment Portfolios Criterion-referenced and curricular-based
Curriculum	Content-related pedagogy Inquiry-based Frameworks by subject area Thematic Cooperative learning Functional and community-based Computer-assisted
Instruction	Lesson planning Instructional objectives Multi-level Multi-method Grouping Tutorial Adaptations

(continued)

Table 2.2 continued

Program Goal Area	Knowledge and Skills
Classroom Management	Interpersonal skills training Conflict resolution Building a classroom community Transitions Active listening and teacher talk
Sociopolitical Context of Schooling	Community expectations Systems change Multiculturalism Effective advocacy Educational rights
Teaming and Collaboration	Action planning Time management Communication strategies School support and community personnel General education and special education teaming Transdisciplinary teaming (OT, PT, Speech, etc.) Working with support personnel
Home-School Collaboration	Culturally inclusive Due process Home involvement Family priorities and the IEP/IFSP Communication strategies
Technology	Adaptive devices Instructional software Internet E-mail
Community	Accessing resources and supports Peer support networks Children's socioemotional needs Friendships Conflict resolution
Reflective Practitioner	Teacher as learner Teacher as inquirer Teacher as problem-solver
Practical Considerations	Professional development School routines Job interviewing Substitute teachers Preparing a resume Being evaluated Unions

placements. This has been an overwhelmingly popular experience and has just been revised to include the first substantive exposure to design of the IEP and the IFSP—again, through the eyes of the family's priorities. Students learn to do an informal interview with the family following "culturally inclusive" guidelines, and to take the family's perspective on educational priorities for a child with disabilities with whom they already have a social relationship (Harry et al., 1995).

By their junior year, students also have completed an early childhood field experience and a guided tutorial placement in an urban elementary school, coordinated in both cases with coursework (see Table 2.3). At that time, they become part of a Professional Development School cadre that remains together through the student teaching semester and graduation. The Professional Development School (PDS) is a collaborative partnership linking Syracuse University, area public schools, and the community in a longitudinal relationship engaging area professional educators in the teacher education process.

As students enter the First Professional Block and begin instruction in mathematics, reading, and language arts methods, they join their PDS cadre. Each cadre consists of approximately 12 preservice teachers and 12 to 15 cooperating teachers (both general and special educators) from two or more schools, at least one urban and one suburban, representing grades K–6. Each preservice teacher education student alternates urban and suburban placements, assignments to either a special or a general educator as cooperating teacher, and grades K–3 versus 4–6 across the three semesters of the professional block and student teaching semesters.

Schools in the cadres—both urban and suburban—were selected for the quality of their general education programs and quality of inclusive programs for students with disabilities. In some instances, these efforts are new developments and our School of Education is involved in mutually supportive capacity-building activities to facilitate quality inclusive schooling in area schools. Various externally funded school-university partnership projects involving Syracuse University faculty and district personnel in mathematics, social studies, science, special education, and other areas have offered direct support for components of quality inclusive schooling during the planning and implementation phase of the PDS.

For example, in one project supported by the Kennedy Foundation, a faculty member in social studies education and area teachers collaborate in the development of multi-level instruction for inclusive social studies education. The results of this work are being infused into our methods courses as well as in social studies instructional practice in selected participating cadre schools (Oyler, 1995). Because each cadre is a cohesive unit that functions as a Collaborative Field Team with school administrators and inclusive program faculty teaching associated coursework, preservice teachers are mentored in an intensive series of placements that can be adapted to meet individual needs and interests.

Table 2.3

Inclusive Program Field Experiences and Professional Development School Placements

Course Title	Program Year/s	Placement	Rationale and Requirements
EDU 303: Teaching & Learning for Inclusive Schooling	2nd Semester 1st yr. or Sophomore year (either semester)	All students placed in one urban K–6 school; 10 weeks, 2 hours weekly (20 hrs.)	■ Structured guided tutorial (1:1) of child supervised by building reading teachers. ■ Urban school experience with children regarded as "at-risk," majority African American and Latino. ■ Three classroom observation assignments on learning/teaching styles, management, and lesson planning.
SPE 311: Perspectives on Disabilities	Sophomore year	Two undergraduates paired with one child with disabilities through community/family support agencies; 10 weeks each semester, 2 hours weekly (40 hrs.)	■ Visits to child's home and community with family as major contact. ■ Respite and recreation focus—seeing things "through the eyes of the child and family." ■ Introduction to the components of the IEP/IFSP; doing a family interview on priority goals
SPE 312: Practicum	Sophomore year		
CFS 322: Early Childhood	Sophomore semester	Inclusive preschool and area day-care settings (30 hrs. total)	■ Practicum connected to early childhood course on development. ■ Opportunity to see special education services delivered in typical preschools and day-care centers.
SPE 346: Methods & Curriculum Severe Disabilities and SPE 347: Practicum—Pre K–3 or SPE 348: Practicum—K–8	Junior and senior year semester; Sophomore, for those planing study abroad.	Middle school or early childhood placement serving students with disabilities in general education; 9 hours weekly for 10 weeks (90 hrs.)	■ Secondary focus to prepare for K–8 special education qualification. ■ Or, Early Childhood focus to prepare for Pre K–3 special education qualification. ■ Interdisciplinary team placement and collaboration teaming. ■ IEP development and focus on severe disabilities in inclusive classes.

(continued)

Table 2.3 continued

Course Title	Program Year/s	Placement	Rationale and Requirements
First Professional Block[a] ■ Math Methods ■ Reading Methods ■ Language Arts Methods ■ Practicum ■ Strategies	Junior Year Semester	Two 3-week, all-day place-ments: 1 urban/1 suburban 1 primary (K–3) and 1 intermediate (4–6)	■ Practice in direct instruction with whole group, specific content and skills (e.g., hands-on math). ■ Lesson plans, integrated content, individualized adaptations, and assignments.
Second Professional Block ■ Social Studies Methods ■ Science Methods ■ Curriculum Adapta-tions for Special Education ■ Practicum	Junior or Senior Year Semester	One 6-week placement, 3 hours a day and visits 1 placement in grade level not previously experienced (urban and suburban)	■ Write, modify, instruct thematic and hands-on content units. ■ Self-evaluation on video (twice across time). ■ Focus on multi-level adaptations.
Student Teaching with Weekly Seminar on Diversity	Senior Semester	Two 7-week all-day placements: 1 urban/1 suburban 1 primary (K–3) and 1 intermediate (4–6) Both inclusive placements, one with GE and one with SPE teacher.	■ Plan and carry out all instruction. ■ Monitor and assess student learning, including authentic assessment. ■ Collaborate and team with personnel and families. ■ Work with students representing full range of diversity. ■ Complete personal portfolio.[b]

[a] Students are assigned to a Professional Development School Cadre prior to their first Block placement. Each Cadre includes approximately 15 teachers from two or more schools (urban and suburban) in grade K–6; teachers, students, and university faculty interact collaboratively on each cadre for four semesters.

[b] Program Portfolio Reviews are conducted at the end of the first Professional Block, the second Professional Block, and student teaching, with Review attended by all Cadre members (teachers, administrators, students, university supervisors, faculty).

In addition to the year-long respite experience with a child with disabilities, our students work with students with disabilities in each of their inclusive field placements (see Table 2.3). These placements include students with labels such as learning disabilities, mental retardation, autism, sensory impairments, multiple disabilities, emotional disturbance, and attention deficit disorders at preschool and elementary-age levels. Specific requirements to adapt instruction and curriculum for students with special needs are incorporated within the various methods coursework and student teaching requirements. Each of our students also completes a dedicated semester-long placement wherein the major assignment is to work with students who have significant disabilities. At present, these placements have been concentrated at middle or high school level to prepare students for a special education credential that extends through secondary level, but in the future, we anticipate student choice between an annotation in early childhood or secondary special education in addition to the elementary school preparation.

Diversity and Multiculturalism

We recognize diversity as the reality of today's schools and world and value the ability and commitment of our graduates to understand and teach all students. Thus, our Inclusive Elementary and Special Education Program has infused special education content throughout coursework and field experiences, modeling inclusion in our walk as well as our talk. In addition, multicultural education is a critical feature of our program. Students enroll in both liberal arts and professional education coursework throughout the 4 years of study focused upon the knowledge and skills needed for the cultural pluralism of today's classrooms. Preparation for cultural diversity includes each of the following:

- Multicultural Literature: Each student must take one 3-credit course in multicultural literature, defined as "non-European/European American," and selected from among many available options.
- Multicultural Understandings: Every Inclusive student also completes one 3-credit course in multicultural understandings from the social sciences, defined as addressing in total or in part social science content concerning non-European/European American cultures/issues.
- EDU 310 The American School or equivalent: Students must complete one course with a major emphasis upon diversity issues in education and/ or learning.
- Field Work Experiences: Inclusive majors complete nine distinct semester-long field experiences working with children and schools, beginning with two during the second through fourth semesters of study, that emphasize preparation for diversity. For many of our students, their SPE 311–312 placement with a child with disabilities is their first experience with disability. As part of the field experience requirement for our

educational psychology course (EDU 303), students tutor a child in an urban elementary school selected for collaboration at this level because of its high proportionate enrollment of children of color. Subsequent field work includes the rotation between culturally diverse urban schools and the less diverse suburban schools, and work with children with and without disabilities.

■ CFE 444 Schooling and Diversity: This seminar-format course accompanies the student teaching semester and is directed at diversity issues, multiculturalism, and tying together theory and practice on these dimensions.

Community Support

The Syracuse community offers further support for inclusive teacher education: As one of New York's "Big Five," the city of Syracuse encompasses an urban school district serving more than 20,000 children and youth. Approximately 50 percent of the school population is African American, American Indian, or Puerto Rican or other Latino nationalities, and smaller numbers are Asian, Pacific Islanders, and native Alaskans.

Further, the City School District has a long history of providing special education programs for students with disabilities within the general education community. One of the earliest media presentations on inclusion—Regular Lives, shown nationally on public television in 1988—was filmed in the Syracuse City School District elementary and secondary schools, showing children with autism and other significant disabilities as full participants in the general education classroom with their age-peers (Biklen, 1988). Surrounding suburban school districts add to the diversity of our student population; many of these districts also are well known for their exemplary special education programs.

Syracuse University is centrally located within the Syracuse community, giving our students ready access to a diverse range of field experiences within a few minutes of campus. Clearly, a strong values base and capacity for program quality existed in nearby schools, and we already had a long history of working closely and collaboratively with area districts (Meyer, Williams, Harootunian, & Steinberg, 1995).

Summary and Recommendations

We are now in the sixth year of our Inclusive Program. Two classes have graduated, assumed teaching positions, or gone on to graduate school, and many changes have occurred to the program content and process. We have carried out several program evaluation activities, including graduate follow-up and an ongoing series of Focus Group meetings with relevant constituent groups on the extent to which we are meeting our program goals (for a succinct statement of this evaluation process, see Krueger, 1994). Based on our data, we can assert confidently that there is general consensus that we are doing what we set out to do. Our students and graduates have been exposed to issues of diversity and inclusion; they are committed to the principle that all children can learn; and they are mastering the practices of collaboration, individualization, and curricular adaptations to make learning possible.

One practical outcome of our program is that virtually all graduates to date are either employed or in graduate school, having made a choice in either case. District personnel recruiters have enthusiastically interviewed our students; our record of interviews and job offers far exceeds that of other teacher education graduates with single certificates graduating from our programs in previous years and from other programs in New York State.

Our evaluation process also has identified areas where ongoing effort is needed. We suspect that the issues that have arisen for us are similar to needs elsewhere.

Teacher preparation programs have to articulate clearly a scope and sequence of knowledge and skills represented in each educational experience. Special education programs historically have specified competencies for students, and general education curricula typically have included a scope and sequence for children across the grade levels. By specifying the information and skills across the framework of the entire sequence of coursework, field experiences, and other learning opportunities, several important outcomes are possible. First, students will have explicit reference points for critical components needed at each level. Second, any possible "drift" in course content would be mediated by the accountability inherent in an explicit scope and sequence: All faculty teaching coursework would be aware of expectations for them and the students. Discussion of any needed changes to the listing is an explicit agenda item at one of the meetings of program faculty each year; the results of each year's discussion with student teachers and their cooperating teachers in the cadres also will be summarized and shared with faculty in written form. Having such a listing can serve the dual purpose of communicating with constituents in the field—building principals, cooperating teachers, future employers, and others—about the design of the program. The listing would provide a reference point for any concerns about program content and, if needed, changes could be made for any skills that were not thought to be covered adequately.

This process also can evoke mixed feelings among faculty. Issues of academic freedom and individual approaches to teaching specific courses are as dear to faculty in the School of Education as they are in the academic content disciplines. A faculty member in special education who regularly teaches one of the core courses advocates intensive pull-out instruction in small group situations for early remediation, and teaches methods appropriate for pull-out approaches. At the same time, other faculty are emphasizing inclusive approaches to address similar needs. Perhaps strategies are available to resolve conflicting approaches, but our feeling has been that diversive perspectives can contribute to the development of critical thinking. Our students will experience conflicting perspectives on appropriate educational practices in the schools, and surely they can accommodate such perspectives here as well.

We have a Scope and Sequence in addition to the broader listing of the Program Goal Areas but have not yet moved to making the former a checklist within student programs. We are in the process of making it a part of each student's file as well as our program records and communications with area schools. At the same time, it is important to view both listings as dynamic and ready to accommodate new ideas and changes in thinking and practice so they do not become obstacles to change as new, inclusive programs push the boundaries of what we know.

Doctoral preparation should be coordinated more closely with teacher preparation programs, particularly innovative programs such as the Inclusive Program. Not all teacher preparation universities also provide doctoral education in teacher education and educational administration. When they do, however, doctoral students frequently serve as field experience supervisors or course instructors as part of their Graduate Assistantship responsibilities. Each year, several doctoral students from both general and special education programs serve in these roles, but their involvement has been episodic rather than longitudinal.

By articulating a longitudinal and developmental involvement with an innovative program such as ours, doctoral graduates would have a better understanding of the process and then would have the overall knowledge to create further change in the colleges and universities that hire them as faculty in teacher preparation programs. This would put them in a better position to develop their own ideas about preparing America's teachers with the benefit of knowledge about the impact of inclusive teacher education on a group of preservice teachers-to-be throughout the process.

Diversity is a reality of schooling that must be reflected in every aspect of teacher education. By providing our students with an inclusive teacher education program with both elementary and special education content, our graduates are being prepared for the realities of diverse student needs. By incorporating required multicultural coursework in both the humanities and social sciences foundation areas as well as in the professional core, our teachers also will be more knowledgeable about the different cultures they are likely to encounter in today's schools. As an urban university, we also have been able to provide preservice teachers with experiences in urban (and suburban) schools enrolling students of color and students with diverse cultural and linguistic backgrounds.

As a university, we are not diverse: The vast majority of our faculty members are monocultural European Americans and do not have disabilities. Our students are quick to point out that the professors and students themselves must become multicultural. Our cooperating teachers, building principals, and even our doctoral students are becoming more diverse, with persons of color and persons with disabilities in key roles. Also, we have increased our enrollment of preservice teachers of color and with disabilities. Commitment is needed, however, especially as our resources for new hires and student aid decline, to increase the diversity of teacher education. We must ourselves do as we say.

References

Biklen, D. (Producer). (1988). *Regular lives* [Video]. Washington, DC: State of the Art.

Harry, B., Grenot-Scheyer, M., Smith-Lewis, M., Park, H. S., Xin, F., & Schwartz, I. (1995). Developing culturally inclusive services for individuals with severe disabilities. *Journal of the Association for Persons with Severe Handicaps, 20,* 99–109.

Krueger, R. A. (1994). *Focus groups: A practical guide for applied research* (2d ed.). Thousand Oaks, CA: Sage Publications.

Meyer, L. H., Williams, D. R., Harootunian, B., & Steinberg, A. (1995). An inclusion model to reduce at-risk status among middle school students: The Syracuse experience. In I. M. Evans, T. Cicchelli, M. Cohen, & N. P. Shapiro (Eds.), *Staying in school: Partnerships for educational change* (pp. 83–110). Baltimore: Paul H. Brookes Publishing.

Oyler, C. (1995, April). *Learning to teach multilevel social studies in the inclusive elementary classroom.* Paper presented at the Annual Meeting of the American Educational Research Association, San Francisco.

The Power of Integrated Teacher Preparation: The University of Connecticut

Kay A. Norlander, Charles W. Case, Timothy G. Reagan,
Pamela Campbell, and James D. Strauch

When considering the hectic academic schedules and already complicated curriculum that are incumbent in a normally functioning classroom, to add students with special needs might seem burdensome and frustrating. But today it is the responsibility of every classroom teacher to become educated and accommodating in order to meet the needs of all students; it is no longer the sole responsibility of the special educator. As a future teacher, I feel it is imperative to embrace the "inclusion" trend. It will be my responsibility to incorporate the needs of students who are challenged into my instruction. Although it will require supplementary resources and additional time in my preparation for class instruction, I need to think of it as my obligation as an educator. (Garrish, future elementary teacher, portfolio entry, December 1993)

The unification of teacher education programs, across grade levels and teaching disciplines, is one viable way to initiate systemic change in how all students are educated equitably in our country's schools. As teacher preparation programs work toward this integration, they must simultaneously link schools to the places traditionally charged with the preparation of teachers. Partnerships between schools of education and the schools where children are taught must be forged to provide teachers in preparation with the opportunity to view real school problems, influence systemic change, and allow students and teachers to work together across teaching disciplines (see Case, Norlander, & Reagan, 1993a; Darling-Hammond, 1994; Fullan, 1993; Goodlad, 1994; Levine, 1992; Sirotnik, 1988; among others).

Committed to the simultaneous renewal of schools and the education of educators (see Goodlad, 1990a, 1994), to the notion that reflective practice must undergird all we do, and armed with the belief that we have a legal and moral obligation to educate all of the nation's youth, the faculty in the School of Education at the University of Connecticut has undertaken a radical reconceptualization regarding how teachers can best be prepared. This process of change, which began in 1987, has resulted in one teacher education program encompassing all of the teaching disciplines and spanning all grade levels; no longer are special education and general education separate programs of study. This chapter tells the story of how this change has transpired, details the course of study involved in the new teacher education program, describes the barriers that we faced and that continue, and, in the voices of the students themselves, provides evidence of the program's impact on the next generation of teachers.

Building a Unified Teacher Education Program: The Context for Collaboration

Over the past 8 years, the School of Education faculty and our school partners created, pilot-tested, evaluated, and refined an integrated bachelor's/master's-degree program, within the School of Education, which was fully implemented in the fall of 1991. Discussions on many levels and with a wide variety of con-stituents—including teachers, school administrators, parents, and community participants—have taken place. In initiating the renewal of the teacher educa-tion program, the faculty in the School of Education began the process in a somewhat unusual way. Having agreed that serious reform was needed, the fac-ulty and administration, together with other constituencies served by the teacher education program, literally began from scratch. The faculty across departments worked together; we collaborated. There were no "turf wars" aimed at protect-ing specific courses, because the existing teacher education curriculum was, in effect, completely scrapped. Rather than focusing on courses, the faculty sought to identify the common knowledge and skills with which they believed all edu-cators should be familiar.

Once that knowledge base had been identified, new courses and field expe-riences were designed to ensure that all graduates of the program would be com-petent with respect to the knowledge base. This process was in many ways the beginning of a radical change in faculty culture. For the first time, faculty members from various departments and program areas, including those not traditionally involved in the preparation of teachers, sat together and honestly discussed curricular issues related to classroom teaching. There were arguments, to be sure, but a surprising degree of consensus emerged. The habits that developed in the process of working together collaboratively to redesign the teacher education program continued to function as the new program was implemented.

The changes that were finally enacted represent a complete change from the way in which teachers traditionally had been prepared, in separate programs of study, without a solid grounding in the liberal arts, with little or no experience in urban settings or with a diversity of learners, and with few clinical experiences other than student teaching (see Case, Norlander & Reagan, 1993b). From the beginning of the reform process, education faculty and students, arts and sciences faculty, and teachers and principals collaboratively defined the elements of the architecture of this new, integrated program. Inquiry, reflective practice, and diversity became the cornerstones of the program. It is important to stress that the changes described herein are based on a total redesign of the program, not simply the tinkering with one or two courses (e.g., the addition of a course on special education for those preparing to be general educators). We now have a single professional teacher education program rather than separate programs of study for elementary, secondary, and special education, and all of our students' clinical work, six semesters, takes place in professional development centers (PDCs). We find evidence that students graduating from the teacher education program believe that a collaborative/unified model of teacher education is a "better" way to prepare teachers. One of these students wrote:

> This year [the master's/internship year] has proven to me, beyond a shadow of a doubt, that collaboration is the direction in which we as teachers (within and outside of special education and across disciplines) are headed. I'm confident that I will be able to provide special education services to my students in whatever environment is least restrictive in meeting their needs. However, I am even more confident that I am an even better special educator when I work with my colleagues. (Pion-Flaherty, future special educator, internship summary, May 1994a)

The University Context

The University of Connecticut, a rural land-grant institution, covering 3,100 acres in and around Storrs, Connecticut, is the state's major research university. The university enrolls approximately 24,000 undergraduates and graduate students at the Storrs campus, at the five regional campuses and at one of the three professional schools. The university strives to provide a high quality education, linking this to public service, and to contribute to society through research. University-wide, there are more than 1,500 faculty members, and 73 of these are in the School of Education. Of these 73 full-time faculty, six are from minority groups and 26 are women.

Even though the university has a large student body, an essential feature of the teacher preparation program at the University of Connecticut is its commitment to admitting a relatively small number of prospective educators in cohort groups. These students have completed their first 2 years of study in a program of general education and have started a major in the liberal arts outside of the School of Education. Students (approximately 125 in each class) enter as juniors and then spend 3 years in the School of Education in an integrated bachelor's/master's-degree program. Thus in any given year, about 375 students are in the School preparing to be teachers. Students who are admitted to the program have strong academic backgrounds in the liberal arts and sciences; most students have a lower division gradepoint average of 3.0 or better and a score of at least 1000 on the SATs. Beyond these academic qualifications, students have had experience working with children, submit three letters of recommendation, and compete in a rigorous interview process. Most important, each of the candidates selected must demonstrate a capacity to care about all children.

The Professional Development Center

A central feature of the redesign of the teacher preparation program at the University of Connecticut has been our determination to foster collaboration between the university and our partner schools. Professional Development Centers (PDCs) provide the real-life context for preparing teachers and are the linchpin of the reform we have undertaken. The PDCs are partnerships that have been nurtured for as long as 8 years, and include 32 schools in parts of nine school districts, representing rural, suburban, and urban settings. These centers for professional development are not simply schools in which student teaching takes place; they are places in which colleagues from the schools and the university, with their respective students, come together for the purposes of preparing future teachers and renewing the teaching profession (including university teaching). These are places with a shared dedication to the improvement of schools. In bringing together these two groups, the major goal and focus is always to enhance the lives of children. These partnerships have influenced not only the preparation program but also the culture that prescribes the life of the university faculty and students, school teachers, and school administrators.

The collaboration we have sought to foster has been manifested in a number of ways. These include the active involvement of university faculty in the daily life of partnership schools, the participation of school-based teachers in the design and operation of the university's teacher preparation program, joint efforts to secure funding for school-based projects, and extensive involvement of teacher preparation students in a wide range of activities in the partnership schools (see Case, Norlander, & Reagan, 1993a).

The relationships between the University of Connecticut and the partner schools have been positive, supportive of school change, and essential in the preparation of new teachers as well as in the renewal of long-time practicing teachers. Comments by teachers and school administrators clearly support the idea of "partnership" in the renewal of schools and the teaching profession and the impact this has on the students in that school. As one teacher commented, "[They] helped to move the school along in terms of renewal and reform." Another teacher articulated this during a discussion about the partnership with a university faculty member in the following manner:

> I really believe that a lot of the projects [undertaken by master's interns] made a huge difference to the teachers and students in the school—they were, for the most part, really targeted on the problems that everyone recognized in the school setting. (Teacher interview, May 1994)

Finally, the partnership arrangements between the university and its PDCs have encouraged and facilitated the integration of special and regular education—in the schools and in the School of Education alike. The director of Pupil Services in Windham, one of the urban PDCs, attests to the need for partnerships between school districts and universities in writing:

> I believe that there is a need for school districts to work closely with universities to ensure that they are in sync with meeting the challenges of educating children with diverse needs and cultural characteristics. (Vannie, letter of support, 1992)

Characteristics of the Integrated Teacher Education Program

Specific components of the University of Connecticut's integrated/unified teacher education program include program philosophy, program structure, and the importance of cohorts.

Philosophical Components

The two philosophical pillars upon which the University of Connecticut teacher education program rests are the commitment to reflective practice and inquiry and the commitment to both celebrating and understanding diversity. Although these two themes are far from uncommon in teacher education programs in the United States today, in the University of Connecticut's case they are not merely slogans that were adopted easily or thoughtlessly. Both have been subject to considerable discussion and debate among faculty, as well as between faculty and school-based colleagues and between faculty and students.

In the period during which the program was being constructed, a working paper on the theme of reflective practice and inquiry was widely circulated and discussed. Since then, faculty members have written a number of articles on this theme and have produced a co-authored book on reflective practice (Brubacher, Case, & Reagan, 1994). Reflective practice by teachers is discussed in the core courses and in seminars and is modeled for students by many of the faculty members, most of whom are now involved in the teacher education program. The theme of diversity has been of similar concern and focus, and, like that of reflective practice, is taught formally, imbedded in seminar discussions, modeled by the faculty, and manifested in the activities and commitments of the School of Education as well as in extensive faculty publications in this area.

Inquiry and Reflective Practice

Undergirding our reform efforts is the commitment to inquiry in schools as the basis for professional practice of both university and school faculty, and to the idea that reflection and inquiry are essential to the renewal of schools and the teaching profession (see Brubacher et al., 1994; Clift, Houston, & Pugach, 1990; Dewey, 1910/1991); Reagan, 1993; Schon, 1987; Sirotnik, 1988; Smyth, 1989). Further, we believe strongly that teachers who are reflective in their practice will collectively have a stronger voice in changing their individual classrooms and the schools in which they work (see Cochran-Smith & Lytle, 1993; Gideonse, 1990; Lytle & Cochran-Smith, 1992; Norlander, Reagan, & Case, 1994). Through the infusion of collaboratively planned and conducted school-based research, we have sought to solidify the partnerships with each of our PDCs. As the Holmes Group (1990) has suggested:

> Inquiry in the Professional Development School should be a way for teachers, administrators, and professors to come together on equal footing. It should help to forge a shared identity in schools and universities. And it should serve as a professional norm around which collaboration can take place, bringing together the many parties who are concerned for improving schools. (p. 60)

One way in which this is manifested in practice is during the internship (master's) year. An important aspect of this year in the teacher preparation program is the planning and conducting of a year-long inquiry project within the context of the student's internship assignment. These inquiry projects are the result of collaborative input from school-based teachers and administrators, university faculty, and the teacher education students themselves. In short, the research projects contribute not only to the individual student's education but also to the renewal and improvement of the setting in which the intern is working. Many of these inquiry projects, by students preparing to be either general or special educators, or both, have focused on the needs of and services for at-risk and special needs students.

At the same time as these inquiry projects provide the teacher in preparation the means to conduct action-based research, they have a direct impact on the schools in which they are undertaken and, as stated earlier, have assisted the partner schools in advancing the integration of general and special education services. Some of the topics of inquiry and research are as follows:

- A Qualitative Study of Students with Emotional Disturbance Working as Teachers' Aides
- How Does Heterogeneous Teaming Affect the Learning Environment of the Tenth Grade at East Hartford High School?
- Collaboration Among Regular and Special Educators: An Ethnographic Study of a New Staff
- The Effects of Computer-Aided Instruction on the Math Skills, Problem-solving Abilities, and Attitudes of Special Needs High School Students
- A Qualitative Study of the Use of Computers as a Tool for Students with Developmental Disabilities
- Writing to Understand: A Study on Integrating Process Writing and Computer Technology to Teach Writing to Students with Special Needs
- The Effects of Team Teaching and Mainstreaming on Regular and Special Education Students' Self-Efficacy Toward Learning and Social and Academic Communication

Throughout the program, students maintain a journal in which they reflect on their learning and experiences. They ask questions, form hypotheses, and propose alternatives—moving from an initial, largely descriptive stage to one that is more thoughtful, analytic, and problem-focused. They use journals to gather fieldnotes, which in turn direct their inquiry. Journal entries are shared with the seminar leader, who responds in ways that encourage and support further reflection and analysis. This written dialogue often serves as the basis for conversations during seminar, especially when several students identify similar themes. Reflecting and inquiring through journal writing and seminars over a period of three years becomes a natural process for these future teachers. Comments from a master's intern exemplifies the importance of journal writing and its interaction with reflective practice:

> I think journals are a tremendous tool generally in terms of your own growth. I think writing for me is closely tied to my own [personal] growth and I think that holds for my teaching as well. Keeping a record of what you do, thinking reflectively about what you might do better, is an important part of professional growth, especially teaching.... [A journal] is a way of unpacking your thoughts. (Future elementary, English, and special educator, student interview, May 1994)

Insights and comments of the master's interns themselves provide evidence of the success of this undertaking. In discussing the importance of reflection and inquiry in their work as teachers, they emphasize how being reflective helps them analyze their work and the work of their students, and how reflection assists them in changing their teaching practice.

Reflective practice to me is...looking at situations that I encounter retrospectively...looking at things that I did to counteract a situation or how I behaved.... Primarily this means looking at myself and how I responded and figuring out whether or not there was a better way I could have handled a situation. What could I have done differently, are the questions I ask myself, in my quiet time, reflecting on what I did so that if a similar situation is ever to occur again, I would handle it better. (Future special educator, student interview, May 1994)

Diversity as a Central Theme

Throughout the teacher education program, there has been a deliberate effort to make diversity a central theme. Specific coursework, taken by all students in the preparation program, such as "Multiculturalism," "Exceptionality," and "School and Society," and specific readings and assignment, address the diverse nature of today's school population. Issues such as the inclusion of special education students in general education classrooms, gender equity, and multiculturalism in school and society are emphasized. More important, these topics are not taught in isolation from the classroom. As all students observe and work in a variety of clinical sites, including urban settings, and interact with students with disabilities, they have the opportunity to confront directly the problems and issues discussed in class.

In addition to content in core courses and experiential learning in the clinical sites, issues of diversity are addressed often and in considerable depth in the seminars that all students attend. The goal of these seminars is not merely to provide a forum for discussions of theory and practice related to diversity issues but, rather, to assist students in becoming increasingly sensitive to and reflective about such matters. One second-year student wrote just prior to student teaching:

The school should be a place to learn, grow, laugh, cry, make mistakes, and soar to new heights. Students should learn about diversity and grow to respect and understand the differences in others, as well as in the world that they will face.... The schools should mirror our hopes for society by giving an equal opportunity to all and focusing on the many abilities that all of us possess. (O'Toole, future special educator, statement of personal philosophy, December 1994)

A point to be emphasized is that when we speak of diversity, our conceptualization is somewhat broader than that often found in the educational literature. We have explicitly articulated a view of diversity, in both multicultural education courses and in special education courses, that includes individuals with disabilities. For example, the initial course dealing with multicultural education includes a unit on the deaf as a cultural and linguistic minority, and students are encouraged in all courses to utilize "difference" rather than "deficit" views of all students. As one of our student stated:

As a future educator, I recognize that the student population I will be teaching is becoming increasingly diverse. My students may have learning and/or physical disabilities. They may also be at-risk, homeless, or gifted. I embrace the challenge of providing the least restrictive environment that stimulates learning for all students. I believe it is important to encourage learners to reach their unique potential, to advocate for themselves, and to learn to appreciate their similarities and differences. (Hawkesworth, future special educator, summative activity in "Exceptionality II," December 1994)

Commitment to Urban Education

Closely related to our concern with diversity, broadly conceived, has been our commitment to urban education. Three of our largest and most active PDCs are in culturally diverse urban districts, characterized by many of the usual challenges and problems that face urban school districts all over the country. It is quite possible, as pointed out by Pugach and Seidl (1995), that university-school partnerships with urban schools have the potential to influence the way children with disabilities are served and to move "...toward a sense of collective advocacy for children and youth" (p. 393). They further stated:

In urban school districts, partnerships for the purpose of both preparing new teachers and supporting the growth of practicing teachers have the added advantage of bringing additional human resources into the schools themselves. For students who have been cast as having mild disabilities, this increase might ease the transition as students move from formal and segregated pullout programs into a classroom-as-community-referenced form of intensive instruction. For students whose disabilities are enduring, the increase might help build the networks necessary to provide the range of services necessary. (Pugach & Seidl, 1995, pp. 392–393)

We believe that our involvement in these PDCs has been beneficial not only to our students and faculty but also to the teachers and students with whom we work. One of the encouraging elements of our collaboration has been the strong support that we, as a teacher education program, have received from teachers and administrators in these three urban school districts. Most important, though, is the effect that working in an urban district has had on our students. As the dean of the School of Education commented in a publication about our program:

I see caring and helping interactions between our university students, most of whom have never been in cities before, and wonderfully diverse students. I listen to our students struggle as their beliefs and understandings change, and as their anger grows because of the callousness and injustice they see surrounding city life. They can never be the same. (Case, 1993, p. 21)

This comment is reinforced by our students with strength and conviction. As one third-year master's intern, working in a large high school in one of the urban PDCs, told us:

Personally, in reflecting on this year as a whole, I have developed greatly as a teacher and a person. Exposure to some of the problems that urban centers face brought to fruition a better understanding of the challenges and roles that a teacher must assume in working with these students. (Broderick, future elementary teacher, internship summary, May 1994)

Another student working in this same high school spoke about his internship experience coordinating a large tutoring program and how this experience has influenced his thinking:

So much of this world tells the student that s/he cannot succeed, or, that s/he is not supposed to succeed. I doubt if I would have had such perseverance if I had to face the onslaught of negative expectations that many of these students face day in and out. Where so many things attempt to suppress the inner-city student (whether these suppressions are conscious or subconscious on the part of the suppressor), this internship has solidified [my understanding of] the need to give each student whatever is necessary in order to succeed. (Keating, future English teacher, internship summary, December 1993)

And in speaking about faculty support and influence on the choice to work in urban schools, one student wrote:

...I never thought I would be successful teaching at the secondary level in an urban setting. On the contrary, I had always imagined that I would teach in a suburban elementary school at the primary level. However, [the faculty] believed in me when I had my share of doubts. As a result, I had a terrific student teaching experience [at Bulkeley High School in Hartford, CT] in which I developed and expanded my teaching ability. The urban setting was both challenging and rewarding. In fact, I am now completing my master's internship placement in the same school.... The remarkable integrity and professionalism she [the faculty member] brings to her teaching, as well as her commitment to both urban education and the simultaneous renewal of schools and the teaching profession, are inspirational. (Pion-Flaherty, future special educator, Presentation of Faculty Teaching Award, April 1994b)

Program Structure and Specific Curriculum Characteristics

The structure of the University of Connecticut's teacher education program is built on several basic and, in our estimation, critical tenets of professional preparation, including:

— a broad liberal arts background and a liberal arts major;
— a series of progressively challenging and diverse clinical experiences (including a mandatory urban experience and work with students with disabilities);
— a common core curriculum for all prospective teachers regardless of intended area of certification;

— a series of integrative seminars as well as pedagogical coursework; and
— an emphasis on analysis and reflection throughout the program.

This model of preparation explicitly rejects the apprenticeship model that has been used most often to "train" teachers (Case, Lanier, & Miskel, 1986). This model of teacher education also relies heavily on the notion of cohorts. As stated earlier, students enter as juniors and spend 3 years in the teacher education program, resulting in both the bachelor's and the master's degrees.

Professional teacher preparation at the University of Connecticut involves five interconnected strands: core, clinic, seminar, subject-specific pedagogy, and a content area major in the liberal arts and sciences, with reflective practice and diversity at the center (illustrated in Figure 3.1). *Core* coursework represents the educational content the faculty has determined collaboratively to be essential for all students regardless of certification area. *Clinic* refers to the carefully designed sequence of increasingly challenging fieldwork experiences in which students are given the opportunity to view, practice, and analyze a wide variety of educational settings in urban, suburban, and rural schools. All students have at least one urban placement, work with students with disabilities at some time

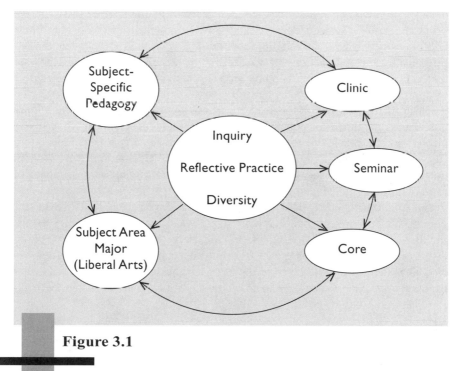

Figure 3.1

Model of Professional Teacher Preparation at University of Connecticut

during their preparation, and have experiences in both elementary and secondary schools. *Seminar* is designed to bridge the gap sometimes found between theoretical content and practice. In seminar students focus on the analysis and reflection of experiences encountered in the field in juxtaposition to coursework. *Subject-specific pedagogy* courses provide students with the necessary specialized preparation for their individual areas of certification. During the master's year, students complete a year-long internship assignment and an inquiry project. The focus of this year is on developing leadership and research skills. Finally, each student has a *solid liberal arts background with an elected subject area major*. As has been noted already, every phase of the program emphasizes analysis and reflection; student diversity is recognized throughout (for further details on the University of Connecticut's program, see Case et al., 1993a; Reagan, Case, & Norlander, 1993; Reagan, Norlander, Case, & Brubacher, 1994).

Coursework: Influence on Collaboration

Coursework provides opportunities for students to be socialized into the process of collaboration. With a strong background in the liberal arts, students bring a breadth and depth of knowledge to share. It is in the content, sequence, and delivery of education courses that students learn from one another and from the program faculty. The sequence of courses gives students time to consider topics and issues over 3 years and to build and expand upon their knowledge and beliefs in a logical and meaningful way. Simultaneous clinic placements each semester provide opportunities for students to observe, apply, and analyze the content of coursework.

During the first year of the teacher preparation program, the content of core coursework is related to subjects and issues that students can observe easily in clinic: how students learn, how students with special needs can be included more fully in schools, the many uses of technology, how teachers measure student performance, current social and community issues, as well as the impact of multiculturalism on educational practice. In the very first semester of the program, students, together, take their first core course on exceptionality. In this course, students are exposed to history and laws, teacher responsibility for the inclusion of students with disabilities, and the characteristics of this diverse population of learners. This course asks these future teachers to confront stereotypes as well as their own attitudes toward people with disabilities. At the conclusion of this course, students are asked to articulate the "most important things learned." A selection of these follows:

- Not all "special children" need to be separated from the mainstream class.
- As a teacher, I need to adjust to individual needs.
- Understanding that all children learn differently is important and should be considered when preparing a lesson, test, or other assignment.
- People are people first; the handicap is secondary.

- Every person has an exceptionality.
- Laws about guidelines, and parent, child, and teacher rights (and responsibilities).
- All kids have different needs.

In the second year, as students move into their area of specialization, pedagogical coursework is taught simultaneously with core courses. The content of coursework, at this point, is connected directly to teaching children in the classroom. During this year of study, students take their second course on exceptionality. This course addresses curriculum and instructional practices and links these to the subject-specific pedagogical coursework being taken simultaneously. During the third year of preparation, coursework focuses on research methods, professional ethics, policy, and leadership. These courses provide the foundation for the student's year-long inquiry project. The opportunity to pursue elective courses in the final year of the program enables students to build additional areas of specialization and to study with graduate faculty having similar research interests. Table 3.1 provides a listing of the core coursework taken by all teacher education students and also illustrates the subject-specific pedagogical coursework taken by students who ultimately will be certified in special education (a similar sequence of subject-specific courses is offered at this time in each of the disciplines). Along with this coursework students have a clinical placement each semester and an integrative seminar (represented in Table 3.1).

Assignments and activities in both core and subject-specific pedagogical courses often include cooperative and group activities in which students learn to depend and rely on others' expertise. Students learn how to teach and learn together through the ways in which coursework is delivered. Instructors represent the broad range of disciplines within the School of Education; as stated earlier, teacher education is a schoolwide responsibility. Even within core classes with groups of more than 100 students, smaller cross-disciplinary groups of students commonly work on case studies or modify lesson or unit plans to accommodate learners with special needs. Many assignments are linked across core and pedagogy courses. For example, secondary students work in groups of four to five to develop interdisciplinary units of study. At the same time, during one of the core courses on exceptionality, these students are joined by a fellow student preparing to be a special educator to integrate instructional modifications into their units. In doing so, they identify strategies that might be used across classrooms and subject areas. The summative activity in this course on exceptionality asks students to articulate their philosophy regarding the education of learners with special education needs, to provide a theoretical rationale for that philosophy and, finally, to suggest how this philosophy might affect their teaching practice. Two students, in their second year of preparation, after completing this second course on "Exceptionality" wrote:

Table 3.1

Course Sequence

Program Year and Semester	Core Coursework	Subject-Specific Pedagogy/Special Education*	Seminar/Clinic
	4 credits		3 credits
Junior/Fall	▪ Learning I ▪ Exceptionality I ▪ Multiculturalism ▪ Technology in Education		*Seminar:* The Student as Learner *Clinic:* One day per week, placement outside certification area
	4 credits		3 credits
Junior/ Spring	▪ Learning II ▪ Assessment of Learning I ▪ Social Context of Schooling ▪ Social and Community Issues		*Seminar:* The Student in the School Context *Clinic:* One day per week, placement outside certification area
	3 credits	9 credits	3 credits
Senior/Fall	▪ Philosophical Tools for Teaching ▪ Assessment of Learning II ▪ Exceptionality II	▪ Teaching Reading and Writing ▪ Diagnosis, Assessment, and Program Planning ▪ Curriculum and Methods for Teaching Students with Disabilities	*Seminar:* Methods of Teaching *Clinic:* One day per week, placement in area of certification

(continued)

The classroom should be a community for all students to be included and feel comfortable. As educators, it is necessary to ensure that those students with special needs are just as much a part of the class as the other students. An environment should be created in which all students are needed and valued! (Papp, future elementary teacher, statement of philosophy, December 1994)

My coursework and clinical experiences over the past year have really opened my eyes to the realities of teaching. No longer are my visions of a classroom full of homogeneous students. The lack of homogeneity in the classroom has not clouded my idealistic views but instead clarified my goals. My vision is now one of diversity including students of all abilities. (Quinn, future history/social studies teacher, philosophy on exceptional learning needs, December 1994)

Table 3.1 continued

Program Year and Semester	Core Coursework	Subject-Specific Pedagogy/Special Education*	Seminar/Clinic
Senior/ Spring		2 credits ■ Instruction of Students with Disabilities	12 credits *Seminar:* Analysis of teaching (3 credits) *Clinic:* Student Teaching (9 credits), 10 weeks, full-time placement in area of certification
Master's/ Fall	3 credits ■ Method of Inquiry for Educational Professionals	3 credits ■ Developmental Foundation of Exceptionality (3 credits of electives within the School of Education or in Liberal Arts and Sciences)	6 credits *Seminar:* Inquiry, Leadership, and the Moral Dimensions of Teaching *Clinic:* Internship, 20 hours, full-year placement
Master's/ Spring	3 credits ■ Professional Ethics for Teachers ■ Teacher Leadership and Organizations ■ Policy Issues for Teachers	(6 credits of electives within the School of Education or in Liberal Arts and Sciences)	6 credits *Seminar:* Inquiry, Leadership, and the Moral Dimensions of Teaching *Clinic:* Internship, 20 hours, full-year placement

* A similar sequence of subject-specific pedagogical coursework is taken at this time in each of the teaching disciplines/areas of state certification.

The importance of being socialized into a profession that embraces the notion of collaboration, to become a teacher who truly cares about all children, cannot be overstated. Students must examine their own beliefs and attitudes—directly confronting issues such as equity, justice, truth, access to knowledge, and integration. Students learn that, frequently, there are no clear-cut or absolute answers—often a disquieting experience. Because these issues, presented in coursework, are clearly evident in their clinic placements, students realize the importance of taking the risks that may be associated in their confronting.

Varied Clinical Experiences: Influence on Collaboration

Students learn about the culture of schools through a series of six clinical experiences in the PDCs. Overall, this planned sequence of experiences is designed to move students from observers and learners about schools to leaders who will assume responsibility for school renewal. Initially students are placed in settings other than those in which they first will gain certification. Placements are planned intentionally to give students experiences across grade levels and areas of specialization. For example, prospective high school teachers spend one day a week for an entire semester in an elementary classroom, and future general education teachers work in special education settings. Similarly, a future special educator might be placed first in a high school English class or on an interdisciplinary middle school team. These first experiences provide an awareness of schools as organizations and stress issues that transcend the boundaries typically imposed by classroom walls. Students often work with school principals, school social workers, speech clinicians, librarians, media specialists, and the like. The importance of these cross-disciplinary experiences is emphasized by two of the program's students preparing to be elementary school teachers:

> Until this semester, a large part of my overall philosophy concerning mainstreaming was based in my coursework. This semester, I have had the unique opportunity to work in a kindergarten with mainstreamed students. These students were real and they gave faces to the theories and speculation I had encountered in class. They are the students who require a little more from me and for whom I will gladly give more of myself. I believe that working with these students has been the most significant element of the development of my philosophy [toward exceptional learners]. (Kittredge, future elementary teacher, final course evaluation in "Exceptionality II," December 1994)

> I think one of the real strengths of this program is how it tests your ability to adapt and the way it throws you into situations that you never anticipated.... The first clinical experience I had was a resource room for high school special education students. There was a boy who had severe cerebral palsy and a girl who had Down syndrome. I was scared to death because at this time I went into the program focusing on elementary education [this student also gained state certification in English and special education]. I wasn't interested in special education or in working with special needs kids, or at least I didn't think I was. It was one of the most incredible experiences of my life...you talk about reflective practice, stepping back and thinking that I was actually doing the things I was doing was just unbelievable. (future elementary, English, and special education teacher, student interview, May 1994)

During the second year of the program, clinic placements enable students to work in their area of specialization with teachers who model effective practice. School and university faculties work together as students assume greater responsibility for teaching in a classroom and move from a one day per week placement into the full-time student teaching experience that takes place during the spring semester. Prior to the student teaching experience, one of the students commented on the importance of these early clinic experiences:

> During our observations [clinical placements] these past three semesters, we have all been exposed to a countless number of experiences that have shaped our growth as professional educators. These have realized and actualized our "book knowledge" and given us an opportunity to interact with the very same students that we will soon be teaching. In my experiences, I have observed many students.... One of these is Rick, a mainstreamed special education student [with developmental disabilities]...who participated fully in a fifth grade general music class.... Though Rick had difficulty manipulating and coordinating the fingerings for some of the pitches [on the recorder], the class encouraged his playing, giving him confidence to participate. With the support of his classmates, the mainstreamed classroom had given Rick more than an inclusive education; it gave him a chance to be accepted and involved. (Pope, future music teacher, portfolio entry, December 1993)

In the third and final master's (internship) year, students integrate all of their previous experiences and expand their role to one of teacher leader and researcher—a role with responsibility for the larger school community. As interns, students become immersed in the culture of the school, spending 20 hours per week in this clinical placement for the entire school year. In providing additional resources to the school, interns serve as program developers and coordinators, consultants, and researchers. Interns also continue to teach and work with children in a variety of ways. Simultaneously, the school provides the intern with the unique opportunity to accept responsibilities related to the broader community of learners.

Internship activities center on a year-long project conceived jointly by members of the school community and the university. Again, interns often step outside of their area of certification, often working on projects in which students with special education needs are the primary recipients. Two such examples are described by interns who eventually will gain certification in mathematics and English respectively:

> As I reflect on this year, I would not trade my internship experience for anything. [This intern coordinated a mathematics/technology lab for students with special education needs.] I am finally computer literate! Furthermore, working with special needs students was a terrific learning experience.... As a result of this year, I feel I gained a better understanding of these students' needs and of them as people. (Panek, future mathematics teacher, internship summary, May 1995)

> Now that the program is almost over [an internship working on process writing in a writing/technology lab with students with special education needs], I am reflecting on my students' progress throughout the program, with both computers and writing. As a facilitator of the computer and writing development, I have learned many things that I can incorporate within my teaching in the future. First of all, I have realized the extreme importance of computer technology in motivating students to

write. I also realize the importance of using process writing approaches to teach writing to all students. As a future English teacher, I plan on empowering my students to develop their unique voice, both verbally and in writing.... An effective teacher should be willing and able to provide instruction which fosters the needs of all students in the classroom. I feel that I am more aware and prepared to teach students with special needs in the regular classroom. (Vezena, future English teacher, internship summary, May 1995)

Seminars: Influence on Collaboration

Seminars provide a forum for debate and discussion throughout the teacher preparation program and are designed such that students achieve a level of scholarship beyond the usual. The focus and activities of seminars are centered around the content of coursework and the simultaneous experiences in each of the clinical placements. As students progress through the program, discussions typically move from observations based solely on personal experience to conversations informed by practice and the professional literature. Authority and responsibility in the seminars are shared among the participants.

The configuration and composition of seminars afford students the opportunity to know many of their peers and faculty in more personal ways. Students meet in small groups of 10–15, often onsite with faculty from the university and the PDCs. In five of the six seminars, seminar cohorts are composed of interdisciplinary groups from a particular PDC. By grouping students by PDC, the content of coursework can be considered in the context of the specific PDC. In the fall of the second year, when students focus on specialized pedagogical coursework, seminar groups are organized according to specializations (elementary, secondary, special, music, and physical education). Seminar groups change each semester, with the exception of the master's year, when students remain in their PDC, and consequently their seminar group, for the entire year. Therefore, in 3 years, as members of five different seminar groups, students may get to know as many as 75 of their peers through quite intense, professional conversations about schools and teaching, teachers and children, families and community, and the like. Students often frame debates, suggest background reading, and then lead discussions. Sessions might focus on teacher expectations versus diverse student populations, homelessness and poverty versus access to knowledge, integration versus inclusion of students with disabilities, or excellence versus equity.

Importance of Cohorts

As stated earlier, the teacher preparation program at the University of Connecticut is committed to admitting prospective educators in cohort groups. The make-up of each entering cohort spans the teaching disciplines and grade levels. A typical junior group has 45 students in elementary education, 25 in special education, 15 in each of the secondary subject areas (English, math, science, and social studies), 10 in music education, and a small number in physical education. Students study together in large and small interdisciplinary and disciplinary groups at the university and in the partner schools.

Every semester students are in small interdisciplinary seminar groups of 10–15 students and, at the same time, in a cohort in a partnership school made up of students from all three years of the program. Although these students are working toward state certification in a specific area, they complete much of their coursework together, across disciplines, during their 3 years in the School of Education. They are preparing to be educational professionals, not simply first-grade teachers, special education teachers, or secondary math teachers.

The power of these cohorts should not be understated. They are proving to be essential in professional preparation and, more specifically, they provide ongoing opportunities for students to collaborate across the disciplines. In the words of the students themselves, we find evidence of the importance of working and learning in cohorts, how being socialized together is making a significant difference in their learning. In interviews with these students and in their writing (journals, internship summaries, and the like), they consistently talk about the need for a community of educators, the importance of working in teams, how collaboration affects their ability to inquire and be reflective, how cohorts have been instrumental in developing "intellectual communities," and, most important, how these teams of educators have been able to provide all children, including those with disabilities, with a better education (see Campbell et al., 1995; Norlander, Reagan, & Case, 1994). As examples, two students working in the same urban high school during their internship (master's) year comment on the importance of cohorts or teams working together:

> As part of the Transition Team [one of the internship assignments], I developed my interpersonal and collaborative skills in working with fellow colleagues [two of which would be elementary teachers and one a special educator]. This was an important experience because it gave me the position of a shared decision maker and a team collaborator. These are invaluable social and interpersonal skills for any future teacher. (Future elementary teacher, student interview, May 1994)

> I profited greatly from my work with other university interns [placed in the same urban high school]. We impressed ourselves with what we were able to do together, much of what would not have been possible had we been working alone. I have a good sense, through this experience, of the power of collaboration. I know that what people can do when they work together far outweighs what happens when people go it alone. (Abrams, future elementary, English, and special educator, internship summary, May 1994)

This same intern, one of 10 master's students working collaboratively at Bulkeley High School in Hartford, CT (half future special education, half future general education teachers), went on to say:

Together the team supported each other, filling in for each other, advising each other, all in the effort of improving the educational situation for as many students as we humanly could. The students were the priority and the focus of all of our efforts. It is a great source of pride for me to have been part of a team that was so dedicated, in a highly moral sense, to the educational welfare of dozens of children. (Abrams, future elementary, English, and special educator, internship summary, May 1994)

Final Analysis

From its initial implementation, the new teacher education program at the University of Connecticut has been the focus of a variety of ongoing evaluation efforts. These efforts included both traditional kinds of program evaluation activities and more naturalistic activities designed to provide a more indepth understanding of the perceptions of program participants (see Reagan, Case, Case, & Freiberg, 1993). Regularly, input is sought from students in the program, teachers and administrators in the PDCs, and faculty members. Surveys, interviews, focus groups, observations, focused discussions, and fieldnotes are among the methods that have been employed consistently. Although some of the evaluations were intended primarily to meet various accreditation requirements, most have been conducted with a central concern for programmatic review to assist the faculty in improving the program. Further, the program has been studied, utilizing extensive interview and survey data, by faculty in the School of Education and by graduate students conducting master's and doctoral-level research studies. The results of these studies and evaluation activities are widely disseminated and discussed, and have been used on numerous occasions to change or modify elements of the program that have worked less effectively than we would have wished.

From these evaluation activities and our reflections on and analysis of them, several areas of change and concern have been identified. We certainly have learned some important lessons about the unification of teacher education programs. In all, collaboration across teaching disciplines and grade levels, among general and special educators and between the School of Education and our partner schools, seems to be meeting with success on many fronts.

Changes in the Culture of the Faculty

The reform and renewal of the teacher education program has had an impact not only on the students in the program, the curriculum, and the schools in which we are working but also on the culture of the faculty in the School of Education. Prior to the reforms begun 8 years ago, the faculty culture in the school was similar to that found in most research universities. Teacher education was not generally seen as the central mission of the school, faculty members tended to have few serious cross-disciplinary relationships and professional interactions, and most faculty members spent relatively little time in the public schools. They were tied to specific teacher education programs that typically entailed little interaction across disciplines in curriculum planning, student supervision, or research activities. These characteristics were not, of course, in any way unique to the University of Connecticut. They are precisely those identified by John Goodlad in *Teachers for Our Nation's Schools* (1990b) and elsewhere, and they have been among the concerns that the Holmes Group (1986, 1990, 1995) has been addressing as well. The problems faced in undertaking the renewal of teacher education at the University of Connecticut, in short, were not unusual. Quite the contrary.

One direct result of program unification is the large number of faculty members now working together across departmental lines. This willingness to cross historically sacred departmental boundaries has been manifested in team-taught courses, faculty members teaching courses in departments other than their own, collaborative work on inservice activities, and a growing body of co-authored research and publications produced by faculty members who in the past might not have worked together. An ongoing series of meetings involving core, seminar, and clinic instructors also helped to maintain this cross-disciplinary approach to the program, as has the faculty's commitment to implementing reflective practice in our own teaching. The result is that for many of the faculty, and especially younger faculty, departmental affiliation is of relatively minor significance. One direct result has been the greater awareness and understanding of each others' responsibility toward students with disabilities in school settings.

Faculty culture has changed in several other ways as well. Although some faculty members in the School of Education have primary (and, in some cases, sole) responsibilities in graduate education and research, this is increasingly rare. The overwhelming majority of the faculty members in the School of Education are involved, often in multiple ways, in the teacher education program. Further, the teacher education program is becoming a major force and focus of the School of Education. Finally, faculty members are involved increasingly in the public schools in a variety of roles. Many faculty members (as well as the dean) spend at least one full day a week in partnership schools. As a result of these changes, what it means to be a faculty member of the School of Education at the University of Connecticut is very different from what faculty members at many institutions would expect; the education of teachers and other school professionals has become a schoolwide responsibility. Yet, a small number of faculty members continue to view their roles as that of a graduate or research faculty member alone. Even in these instances, the overarching focus of the School of Education on teaching and learning, with a special and pervasive commitment to public schools, continues to influence faculty thinking quite broadly.

A few faculty members in special education also have continued to advocate for specialized programs of study for special education teachers. This constituency has consistently viewed the changes as too faculty-intensive, too school-based, and not tied sufficiently to their areas of specialization. They go further in believing that the broader conceptualization of the education of special educators is detrimental to the education of special education students. This last concern stems from the fact that the program of study for special educators is no longer separate and "specialized"—that we have integrated the special and general teacher education programs. This split in philosophy in essence has created two special education faculties. These concerns, though not taken lightly, have not hindered the overall progress of the unified teacher education program.

Changes in the Practice of Inclusion

Inclusion is becoming a matter of urgency in the public schools and is very much a topic of discussion and debate locally and nationally. This urgency has been reflected back to the university, both by students and by classroom teachers working with university faculty. It has led to a greater focus on inclusion and inclusive education in university coursework, as a recurring topic in seminars, and as an ongoing emphasis of many jointly planned and conducted inservice sessions in the partnership schools. One of the urban high schools now has a number of co-taught classes and several ninth grade cross-disciplinary clusters that include a special educator. Many of the internship projects (upward of 115 each semester) have focused on the integration of and services for students with special education needs in mainstream settings.

One of the urban districts (PDCs) has adopted a schoolwide model of "inclusive" educational practices. In this case, the partnership with the university has been beneficial both to the partnership schools implementing this practice and to preparing teachers from the university placed in these clinic settings. As stated earlier, the faculty working in these PDCs come from all departments in the School of Education, including faculty from special education, who have been available, in a wide variety of ways, to these schools.

Concerns

Of course, all is not perfect. A number of concerns, some more systemic than others, persist. Some of these concerns and problems come from outside the university itself, others from within our own tent.

Anti-teacher education political dynamics at both the state and the national level must be contended with forcefully and directly. For example, when we began our own program redesign, the State Department of Education also was reconstructing the way teachers were licensed. Their focus was on "testing," and a competency-based model was instituted. Teacher behaviors such as "closure" and "preinstructional set," as well as consequent student outcomes such as "time-on-task" were the focus of their assessments. As our program was concentrating on the themes of leadership, reflective practice, inquiry, and diversity, we found ourselves at odds with the State Department. In addition, as we moved to a 5-year integrated bachelor's/master's degree program, instituted the policy of a subject-area major in the liberal arts, and required numerous clinical experiences (including a mandatory urban placement and experiences with exceptional learners), our fellow education institutions, public and private, were, to say the least, threatened, and they continue to prepare teachers in fairly traditional 4-year programs. Further, the state continues its practice of very separate certifications for each discipline and grade level(s) with special education being a noncategorical K–12 certificate. On the other hand, the State Department has moved to requiring a subject-area major of all prospective teachers, including special educators, and has given our program complete state approval. It seems as though in coming to some common understandings, we have reached a truce, a least momentarily.

Concerns within the partner schools at first centered on mutual trust and the inability to envision large numbers of our faculty and students working collaboratively in their schools. The initial hesitation was quite realistic and expected. In the past, their experience had been of a university coming in for a brief time to conduct research or to place student teachers in their school with little supervision or interaction with the regular university faculty. If involvement was of a more sustained nature, it typically was grant-funded and when the grant monies dried up, the involvement ceased. Further, placing each of our students at all grade levels and with a wide variety of students and types of classes caused some concern in the beginning. For example, someone who eventually would be certified in special education might be placed first with a high school biology teacher. Initially, many of the teachers working with our students did not fully understand the importance of this practice. This misunderstanding now has been replaced for the most part, with enthusiasm. To some extent, the above concerns recur as teachers or school administrators change; yet, largely, we have overcome many of these problems.

Last, institutionalization of the redesigned teacher preparation program is of prime concern. As the state and university face serious budget cuts, resources, scarce to begin with, have become an even greater concern. In addition, the changing leadership at the university and within school districts force us to "reeducate" new leadership regularly. Of course, as leadership changes, reallocation of resources, or a change in overall commitment or philosophy is always possible. And, finally, some among our own ranks, faculty, administrators, and teachers remain "untransformed." Some continue to place less value on teacher education than on traditional research, narrowly focused.

The Lessons Learned in Unifying Teacher Education Programs

What are the primary lessons we have learned during the past 8 years? First, reflective practice and inquiry must be pervasive in all that we do. Everyone must be involved in doing this. As a result, we have been able to question our own process of renewal, not simply evaluate our students or isolated parts of the teacher education program.

We also have found that issues of diversity must be confronted in every aspect of the program. This confrontation takes place in coursework, in clinical settings, in seminars, and on very personal levels. Changing attitudes is not easy and often is quite unsettling. Yet, through the wide variety of clinical work, students are able to view, and therefore better understand, the many issues related to the multicultural make-up of our schools, gender equity, integration of students with disabilities, and so forth. Here lies yet another example of the need for strong professional partnerships with schools. Professional development centers indeed are a cornerstone of the teacher preparation program. Reflecting on the importance of PDCs, we believe the entire program would be inconsequential without these strong professional relationships. Certainly, without these partnerships, the renewal we are seeking would be, at best, one-sided.

Throughout, socialization into the teaching profession rests on cohorts, groups of students and faculty who learn and mature together as professional educators. The interdisciplinary nature of these groups, as well as the cross-departmental work of the faculty in curricular areas, make these cohort groups quite powerful. By working in these groups, students are gaining the inquiry, collaborative, and leadership skills necessary to shape the future of schooling.

The commitment of faculty is essential, and visible leadership is critical. When the deans and department chairs spend considerable time in the designing of the program, in the partner schools, and in teaching coursework at all levels of the program, the faculty seems to be much more committed to do the same. Having strong, committed, and involved leadership cannot be stressed strongly enough. And, in the final analysis, change of this sort takes considerable time and nurturance. First and foremost, we must care about children, who they are as individuals and how each of them learns (Noddings, 1984, 1992). In caring about all children, we then are able to care about our schools and our profession. If we work and learn from one another—we can, as Seymour Sarason (1993) suggested, raise our "expectations" for change:

> Of course, some will be allergic to the idea [of change] and will say no thank you. But there will be others who will be grateful for the opportunity to change their lives, those of their students, and those of school children. (Sarason, 1993, p. 125)

The unification of teacher education programs will take time and the human resources from many fronts, but it appears possible. Teachers who are prepared together, in integrated programs, where the primary focus is on reflection and diversity, possibly could be the force required to change schooling as we know it.

> ...the program has made us want more, and you need a population of educators who are more powerfully trained and who are really interested in changing the system.... [The program] mobilizes a great number of people, together, who are going to be very educated and want to change the system. (Future English teacher, student interview, May 1995)

Given that this chapter opened with the words of a future educator, we think it appropriate to close in the same manner. It is our belief that these two future educators summarize the power of integrated teacher preparation.

> The question, whom is responsible for the education of their students [with exceptionality], is not one easily answered. I do not believe you can designate any one person as responsible for the education of any student, exceptional learner or not. Teachers, peers, parents, the community, everyone is responsible for the education of our children and it takes an effort from all to make it successful.... I would like to think that my philosophy, equal and fair treatment for all students and [respectful of] their individual needs, would be the backbone of my teaching. Diversity is what makes this world such an exciting and interesting place and thus I hope my philosophy will develop into a reality. I believe as a society we look too much at what people cannot do. If we can get beyond what people can't do and change our focus toward individuals' strengths, we can eliminate many of the misconceptions and stereotypes [people have] of exceptional students. Then we can begin to treat diversity in the manner that it should be, positively. (Quinn, future history/social studies teacher, philosophy of exceptional learning needs, December 1994)

> We are not, after all, solitary teachers but members of a community of learning and ideas; through the thoughts of others I may find solutions for my own needs. (Pearce, future history/social studies teacher, assignment in "Exceptionality II," December 1994)

References

Abrams, R. (1994). Internship summary. Unpublished student work, University of Connecticut, Storrs.

Broderick, D. (1994). Internship summary. Unpublished student work, University of Connecticut, Storrs.

Brubacher, J. W., Case, C. W., & Reagan, T. G. (1994). *Becoming a reflective educator: How to build a culture of inquiry in the schools.* Thousand Oaks, CA: Corwin Press.

Campbell, P., Norlander, K. A., Reagan, T. G., Case, C. W., DeFranco, T., & Brubacher, J. W. (1995). Ensuring identification with an "other-oriented" culture of teaching: Socialization into a caring profession. *Record in Educational Leadership, 15*(2), 72–78.

Case, C. W. (1993). The view from here: Correspondents from NNER sites reflect on the situation as they see it. *Center Correspondent, 5,* 4–22.

Case, C. W., Lanier, J. E., & Miskel, C. G. (1986). The Holmes Group report: Impetus for gaining professional status for teachers. *Journal of Teacher Education, 37*(4), 36–43.

Case, C. W., Norlander, K. A., & Reagan, T. G. (1993a). Cultural transformation in an urban professional development center: Policy implications for school-university collaboration. *Educational Policy, 7*(1), 40–60.

Case, C. W., Norlander, K. A., & Reagan, T. G. (1993b). Reflections on reflection—Looking back over six years: The design of the University of Connecticut's teacher preparation program. *Center Correspondent, 5*(2–3), 25–31.

Clift, R. T., Houston, W. R., & Pugach, M. C. (1990). *Encouraging reflective practice in education: An analysis of issues and programs.* New York: Teachers College Press.

Cochran-Smith, M., & Lytle, S. (1993). *Inside-outside: Teacher research and knowledge.* New York: Teachers College Press.

Darling-Hammond, L. (1994). Developing professional development schools: Early lesson, challenge, and promise. In L. Darling-Hammond (Ed.), *Professional development schools: Schools for developing a profession* (pp. 1–27). New York: Teachers College Press.

Dewey, J. (1910/1991). *How we think.* Amherst, NY: Prometheus Books.

Fullan, M. (1993). *Change forces: Probing the depths of educational reform.* Bristol, PA: Falmer Press.

Garrish, K. (1993). Portfolio entry. Unpublished student work, University of Connecticut, Storrs.

Gideonse, H. D. (1990). Organizing schools to encourage teacher inquiry. In E. F. Elmore & Associates (Eds.), *Restructuring schools: The next generation of educational reform* (pp. 97–124). San Francisco: Jossey-Bass Publishers.

Goodlad, J. I. (1990a). Studying the education of educators: From conceptions to findings. *Phi Delta Kappan, 71*(9), 698–701.

Goodlad, J. I. (1990b). *Teachers for our nation's schools.* San Francisco: Jossey-Bass Publishers.

Goodlad, J. I. (1994). *Educational renewal: Better teachers, better schools.* San Francisco: Jossey-Bass Publishers.

Hawkesworth, K. (1994). Summative Activity in "Exceptionality II." Unpublished student work, University of Connecticut, Storrs.

Holmes Group. (1986). *Tomorrow's teachers.* East Lansing, MI: Author.

Holmes Group. (1990). *Tomorrow's schools.* East Lansing, MI: Author.

Holmes Group. (1995). *Tomorrow's schools of education.* East Lansing, MI: Author.

Keating, B. (1993). Internship summary. Unpublished student work, University of Connecticut, Storrs.

Kittredge, J. (1994). Final course evaluation: Exceptionality II. Unpublished student work, University of Connecticut, Storrs.

Levine, M. (1992). A conceptual framework for professional practice schools. In M. Levine (Ed.), *Professional practice schools: Linking teacher education and school reform* (pp. 8–24). New York: Teachers College Press.

Lytle, S., & Cochran-Smith, M. (1992). Teacher research as a way of knowing. *Harvard Educational Review, 62*(4), 447–474.

Noddings, N. (1984). *Caring: A feminine approach to ethics & moral education.* Berkeley: University of California Press.

Noddings, N. (1992). *The challenge to care in schools: An alternative approach to education.* New York: Teachers College Press.

Norlander, K. A., Reagan, T. G., & Case, C. W. (1994). *Creating "centers of inquiry": Fostering reflective practice and inquiry in the teaching profession.* Monograph, School of Education, University of Connecticut, Storrs.

O'Toole, K. (1994). Statement of personal philosophy. Unpublished student work, University of Connecticut, Storrs.

Panek, C. (1995). Internship summary. Unpublished student work, University of Connecticut, Storrs.

Papp, M. (1994). Statement of philosophy. Unpublished student work, University of Connecticut, Storrs.

Pearce, D. (1994). Assignment in "Exceptionality II." Unpublished student work, University of Connecticut, Storrs.

Pion-Flaherty, P. (1994a). Internship summary. Unpublished student work, University of Connecticut, Storrs.

Pion-Flaherty, P. (1994b). Presentation of faculty teaching award. Unpublished speech, University of Connecticut, Storrs.

Pope, J. (1993). Portfolio entry. Unpublished student work, University of Connecticut, Storrs.

Pugach, M. C., & Seidl, B. L. (1995). From exclusion to inclusion in urban schools: A new case for teacher education reform. *Education and Urban Society, 27*(4), 379–395.

Quinn, J. (1994). Philosophy of exceptional learning needs. Unpublished student work, University of Connecticut, Storrs.

Reagan, T. G. (1993). Educating the "reflective practitioner": The contribution of philosophy of education. *Journal of Research and Development in Education, 26*(4), 189–196.

Reagan, T. G., Case, K. I., Case, C. W., & Freiberg, J. (1993). Reflecting on "reflective practice": Implications for teacher evaluation. *Journal of Personnel Evaluation in Education, 6*(3), 263–277.

Reagan, T. G., Case, C. W., & Norlander, K. A. (1993). Toward reflective teacher education: The University of Connecticut experience. *International Journal of Educational Reform, 2*(4), 399–406.

Reagan, T. G., Norlander, K. A., Case, C. W., & Brubacher, J. W. (1994). Teachers for Connecticut's schools: Postulates, problems and potential at the University of Connecticut. *Record in Educational Leadership, 14*(2), 27–31.

Sarason, S. B. (1993). *Letters to a serious education president.* Newbury Park, CA: Corwin Press.

Schon, D. A. (1987). *Educating the reflective practitioner.* San Francisco: Jossey-Bass Publishers.

Sirotnik, K. A. (1988). The meaning and conduct of inquiry in school-university partnerships. In K. A. Sirotnik & J. I. Goodlad (Eds.), *School-university partnerships in action: Concepts, cases, and concerns.* New York: Teachers College Press.

Smyth, J. (1989). Developing and sustaining critical reflection in teacher education. *Journal of Teacher Education, 40*(2), 2–9.

Vannie, D. (1992). Letter of support. Support letter for personnel preparation grant, University of Connecticut, Storrs.

Vezena, A. (1995). Internship summary. Unpublished student work, University of Connecticut, Storrs.

A Merged Elementary/ Special Education Program in a 4-Year Liberal Arts College: Providence College

Lynne Ryan, Jane Callahan, Junean Krajewski, and Thomas Flaherty

When I first came to Providence College, I didn't really want special education. I just wanted to be an elementary teacher. But you wouldn't let me do that. Now I am so glad I have both. I talk to students from other colleges and they don't understand how to work with children with special needs or how to use approaches like assessment or modifying methods the way I do. I still want to teach in an elementary classroom, but now I know I am so much better prepared. (Comment from a senior during exit interview after student teaching)

Providence College's merged elementary/special education program was approved by the college's Faculty Senate in March 1986, slightly more than 10 years after passage of Public Law 94–142, the Education for All Handicapped Children Act. The first class of dual-certified students graduated in May of 1989. As the above student's comment suggests, the program originally was developed to prepare teachers who could teach all children in an elementary classroom. This chapter explores the development, evolution, and future direction of this program.

Institutional Context

Providence College (PC) is a coeducational, 4-year, undergraduate college of the liberal arts and sciences serving approximately 3,600 students. It originally was entrusted to the Dominican Order of Preachers in the early 1900s to provide an equal educational advantage to Catholics, including the sons of immigrants, in the Diocese of Providence. Although the college has evolved and expanded considerably over the more than 75 years of its existence, it has remained dedicated to its mission of the "intellectual development of its students through the disciplines of the sciences and humanities, equipping them to become productive and responsible citizens of a democratic society." It also has remained dedicated to providing service to the community, as exemplified most recently in its establishment of the Feinstein Center for Public and Community Service. The administration views the education of teachers as giving further witness to its mission of service and has provided strong support to the teacher preparation program.

A strong liberal arts foundation provides prospective teachers at Providence College with a basic background of knowledge as well as the literacy and critical thinking abilities identified as essential elements in the education of educators (Goodlad, 1990). The cornerstone of PC's liberal arts tradition is a program called the Development of Western Civilization (DWC). This unique, nationally recognized program, which uses a thematic, interdisciplinary approach, is required for all freshmen and sophomores. It is taught 5 days a week by four faculty members and addresses the disciplines of English, history, fine arts, philosophy, and theology.

The DWC program addresses non-Western civilizations through their relationships to Western civilization. The adequacy and appropriateness of this approach have fostered some debate and discussion on campus, which is likely to intensify as the college embarks on the first substantial review of its curriculum since the inception of the DWC program 25 years ago. In addition, students in the merged elementary/special education program have 18–21 hours of electives, which affords them the opportunity to have a minor concentration.

Development of the Merged Program

Originally the college was an all-male institution and offered its first education program in secondary education. When the college became coeducational in the 1970s, it added a special education major, preschool–12, which coincided with passage of PL 94–142. From its inception the special education program was part of one, singular Education Department with courses taught by Education Department faculty.

In the 1980s the state required a general education teaching certificate as a prerequisite for obtaining a special education certificate. The special education license no longer would be K–12, but, instead, would be aligned with the general education level (elementary or secondary). Because Providence College had only the secondary education program, it was decided to direct the program to secondary special education. Many students who were in the special education program, however, were dissatisfied, as they were more interested in teaching at the elementary level.

At that time, coincidentally, the special education program had a complete turnover. The two new faculty members both had begun their teaching careers as general education teachers, both had studied special education at the graduate level, and both had experienced firsthand the pedagogical demands placed on classroom teachers through implementation of state and federal special education laws advocating the education of students with disabilities in the least restrictive environment. They appreciated the value of the curriculum focus in their general education coursework and the personalized instruction focus provided by their special education coursework. They also had found the teaching strategies and content provided in their special education courses to be invaluable in their general education positions. In addition, one of the faculty members had obtained her certification in general education at the primary level in Great Britain in the early 1970s and subsequently maintained a commitment to a structured, child-centered curriculum for all students.

A significant factor throughout the restructuring of the department was the philosophical commitment on the part of all faculty, special and general education alike, to the education of all children in the least restrictive environment as well as the development of professionals competent to work in inclusive settings. Although the state required a mainstreaming course at both the preservice and the inservice levels, periodic needs assessments conducted by the state's Comprehensive System of Personnel Development Advisory Board repeatedly identified the continued need to prepare general educators who could teach children with special needs.

A planning team, composed of the department chair and another faculty member, began developing a proposal for a program preparing teachers at the elementary level. Conceptually, the planning team wanted a program that would educate prospective elementary teachers in the competencies needed to teach all children, including those with special needs, in the general education classroom, but that would not offer two separate tracks—one elementary, the other special education. The program would provide the students with a common knowledge base that would enable them, upon graduation, to assume positions as either elementary or elementary special education teachers of students with mild/

moderate disabilities. About this time, a number of researchers were advocating the merging of special and general education at various levels (Pugach & Lilly, 1984; Reynolds & Wang, 1983; Skrtic, 1991; Stainback & Stainback, 1984). Using the concept of a merger as the framework in the fall of 1985, the proposal for the elementary/special education program was presented to the members of the Education Department, who endorsed it unanimously.

The first major hurdle to the program's acceptance was the Academic Affairs Committee of the Faculty Senate, which had to approve the program prior to approval by the Senate. In a liberal arts institution, tension often exists between faculty in the liberal arts and sciences programs and faculty in professional programs, particularly professional programs in education (Soder, 1994). Members of the Academic Affairs Committee supported the concept of a program designed to prepare teachers to educate all children. They were familiar with national reports such as *A Nation at Risk* (National Commission on Excellence in Education, 1983) criticizing the state of American education, and teacher preparation in particular. Heralding the recommendation for increased preparation in academic areas at the expense of pedagogical preparation, the committee stipulated that coursework for the program be restricted to a minimum essential core of courses required by the state accrediting agency.

The challenge for the Education Department's planning team was to integrate the liberal arts program with identified components of a professional education program within a 4-year curriculum. Discussions on what is essential for a beginning teacher to know and be able to do and where and how best to include it within a minimum number of courses were lively, exhausting, and painful. Initially the discussions were guided by the program's mission statement, state accreditation standards, the research literature, faculty experiences, and feedback from students within the department and from teachers and administrators in partner schools. The issues of program outcomes and, more recently, assessment continue to be among the program's greatest challenges and require ongoing communication, debate, monitoring, review and revision. As an example, in the next few years discussions will ensue on how to incorporate performance standards adapted from the Interstate New Teacher Assessment and Support Consortium (INTASC).[1]

The program was approved in the spring of 1986. In the fall of that same year, Madeline Will's paper, *Educating Children with Learning Problems: A Shared Responsibility*, was published, further supporting the concept of the program. The program was reviewed by the state licensing agency in the spring of 1988. The elementary-school members of the visiting team expressed concern that the program was emphasizing special education at the expense of elementary education, particularly because a number of courses that traditionally were considered elementary school methods courses had been combined. Nevertheless, after reviewing syllabi, visiting classes and field sites and receiving positive reports from faculty, alumni, students, cooperating/practicum teachers and school administrators, the team awarded the program a full 5-year approval, which was unusual for a new program.

Theory and Knowledge Base of the Merged Program

The program's unifying theme is the preparation of teachers to teach all children. As the faculty explored the theoretical and knowledge base needed to address this theme, they identified four basic areas: (a) a philosophy of diversity, (b) a culture of collaboration, (c) the development of a teacher as a professional, and (d) a reliance on effective teaching practices (Peters et al., 1989). These features and the ways they are infused within the program will be addressed below.

Diversity

The structure of the merged program at Providence College was developed to provide a common knowledge base to educate professionals who could identify and respond to the unique needs of all children within the least restrictive environment and who believe this is the shared role and responsibility of each and every teacher in the school community. Within current school organizations, teachers are required to assume certain roles—the roles of special education or general education teacher. We hope that a unified system of professional development, such as the merged program, will enable teachers to appreciate the commonality of their knowledge and skill base. The background needed by teachers to address excellence and equity in today's heterogeneous classrooms is needed by all teachers.

As the program was developed and implemented, however, the faculty soon realized that the commitment to diversity by accommodating individual differences did not address adequately the issues of cultural, racial, and linguistic diversity. Shapiro, Sewell, and DuCette (1995) have referred to diversity constructs of culture, race, and gender as differences of kind rather than differences of degree represented by the continuum in areas such as cognitive development. Both contribute to the learner's diversity and uniqueness, and both must be addressed in a teacher preparation program committed to a philosophy of diversity.

The initial response to better address diversity of kind was to require that at least two of the students' six field experiences would be placements in urban schools with a majority of culturally and linguistically diverse youngsters. Because these practicums were linked to methods classes or student teaching seminars, the preservice students' experiences in these multicultural settings provided a contextual basis for discussions of effective teaching strategies for diversity including culturally and linguistically diverse youngsters, as well as the nature of schools, children, and learning (Milk, Mercado, & Sapiens, 1992). Working with the faculty from these multicultural field sites and as part of a tricollege collaborative (Landurand, 1995), the program faculty members now are studying competencies for teaching youngsters who are culturally and linguistically diverse and reviewing the program's curriculum to ensure that these competencies have been infused into coursework (Burstein, Cabello, & Hamann, 1993; Howey, Arends, Galluzzo, Yarger, & Zimpher, 1994).

Collaboration

Sharing the responsibility for all children within the school organization implies that faculty and staff will support each other in finding solutions to problems encountered. Another essential feature in the preparation of teachers who can teach all children is the recognition that each teacher needs support to meet the needs of all children. One important vehicle for providing support is a culture of collaboration (Idol & West, 1991; Pugach & Lilly, 1984). The collaborative model encourages teachers with diverse expertise to generate creative solutions to mutually defined problems (Bauwens, Hourcade, & Friend, 1989).

In addition to the study of collaboration through coursework, the merged program fosters the development of preservice teachers' knowledge, skill, and appreciation of collaboration through a variety of activities.

1. Collaborative planning is modeled in core curriculum courses such as DWC and in education courses such as classroom management, which is team-taught by faculty from education and psychology.
2. Students have four practicums prior to student teaching. In three of the practicums, students work in groups of two to four, collaboratively planning and implementing lessons for these classrooms. Ideally these co-taught lessons will help preservice teachers develop the collegial, experimental environment identified by Little (1982) and deemed so essential to the school reform movement.
3. Most of the field experiences are in settings in which collaborative teaching between the support teachers—for example, special, Chapter 1, English as a Second Language (ESL)—and general education teachers is occurring to some extent.
4. Collaboration can be viewed as the application of cooperative learning to adult planning groups (Thousand & Villa, 1988). By using cooperative learning groups in the college classroom, faculty not only are "practicing what they preach" in modeling an effective teaching strategy (Watson, 1995) but also are able to monitor the development of essential social skills such as communication, cooperation, team planning, problem solving, and group decision making.

The Teacher as a Professional

Darling-Hammond (1994) argued that if we are to transform teaching and learning in our nation's schools, we have to abandon the model of the teacher as a technician and adopt the model of the teacher as a professional. The Providence program strives to develop the teacher as a professional by requiring preservice students to reflect continually on the needs of the learner and to make decisions on appropriate responses to those needs. For example, in each field experience, preservice teachers are required to keep a reflective log on what they have learned about teaching, learning, children, and schools. Through these logs, their field experiences, and case studies, students have opportunities to apply their professional and subject matter knowledge and skills base individually or collaboratively to assess needs, develop appropriate creative, instructional units and lessons based on needs, evaluate their effectiveness, adjust instruction as required, and, when necessary, research alternative instructional approaches.

Although the program provides preservice teachers with a repertoire of strategies, children come to school with such a diversity of learning needs, interests, and abilities that this repertoire alone will be necessary, but not sufficient, to address the range of individual differences these prospective teachers will encounter. In addition, teachers must be able to decide when to implement a certain strategy. No recipe is available to use in meeting the learner's complex needs. Teachers as professionals must be educated as reflective practitioners, problem solvers, and decision makers if they are to assess each learner's needs through the child's responsiveness to instruction and to develop alternative approaches (Darling-Hammond, 1992; Milk, Mercado, & Sapiens, 1992; Pugach & Lilly, 1984; Skrtic, in Thousand, 1990).

Effective Teaching Practices

The body of research on effective instruction is not specific to "regular" or "special" children but, as Bickel and Bickel (1986) noted, has relevancy for all children. Research-based teaching methods in areas such as direct instruction (Gersten, Woodward, & Darch, 1986; Rosenshine, 1986), classroom management (Brophy, 1983), cooperative learning (Johnson, Johnson, Holubec, & Roy, 1984; Slavin, 1983), and metacognition (Palinscar, 1986) are infused within the various courses in the program to provide the preservice teacher with a repertoire of strategies from which to choose when teaching all children.

Key Program Components

The key features of the program are merged competencies and developmental progression of courses, sequential field experiences, professional development partnerships, service learning pedagogy, merged faculty, and dual certification. Next we will discuss the components that have evolved and are evolving as important characteristics of Providence College's merged program.

Merged Competencies and Developmental Progression of Courses

Two critical components of the merged program are the infusion of competencies and the developmental progression of the courses. As noted earlier, faculty members in the program identified the professional knowledge and skills they believe all teachers need to know and be able to do to teach all children in the least restrictive environment. They did not develop a separate knowledge base for elementary courses and another list for special education courses. Once these were identified, the faculty determined in which courses the knowledge and skills would be introduced, reviewed, and applied. Thus, competencies were infused based on a developmental progression through the 4 years of the program and culminating in student teaching.

For example, accommodations are introduced and applied as an integral part of each methods course, such as reading or math/science, not as separate topics in a mainstreaming or a special education course. Then, in the assessment and curriculum course, modifications from the methods courses are reviewed and applied in designing holistic, individualized programs for children. Knowledge and skills related to parental involvement and communication with home and community are addressed initially through the resource/home school course. Although this course could be thought of as a special education course, the focus in this program is on communication among home, school, and community about *all* children. Even though formal assessment is covered in the assessment course, informal and authentic assessment models and strategies are infused into all methods courses, and integration of the two types of assessment occurs in the assessment and curriculum courses. In this way, students are provided with a view of assessment as an essential component of all instruction rather than a separate entity focusing on students with "special" needs.

A listing of the course requirements by year is provided in Table 4.1. The course names are consistent with the names required by the state accreditation agency to assure the college's Faculty Senate and the state accreditation agency that the program is providing the required coursework. The names of the courses, however, do not reflect the merged nature of the program.

Sequential Field Experiences

Another important characteristic of the program is structured, sequential field experiences that provide preservice teachers with opportunities to observe and interact with children in a variety of schools and classrooms. Prior to student

Table 4.1

Requirements by Year

Year	Core	Major	Other	Credits
Freshman	▪ DWC (10) ▪ Eng. Profi- ciency (0)/ Eng. 101 (3) ▪ Math (3) ▪ Intro. Psych. (3) ▪ Fine Arts (3)	▪ Intro. to Characteristics of Individuals with Special Needs (3)	▪ Elective (3) or (6)	28
Sophomore	▪ DWC (10) ▪ Nat. Sci. I biological (3) ▪ Nat. Sci. II physical (3)	▪ M&M Math and Sci. (4) P ▪ Communication Disorders (3)	▪ Elective (3) ▪ Elective (3)	29
Junior	▪ Philosophy (3) ▪ Theology (3) ▪ Child Psych. (3)	▪ M&M Reading (4) P ▪ Classroom Management (3) ▪ M&M Lang. Arts/ Soc. St. (4) P ▪ Res/Self- Contained (3) ▪ Art/Music/Health/ PE (4)	▪ Elective (3) ▪ Elective (3)	33
Senior	▪ Philosophy (3) (Ethics) ▪ Theology (3)	▪ Assessment (3) ▪ Curriculum (4) P ▪ Foundations of Ed. (3) ▪ St. Teach. Elem. (6) St. Teach. SpEd (6)	▪ Elective (3)	31
Total Credits	Core = 53 (or 50 if students do not need to take Eng. 101)	Major = 50	Electives = 18 (or 21 if students do not need to take Eng. 101)	121

P = three credits coursework; one credit practicum.

teaching, students have four field experiences in elementary classrooms, including at least two in urban schools. These field experiences are integral components of methods courses. Starting with a math and science methods course the sophomore year, and continuing for each semester during the junior year and the first semester of the senior year, the students: (a) are introduced to the culture of the school and nearby community, (b) observe classroom instruction, and (c) teach one-to-one, small groups, and the whole class in collaborative teams and individually.

The student teaching experience, the merged program's capstone course, covers 16 weeks during the second semester of the senior year. To meet state licensing requirements preservice teachers are assigned to two different cooperating teachers—one considered a general educator and the other a special educator. As a merged program, our philosophical goal would be to have schools in which all teachers are qualified and prepared to work with all children. Therefore, we do not like to make a distinction between a general educator and a special educator. Because schools and certification structures do make this distinction, however, we used the word "considered." During student teaching, prospective teachers are expected to apply the knowledge and skills developed throughout the program. More specifically, they are expected to act as professionals, to demonstrate their ability to accommodate individual differences in the classroom, to collaborate, and to use effective research on teaching.

Critical to the success of the field experience is the selection of placements. Practicum students and student teachers usually are placed in cohort groups in schools that emphasize education of children within the least restrictive environment.

Faculty members who teach methods courses develop school practicum sites, match preservice teachers to cooperating teachers, and supervise the practicum students for their sections. All full-time program faculty members are student teaching supervisors. Based on their knowledge of the schools and teachers, the student teaching supervisors meet each May to match prospective student teachers with cooperating teachers for the following January placements.

Program faculty members consider their interaction in the schools an essential part of the program, particularly because it affords them firsthand opportunities to monitor the preservice teacher's attainment of program competencies and to identify master teachers for future placements for practicums and for student teaching. In addition, through their presence in the schools, college faculty members have been able to establish relationships with the school faculties and to learn the culture of the school and the curriculum. College and school faculty communicate frequently about the college students, elementary school children, and their professional practice. Discussions in the college classroom have become richer because of this shared understanding.

Practicum students and student teachers both are required to reflect on and discuss teaching with colleagues through reflective logs and discussions in methods classes or weekly student teaching seminars. The fostering of thought and discussion on teaching with colleagues is yet another way the program is attempting to instill a spirit of collegiality that acknowledges the importance of experimentation and dialogue in the teaching profession (Johnston, 1994; Little, 1982).

Professional Development Partnerships

In recent years a number of educational reports have advocated for partnerships between schools and colleges of teacher education as the vehicle for reform (Holmes Group, 1986, 1990; Wise et al., 1987). With professional development partnerships as a goal, program faculties have entered into a planning process with two urban elementary schools. The purposes of initial discussions between college and school faculties are to establish trust and to define early steps toward meaningful partnerships. The objectives of the partnership are to enhance the teacher preparation program, to encourage professional development of the school staff, and to facilitate plans for school improvement. At both sites teachers and staff have been working with individual college faculty members and have offered sites for student teaching and practicums. They agree that a closer and more fully developed partnership will help to meet the goals of the college's and schools' programs and to provide benefits beyond those currently being realized.

The schools were chosen for a variety of reasons, among them, size, the ethnic and cultural diversity of their students, expertise of their teachers, willingness of the staff and administration to engage in collaboration around a common set of goals, and commitment of faculty from both schools to engage in a process of school renewal. In each school the staff could envision personal and professional benefits to the partnership and were willing to set aside time for joint discussions and planning. Examples of activities in various stages of implementation are review and revision of supervision strategies, co-taught classes, student mentoring projects, development of activities and materials at the preservice and inservice level to enhance opportunities for success for all children, and assignment of graduate interns who spend 3 days a week in the schools, to act as school/college facilitators. Faculty from the schools and colleges alike are working to define roles, explore possibilities, and provide meaningful opportunities for preservice teachers to become more involved in professional experiences as members of the school community.

Service Learning Pedagogy

Service learning is becoming recognized as an authentic method of instilling information, strengthening academic skills, providing a context for learning, and offering opportunities for practice in problem solving and decision making with meaningful activities (Conrad & Hedin, 1991; Kinsley & McPherson, 1995).

During the 1993–94 academic year, a department member from the merged program was part of an interdisciplinary faculty research team involved in development of the college's Feinstein Institute of Public and Community Service. Through this involvement, faculty from the Education Department became increasingly aware of the potential of service learning to transform the teaching/learning process in schools to better meet the needs of all students.

The Education Department, in collaboration with the Feinstein Institute, applied for and was awarded a Learn and Serve America higher education grant. The 3-year grant has a primary goal of developing and infusing theories and pedagogy of service learning into the elementary/special education teacher preparation program. It also was designed to prepare preservice teachers sequentially to develop and use strategies to enhance service learning and also to understand the school's role in the community and to be empowered to take a role in school improvement and reform.

In collaboration with teachers in the two urban elementary schools described in the previous section, service learning theory and pedagogy currently are being designed and integrated sequentially into selected sections of methods courses. A cohort of students has applied and been selected to enroll in these sections and to register concurrently for courses that fulfill requirements for the minor in Public and Community Service. Courses such as Community Studies and Race and Ethnic Relations will provide these preservice students with an increased understanding of the role of the school within the community and with an understanding of the changing demographics of today's schools and communities.

Initially, preservice teachers will engage in designing and teaching lessons that involve service to the school. As their conceptual understanding, knowledge, and skills develop, service and service learning projects will be expanded to include the community and, ultimately, schoolwide projects will be developed and implemented. Ideas for increasing the learners' participation and ownership will be explored along with project assessment and evaluation plans. The development of reflection, critical thinking, and decision making will be tied to specific school curriculum areas. Although it is only in its first year, this project is expected to result in a program component that will strengthen the commitment of students and faculty to greater understanding of diversity and to expand the knowledge, skills, and attitudes needed to teach all children.

Merged Faculty

Faculty hired to teach in the merged program must have a philosophical commitment to the education of teachers who are prepared to identify the diverse learning needs, interests, and goals of their students and to develop and implement instruction designed to meet these diverse learning needs. All faculty members receive appointments in the Education Department, and the following factors, it is hoped, will contribute to the view of a unified, not dual, system of professional development:

1. No distinction is made between faculty relative to either elementary or special education degrees or background. All faculty members are identified as education faculty.
2. Recruitment of new faculty focuses on attracting individuals with experience and knowledge of both general and special populations and a commitment to inclusion. In addition, demonstrated effectiveness in teaching as it relates to the above is critical.
3. In all methods courses faculty members are required to emphasize appropriate adaptations to meet all children's individual needs.

Dual Certification

Upon graduation, students are eligible to apply for certification as an elementary teacher and an elementary teacher of students with mild/moderate disabilities in Rhode Island and states that are part of either the Northeast Regional Credential Contract or the Interstate Teacher Certification Compact.[2] Because of their dual certification and their merged theory and knowledge base, these students are attractive to school districts, particularly as schools are moving to more inclusive educational systems.

Future Challenges

As the program moves into its second decade, the following issues have emerged as critical to its ability to develop effective teachers to meet the challenges of tomorrow's schools:

- Establishing a program evaluation system that focuses on the performance of its graduates as teachers.
- Providing more opportunities for articulation between education faculty and faculty in the arts and sciences.
- Continuing to develop college/school partnerships.
- Recruiting qualified faculty to meet the demands of increasing enrollment.
- Fitting it all into a 4-year program.

Each challenge will be discussed in more detail below. Evaluation within the program currently occurs in four ways.

1. Evaluations of individual courses.
2. Constant and ongoing feedback from students in the program and from

school administrators and teachers who work with the preservice teachers at field sites.

3. A survey each fall of the recent graduating class's job/graduate school placements.
4. Surveys of alumni every 5 years or so to determine satisfaction with the program and areas for improvement.

A survey of graduates of the merged program has just been completed, and a preliminary review of results reflects positive responses. For example, 97% of the respondents rated the quality of their education in the teacher preparation program at Providence College as good, very good, or excellent. The written comments presented below indicate satisfaction with their competence and preparation to teach.

> I found my education at PC to be of superior quality. Compared to other teachers, I feel I was well prepared. The practicums required with every course are a definite strength.

> I felt my educational background has greatly helped me through the first few years. I'm constantly looking through old PC notebooks.

> Entering my third year of teaching, I always reflect on the superior training and education I received at Providence College. I feel I was very prepared for my teaching career. At my interview, the principal and Special Education Director were very interested and impressed with Providence College. We discussed the program in detail. The best part is I got the job!

With the emphasis on performance-based assessment, however, program faculty members have expressed a need to develop a more systematic evaluation process that will better provide them with the data needed to improve their practice. The state's movement to adopt an adaptation of the INTASC standards as the mechanism for approval of teacher education programs is providing an additional incentive to develop a more systematic, performance-based evaluation process. During the next few years the program faculty will be working with state Department of Education staff to develop and implement this process.

Second, both Tyson (1994) and Howey and Zimpher (1989), in their studies of exemplary teacher preparation programs, identified the lack of cohesiveness of content, theory, and pedagogy as an area of concern and advocated for better articulation between the arts and sciences and teacher education. Faculty in the merged program currently do not have a mechanism for ongoing dialogue with members of the arts and sciences faculty. A few instances of articulation have occurred, such as a co-taught psychology and education course on classroom management, a course developed on computers in education by a member of the math and computer science department in collaboration with faculty from the education department, and the collaborative service learning program between the Feinstein Institute of Public and Community Service and the Education Department. Those efforts, however, should be broadened to other disciplines.

The collegewide community presently is engaging in an indepth review of the college's curriculum. The faculty in the Education Department looks forward to the opportunity that the review will provide to engage in dialogue with colleagues on questions such as, "What is the nature of an educated person?" and "What implications do these characteristics have for instruction and assessment in the core, department, and program curricula?"

Third, the program has established a number of strong relationships with local public schools and districts, and at least two of these are evolving into a professional development relationship. A long-term goal is to strengthen relationships with selected schools that demonstrate examples of good practice so all of the students will be able to do their field placements in professional development schools. This will enable students to practice in exemplary school communities and will provide program faculty the opportunity to collaborate with school faculty on developing effective teaching/learning practices and on furthering their school reform efforts.

Fourth, the program's first graduating class in 1989 had 25 students. Thus far, there are 85 matriculating students in the merged elementary/special education program in the class of 1999. From a faculty of two, the program has expanded to a faculty of eight full-time, and three to four more faculty members likely will be hired during the next 2 years. During this process the search committee has had difficulty recruiting doctoral-level faculty members who are committed to the philosophy of inclusion and also are able to provide preservice teachers with the knowledge and skills needed to teach children who are academically, cognitively, linguistically, and culturally diverse.

Finally, although evaluations have indicated that we are preparing teachers who are satisfied with their preparation and feedback from professionals in schools indicate that our graduates are well prepared, it has been difficult to "fit it all into a 4-year program." Program faculty members are continuously reviewing and discussing the components of an essential curriculum for preservice elementary/special education teachers and attempting to concentrate on those components within the program's curricula. It is a constant, yet exciting challenge.

The program faculty views this teacher preparation program as only the first step in a lifelong career of a teacher's professional development. The faculty from the program has been involved actively in regional, state, and local mentoring projects such as the Northeast Regional Laboratories Mentoring Network and Rhode Island's Mentor Consultants, and various certification and staff development advisory boards conducted by the Rhode Island Department of Education to assist in formulating the next steps in the continuum of professional development for teachers.

Conclusions

Recently much has been written in the professional literature regarding new paradigms for staff development. Study groups and networking are just a few models of effective staff development that are replacing the "one-shot" workshop/ "talking head" models (Lieberman, 1995). Not only do teacher education programs have to develop new designs to prepare teachers for tomorrow's schools; they must model effective practices as well. In the early stages of this merged program's development, the program faculty had opportunities to network and to participate in research and study groups with other faculties who were exploring creative alternatives to Will's shared responsibility theme[3] (Peters et al., 1989). These interactions were essential to early evolution of the program, but finding avenues for continuing dialogue has been difficult. As the program moves ahead to meet the challenges of the next century, additional opportunities to network must be available and pursued actively.

References

Bauwens, J., Hourcade, J., & Friend, M. (1989). Cooperative teaching: A model for general and special education integration. *Remedial and Special Education, 10,* 17– 22.

Bickel, W., & Bickel, D. (1986). Effective schools, classrooms, and instruction: Implications for special education. *Exceptional Children, 52,* 489–500

Brophy, J. (1983). Classroom organization and management. In D. C. Smith (Ed.), *Essential knowledge for beginning educators* (pp. 23–37). Washington, DC: AACTE.

Burstein, N., Cabello, B., & Hamann, J. (1993). Teacher preparation for culturally diverse urban students: Infusing competencies across the curriculum. *Teacher Education and Special Education, 16,* 1–13.

Conrad, C. W., & Hedlin, D. (1991). School based community service: What we know from research and theory. *Phi Delta Kappan, 72,* 743–749.

Darling-Hammond, L. (1992). Perestoika and professionalism: The case for restructuring teacher preparation. In R. McClure (Ed.), *Excellence in teacher education: Helping teachers develop learning centered schools* (pp. 19–27). Washington, DC: National Education Association.

Darling-Hammond, L. (1994). *The current status of teaching and teacher development in the United States.* Available from National Commission on Teaching and America's Future, Teachers College, Columbia University, New York, NY 10027.

Gersten, R., Woodward, J., & Darch, C. (1986). Direct instruction. A research based approach to curricular design and teaching. *Exceptional Children, 53,* 17–31.

Goodlad, J. (1990). *Teachers for our nations schools.* San Francisco: Jossey-Bass Publishers.

Holmes Group. (1986). *Tomorrow's teachers: A report of the Holmes Group.* East Lansing, MI: Author.

Holmes Group, (1990). *Tomorrow's schools: Principles for the design of professional development schools.* East Lansing, MI: Author.

Howey, K., Arends, R., Galluzzo, G., Yarger, S., & Zimpher, N. (1994). *Rate VII: Teacher preparation in the urban context.* Washington, DC: AACTE Publications.

Howey, K., & Zimpher, N. (1989). *Profiles of preservice teacher education: Inquiry into the nature of programs.* Albany: State University of New York.

Idol, L., & West, F. (1991). Educational collaboration: A catalyst for effective schooling. *Intervention in School and Clinic, 27,* 70–78.

Johnson, D. W., Johnson, R., Holubec, E., & Roy, P. (1984). *Circles of learning.* Arlington, VA: Association for Supervision and Curriculum Development.

Johnston, S. (1994). Experience is the best teacher: Or is it? An analysis of the role of experience in learning to teach. *Journal of Teacher Education, 45,* 199–208.

Kinsley, C. W., & McPherson, K. (Eds.). (1995). *Enriching the curriculum through service learning.* Alexandria, VA: Association for Supervision and Curriculum Development.

Landurand, P. (1995). *The multicultural inclusion college/schools collaboration.* Unpublished manuscript, Rhode Island College.

Lieberman, A. (1995). Practices that support teacher development: Transforming conceptions of professional learning. *Phi Delta Kappan, 76,* 591–596.

Little, J. W. (1982). Norms of collegiality and experimentation: Workplace conditions for school success. *American Educational Research Journal, 19,* 325–340.

Milk, R., Mercado, C., & Sapiens, A. (1992). *Re-thinking the education of teachers of language minority children: Developing reflective teachers for changing schools.* Washington, DC: National Clearinghouse for Bilingual Education.

National Commission on Excellence in Education. (1983). *A nation at risk: The imperative for educational reform.* Washington, DC: U.S. Department of Education.

Palincsar, A. S. (1986). Metacognitive strategy instruction. *Exceptional Children, 53,* 116–124.

Peters, S., Aksamit, D., Fisher, V., Hall, S. P., Ryan, L., & Skrtic, T. (1989). *Case study: Merged elementary and special education program.* Unpublished manuscript.

Pugach, M., & Lilly, M. S. (1984). Reconceptualizing support services for classroom teachers: Implications for teacher education. *Journal of Teacher Education, 35,* 48–55.

Reynolds, M. C., & Wang, M. C. (1983). Restructuring "special" school programs: A position paper. *Policy Studies Review, 2,* 189–212.

Rosenshine, B. (1986). Synthesis of research on explicit teaching. *Educational Leadership, 43,* 60–69.

Shapiro, J . P., Sewell, T. E., & DuCette, J. P. (1995). *Reframing diversity in education.* Lancaster, PA: Technomic Publications.

Skrtic, T. M. (1991). The special education paradox: Equity as the way to excellence. *Harvard Educational Review, 61,* 148–206.

Slavin, R. E. (1983). *Cooperative learning.* New York: Longman.

Soder, R. (1994). Underlying tensions in creating new kinds of school-university partnerships. *Record in Educational Leadership, 14,* 11–14.

Stainback, W., & Stainback, S. (1984). A rationale for the merger of special and regular education. *Exceptional Children, 51,* 102–111.

Thousand, J. S. (1990). Organizational perspectives on teacher education and renewal: A conversation with Tom Skrtic. *Teacher Education and Special Education, 13,* 30–35.

Thousand, J. S., & Villa, R. A. (1988). *Enhancing success in heterogeneous classrooms and schools.* (Monograph No. 8–1). Burlington, VT: Center for Developmental Disabilities University Affiliated Program.

Tyson, H. (1994). *Who will teach the children: Progress and resistance in teacher education.* San Francisco: Jossey-Bass.

Watson, B. (1995). Relinquishing the lectern: Cooperative learning in teacher education. *Journal of Teacher Education, 46,* 209–215.

Will, M. (1986). Educating children with learning problems: A shared responsibility. *Exceptional Children, 52,* 411–416.

Wise, A. E., Darling-Hammond, L., Berry, B., Berliner, D., Haller, E., Prasac, A., & Schlechty, P. (1987). *Effective teacher selection: From recruitment to retention.* Santa Monica, CA: Rand Corp.

Authors' Note

The authors gratefully acknowledge the influence on the evolution of Providence College's program of the Merged Program Study Group initiated by National Inquiry Study into the Future of Students with Special Needs—Susan Peters, Donna Aksamit, Virginia Fisher, S. Pike Hall, Lynne Ryan, and Thomas Skrtic and the faculty of the Merged Elementary/Special Education Program at LaSalle University.

Notes

1. A consortium of more than 30 states working together on licensing standards and assessment.
2. The Northeast Regional Credential is a contract among states in the Northeast that enables teachers certified initially in one member state to obtain initial certification in another member state for up to 2 years, during which time the teacher would satisfy any additional certification requirements of that state. The Interstate Teacher Certification Compact is a contract among approximately 35 states that provides for reciprocity for teacher certification among member states.
3. The Merged Program Study Group initiated by the National Inquiry Study into the Future of Students with Special Needs was sponsored by the Teacher Education Division of the Council for Exceptional Children and headed by Preston Feden of LaSalle University.

The Unified PROTEACH Early Childhood Program at the University of Florida

Vivian I. Correa, Mary Jane K. Rapport, Lynn C. Hartle, Hazel A. Jones, Kristen M. Kemple, and Tina Smith-Bonahue

Like an increasing number of students in colleges of education, preservice students of the Unified Early Childhood Program at the University of Florida are receiving an education that unifies the fields of general and special education. Now in its fourth year, the program is preparing its second cohort of preservice students. Through extensive collaboration, the faculty of the Unified Early Childhood Program has designed a program that

— integrates early childhood and early childhood special education content;
— systematically sequences courses and field experiences in a blocked manner;
— functions within the college's 5-year PROTEACH[1] teacher education model; and
— culminates in a graduate internship in the final year of a 5-year preservice program.

Students exit the program after 5 years with a bachelor's degree from Special Education and a master's degree from Instruction and Curriculum. The departments confer these degrees simply by virtue of the need to delineate full-time equivalence (FTE) equitably. The students receive two early childhood teaching certificates (birth to age 4 and age 3 to grade 3) with an imbedded PreK Handicapped endorsement.

In this chapter we first provide a brief rationale for unification of teacher education in early childhood and a description of the university context in which the program functions. Then we outline the chronology of program development, the program features (including the course sequence and specific course highlights) and the issues that emerged in the process of unification. We provide insight into the complex task of unifying teacher education programs in early childhood and early childhood special education so others will be able to replicate or restructure their own programs.

Rationale and Mission of a Unified Early Childhood Program

The need for early childhood educators who can serve diverse groups of young children is evidenced in the literature (Burton, Hains, Hanline, McLean, & McCormick, 1992; Kagan, 1989; Miller, 1992), national organization reports (National Association of State Boards of Education, 1988; National Commission on Children, 1991), and Florida's state comprehensive plan for personnel development (FDOE, 1991). In addition, there has been a need to examine "the relationship between what often has been seen as the separate fields of early childhood education and early childhood special education" (NAEYC, 1995, p. 19).

In recent years, the call for unification and collaboration of teacher education programs in early childhood and early childhood special education has come from a joint task force from the Association of Teacher Educators (ATE), Division of Early Childhood of the Council for Exceptional Children (DEC), and the National Association for the Education of Young Children (NAEYC). The three organizations have developed guidelines for personnel standards of early childhood and early childhood special education teachers (ATE, DEC, & NAEYC, 1994).

The need for this type of professionalism is particularly critical in Florida, with its dramatic increases in population growth and educational risk factors for children (Hodgkinson, 1991). Florida represents a diverse cultural community with ever larger populations of Hispanics, Haitians, and African Americans. A study by the Center for the Study of Social Policy and the Annie E. Casey Foundation (1993) ranked Florida amongst the lowest of the 50 states: 34th in low birthweight, 32nd in infant mortality, 36th in births to single teens, and 39th in children in poverty. To meet the challenges of serving this young, at-risk population, appropriate preparation of future early childhood educators is critical. The State Department of Education has responded by designing and implementing two early childhood certificates that emphasize integrated knowledge and skills necessary for working with this diverse population.

To this end, the faculty of the Unified Early Childhood Program has developed a set of assumptions that guide the direction of the program. We believe that teachers should provide young children with the opportunity for educational experiences in inclusive environments where the needs of all students are accommodated, success is fostered, and peer relationships among students with differing abilities are encouraged. We further believe we should instill in our future teachers the values of collaboration, consensus building, and shared leadership. Equally important is the assumption that teachers must view the family as an integral part of the educational experience and, in doing so, be sensitive to diversity in society. These assumptions have helped guide the mission of the Unified program by reflecting the unique needs of personnel in the fields of early childhood and early childhood special education.

The mission of the Unified Early Childhood Program is to prepare early childhood professionals who have the competencies to provide for the education and care of a diverse group of children within developmentally and individually appropriate programs. Graduates of the Unified Early Childhood Program will be professionals who have the competencies to design and implement culturally sensitive inclusive early education programs for young children (birth through age 8) with and without disabilities and their families. Achieving the mission of the Unified Early Childhood Program requires an extensive infrastructure with resources from the college and the university. To this end, understanding the context in which preservice students are prepared at the University of Florida will be useful.

The Context of the University of Florida

The University of Florida (UF) is the flagship university of Florida's state university system and is recognized as one of the nation's top universities by the Carnegie Commission on Higher Education. It is located in the rural community of Gainesville, which has a population of 100,000. Currently, UF has a total enrollment of more than 38,000 students and over 2,000 faculty in 20 colleges and schools and 100 interdisciplinary research and education centers, bureaus, and institutes. By its membership in the Association of American Universities (AAU), UF is recognized for its preeminence in graduate and professional education and research. The Graduate School coordinates 123 master's and 76 doctoral programs in 87 of the 137 academic departments.

Five departments comprise the College of Education: Counselor Education, Educational Foundations (EF), Educational Leadership, Instruction and Curriculum (I & C), and Special Education (SE), with a combined faculty of 120. The

Department of Special Education currently is composed of 18 faculty members, 12 in tenure-track positions. The Department of Instruction and Curriculum at present has 40 faculty members, 35 in tenure-track positions. The unified faculty has three faculty housed in SE, two housed in I & C, one in EF, and a graduate assistant (supported by grant funds).

Chronology of the Unified Early Childhood Program

The first meetings concerning unification were held in 1991. Now, some 5 years later, the program has been institutionalized in the College of Education. The steps were many and the challenges painstaking, but the momentum to pursue unification was ceaseless.

Teacher Preparation Before Unification

Since 1988, the Department of Special Education, with the support of four Office of Special Education and Rehabilitative Services (OSERS) personnel preparation grants, has been preparing master's-level preservice early childhood special education (ECSE) personnel in two areas: infant specialists (0–2 years) and preschool interventionists (3–5 years). As part of this preparation, the ECSE program required that extra courses be taken in early childhood (EC) as an add on component to the program plan. In addition, the Department of Special Education was awarded two Florida Department of Education grants to train inservice teachers for the state's PreK handicapped endorsement. A summer institute was conducted in 1990, and a collaborative distance education project with three other institutions of higher education (IHEs) was conducted in the summer of 1991.

Preparation of early childhood educators took place simultaneously in the Department of Instruction and Curriculum. These students had the option of taking two additional courses in EC along with their elementary education coursework to seek the then existing early childhood certificate in Florida. Another option involved more extensive early childhood coursework culminating in a 12-hour specialization in early childhood within the elementary education program. Despite some cross-departmental course requirements, collaboration with EC faculty was almost nonexistent. Interactions between the EC and ECSE faculties were cordial and informal and involved occasional guest lecturing.

The Early Stages of Unification

In the spring of 1991, the EC and ECSE faculties began to talk about unification and initiated a series of planning meetings to explore the possibilities of restructuring and integrating the existing programs. These meetings were attended by key members in the college: the associate dean, the assistant dean of student services, the chairperson of instruction and curriculum, the chairperson of special education, and early childhood and early childhood special education faculty. By involving college and departmental administrators, ownership and support for the program was developed early and has been maintained through continued communication.

The core of the work involved in designing and later implementing the program, however, came from the EC and ECSE faculties and has been described in an article by Kemple, Hartle, Correa, and Fox (1994). By forming a close collaborative team early in the process of program development, faculty members interested in unifying the programs developed presentations that were well organized, cohesive, and united from the start.

Early in the fall of 1991, the group's attention focused on writing and submitting an OSERS personnel preparation grant to support unified student stipends. It was anticipated that grant funds would allow us to pilot-test the new program and give us time to fine-tune the content of the curriculum. The grant, awarded in the spring of 1992, allowed us to begin implementing the unified curriculum and continue the process of fine-tuning the program for institutionalization.

Institutionalization of Unified Early Childhood Program

Early in the stages of institutionalization, various dyads of unified faculty made presentations at more than 25 meetings at the departmental, college, and university levels. These meetings helped to inform faculty in the college of the nature and content of the proposed program. Eventually the meetings began to focus on seeking official departmental approval of the program in the departments of I & C and SE. This stage of development became challenging to the unified faculty. With each presentation, our colleagues suggested revisions. Some revisions clearly helped improve the original design of the program. Other revisions only supported "business as usual" and maintained the more traditional and separatist focus of teacher education in the college. For example, some I & C faculty members wanted us to continue to offer content such as science, social studies, math, music, art, and physical education as single courses, maintaining what we believe was the traditional elementary model. Much diplomacy and education was needed to convince "traditional" elementary education faculty that developmentally appropriate practices in early childhood required that we rethink segregated curriculum and begin to implement integrated content courses.

At each stage of program approval, consensus was difficult to achieve. Although the faculty in special education was not as resistant to the ideas of integrated curriculum, it wanted assurance that unified early childhood students would get "enough" special education pedagogy, including classroom management, direct instruction, and applied behavior analysis. Once again, the unified faculty found itself educating special education faculty on developmentally appropriate practices, inclusion, and preparation of preservice teachers to teach *all* young children. Once we had received departmental approvals, the next step involved college-wide approval.

The Unified Early Childhood Program was presented to the college curriculum committee in the fall of 1994, over 3 years after the first steps of development. The committee was composed of faculty representing all departments in the college, including Educational Foundations. Interestingly, the unified program had become so full that courses such as social and historical foundations of education and learning and cognition were at risk for remaining in the required course of study. Although ongoing dialogue with the chairperson of the Department of Educational Foundations had addressed the professional education core of courses (educational foundations, child development, learning and cognition, and measurements), unified faculty met with much resistance when core foundation courses were recommended for deletion.

Unified faculty thought the content related to social and historical foundations of education would have to be altered to focus on early childhood and early childhood special education. Similarly, the content related to learning theory and development would have to be taught with an early childhood emphasis and could be taught by the unified faculty within the early childhood courses, thus avoiding duplication of content. More negotiations that included individual and small-group meetings with faculty and administrators resulted in the rearrangement of several courses. The faculty of Educational Foundations agreed to teach special sections of social foundations, child development, and measurements with an early childhood focus. The course on learning and cognition was deleted from the program. Finally, after some additional debate and a vote, the college curriculum committee unanimously approved the program in the fall of 1995.

During the final stages of the institutionalization process, the associate dean of the College of Education was responsible for presenting the program to the university curriculum committee. The associate dean and unified faculty met with this committee, and once again much discussion was devoted to the total number of course hours, required summer courses, and limited number of electives in the program. The status of permanent institutionalization of the Unified Early Childhood Program was granted in the fall of 1995. Although external funding supports part of the program presently, the complete Unified program will continue solely on state-supported funds.

The first cohort of students began classes in the unified program in the fall of 1992 during the time that deliberations regarding institutionalization were continuing. The students, who entered the College of Education in their junior year as elementary education majors, had been recruited quickly during the first few days of classes following brief descriptions of the new program. Initially, 17 students received federal support for participating in the experimental program. Fourteen students remained with the program through graduation in the spring of 1995.

The second cohort of unified students began the program in the fall of 1995, after institutionalization had taken place. They are expected to complete the graduate year of the unified program in the spring of 1998. Because the new Florida early childhood certification took effect in July 1995, the second cohort of unified graduates will receive the birth to age 4 Preschool certificate, the age 3 to grade 3 PreK/primary certificate, and the embedded PreK Handicapped endorsement for educating students ages 3 to 5 with disabilities.

The unified portfolio was submitted to the Florida Department of Education (FDOE) in the summer of 1995 and received official approval during late fall 1995. Interestingly, a unified faculty member had been involved on a state advisory council for the development of the new certification and the associated competencies while program development proceeded at the university. This collaborative relationship with the FDOE and the key members of state certification proved to be most advantageous for the unified faculty and reinforced the development of a truly integrated program that would culminate in the state's new certificates.

The next step in institutionalizing the unified program is gaining NCATE approval, which should be complete in 1997. Currently, unified faculty are working closely with the departments of I & C and SE to develop the unified early childhood portfolio. The Unified Early Childhood Program provides a unique opportunity for approval of a NCATE program that crosses departmental lines.

Other Procedural Elements

Part of the institutionalization process involved phasing out the previous EC teacher education programs and securing new course names and numbers. In preparation for institutionalization of the unified program, the COE placed a moratorium on offering courses for the old early childhood certification beginning in the fall of 1994. This provided faculty and students with a way to begin transitioning the college toward the new certification and the newly approved Unified Early Childhood Program.

An additional procedure facing the unified program was to apply for undergraduate course numbers for core EC and ECSE courses. This process of presenting new course names and numbers to the faculties in the Departments of Special Education and Instruction and Curriculum, the college curriculum committee, and the teacher education committee at the university level has begun and continues at this time.

Program Features and Curriculum

As stated earlier, the mission of the Unified Early Childhood Program is to prepare early childhood educators to meet the diverse needs of young children and their families within a developmentally and individually appropriate context. To this end, the curriculum for the unified program was conceptualized from our philosophical orientation and based on state certification requirements and professional standards from two national organizations, DEC and NAEYC. The content and organization of the program facilitate attainment of knowledge and skills in the following ways:

- Each course is competency-based. Students will not complete each course successfully unless they demonstrate mastery-level performance of each competency.
- The coursework provides a strong foundation in both early childhood education and special education in an integrated fashion.
- The program is designed to provide students with an intensive relationship with program faculty for the purpose of academic advisement, supervision and feedback, and post-graduation placement and follow-up.
- The students will move through the program in a cohort that will encourage the development of collegial and mutually supportive relationships.
- The program provides for continuing growth and adaptation of the curriculum through ongoing evaluation of the syllabi and course experiences by faculty, students, and cooperating teachers in practicum and internship school sites.
- The program provides for multi-setting practicum experiences to permit preservice students to display mastery of early childhood and early childhood special education skills across settings.

In the Unified Early Childhood Program, within each course the faculty infuses themes of diversity, inclusion of children with disabilities, collaboration, integrity of the content of the disciplines, the role of family, the assessment cycle, and developmentally appropriate practices, while certain strategically planned courses emphasize a single topic or theme. Each course or experience is designed to guide students to higher levels of understanding of those major themes by helping them revisit and expand upon their previous learning.

To encourage lifelong professionalism, all required courses, the internship, and the seminar require students to reflect on the complexities of teaching. Throughout their program students compile a working portfolio, which includes but is not limited to metacognitive letters written to their faculty advisor each semester, journals for specific courses, and brief reaction papers to specific experiences in their program. The courses and field-based experiences were grouped together for each semester to help students build on and extend competencies.

Table 5.1 presents the full program plan for the junior, senior, and graduate (fifth) year. Students have moved through the program in cohorts of peers, which provide opportunities to build supportive as well as productive relationships.

Course Sequence

During the freshman and sophomore years, students take courses in general and preprofessional education. Courses in the preprofessional area include Introduction to Education, Teaching Diverse Learners, and Technology in Education. Students enter the College of Education in their junior year after taking 60 credit hours of basic education. In the first semester of their junior year, students are introduced to the fields of early childhood and early childhood special education with the intent of helping them understand the diverse needs, interests, and abilities of young children at various ages and stages. As noted in Table 5.1, the Foundations of ECSE and Professional Studies in EC courses are team-taught and include a combined and integrated field-based experience. The thematic areas for this semester are an introduction to young children, recommended practices in integration of EC and ECSE, an orientation to developmentally appropriate practices and inclusive education, family-focused involvement, and the diverse learning needs of children with disabilities. The courses provide students with models of teaming and collaboration across the disciplines of EC and ECSE.

Courses scheduled in the second semester of the junior year focus on the cycle of teaching, learning, assessment, and revision of the content of each discipline. During this semester students also begin to integrate an understanding of multicultural and linguistic diversity with the impact of children's learning and families' involvement in the educational process. A practicum course in this semester provides students with opportunities to observe and to engage diverse groups of children at the kindergarten and primary levels (ages 5 to 8) in appropriate learning experiences. In addition, an integrated math and science course for young children gives unified students the opportunity to understand thematic education and develop integrated curriculum.

In the fall of the senior year, the courses assist students in integrating their understanding of the impacts of social contexts, social competence, and education programs for infants and toddlers ages birth to 3. This semester also includes coursework and practicum experiences in working with students with disabilities ages birth to 5. An emphasis on medical and early intervention models supported by Public Law 99–457, Part H, are infused into the curriculum. Providing students with specific information on etiology and infant intervention models are the focus of this semester.

In the spring of the senior year, courses offered provide a review and synthesis of the design and evaluation of appropriate curriculum for all children,

Table 5.1

Unified Early Childhood Course of Study

Junior Year
31 hours

Fall:		Spring:	
*Early Childhood Special Education	2	EC Mathematics & Science	3
*Professional Studies in EC Education	2	Assessment in EC Special Education	3
The Young Child	3	Clinical Seminar in	
Exceptional People	3	Kindergarten/Primary	3
Language Acquisitions	3	Emergent Literacy	3
Family Focused Involvement	3	Multicultural Issues EC	
		Special Education	3

Senior Year
29 hours

Fall:		Spring:	
Social Foundation of EC Education	3	EC Science & Social Studies	3
Social Competence in EC	3	Educational Measurement	
Educational Programs for		and Evaluation	2
Infants/Toddlers	3	EC Children's Literature	3
Clinical Seminar in EC		*EC Special Education Curriculum	3
Special Education	3	*EC Curriculum	3
Children with Severe/Multiple			
Disabilities	3		

Graduate Year
36 hours

Summer:		Fall:		Spring:	
EC Background and		Internship in EC/ECSE	12	Creativity in EC	
Concepts	3	Transdisciplinary		Curriculum	3
Reading/Primary		Teaming	3	Day Care/Young	
Grades	3			Children	3
				Master's Action	
				Research	3
				Child Health	3
				Communications	
				Disorders	3

*Courses that are blocked and co-taught

including those with disabilities and diverse cultural backgrounds. The concept of integrated academic content is expanded in courses such as science and social studies, along with an integrated team-taught course on early childhood and early childhood special education curriculum. These courses strengthen students' abilities to integrate curriculum for inclusive early childhood settings. Educational measurements and evaluation content provide students with the knowledge necessary to understand standardized and norm-referenced assessments and enhance students' abilities to evaluate and assess children's progress through contemporary assessment practices (e.g., authentic assessment, curriculum-based assessment, and portfolio assessment).

The following summer begins the graduate and final year. One additional course prepares students for internship by building on their understanding of current trends and issues in early childhood education, including the micropolitics of teaching. Students also receive additional coursework on teaching reading, an important curricular area in the primary grades. In a 2-week teaming and transdisciplinary course in the fall semester, prior to internship, these future teachers experience the additional role they will play beyond their role with children who are developing typically. This course helps to prepare them further for working with children with disabilities. During the supervised internship, students have the opportunity to apply the knowledge constructed over the past 2 years. In their final spring semester, through action research, students explore questions that emerged as they participated in the internship, especially questions regarding inclusive education. Students, often working in pairs, collect and analyze data to answer those specific questions and, hence, learn skills and dispositions for researching the ever-emerging questions surrounding appropriate teaching and learning.

Another course also helps students explore questions specifically about the creative, artistic, and musical potential of young children. Students also are encouraged to extend their career options beyond primary teaching to directing child care through an additional course offering. Finally, two out-of-college courses are required by the Graduate School, and certain courses are recommended to fulfill additional certification requirements.

Course Highlights

Providing the sequence and brief descriptions of the courses can be a foundation to begin program and curriculum development for faculties in other teacher education programs. More detail, however, may be valuable in describing the unified curriculum. The unique course features and descriptions are highlighted in Table 5.2. The courses designated by an asterisk represent contemporary practices in early education, including inclusion, diversity, teaming and collaboration, developmentally appropriate curriculum and assessment, and family-focused involvement. Courses at the end of the program emphasize application of

Table 5.2

Unified Early Childhood Course Highlights

Course	Description
Early Childhood Special Education and Professional Studies in ECE Education	In these two courses students are introduced to the development and implementation of developmentally appropriate intervention programs. The courses provide an overview of the components of early childhood and early childhood special education programs, introduce the student to current issues and practices, and provide a foundation in teaming and multi-disciplinary approaches to intervention. Students begin the development of their own evaluation portfolios, spend 10 hours a week in field observations, and begin writing reflections on teaching.
The Young Child	Although child development appears in almost every teacher education program, the content of this course focuses on development of children from birth to age 8. The course, taught by an early childhood faculty member in the Department of Educational Foundations, presents an expanded study of growth and development during infancy and early childhood.
Exceptional People	This course is taken with students in the Department of Special Education and provides the unified students with the more traditional but necessary aspects of special education. Incidence, causes, diagnosis, agencies for referral, and recommended teaching procedures for children with the types of disabilities found in public schools are considered. In addition, special education school law, cultural diversity, and family-focused involvement are emphasized. This course provides the students with an opportunity to begin peer collaboration with students who are experiencing a more traditional teacher education special education program.
Family Focused Involvement	In this course students are provided with content in family systems theory and interaction, community resources, service coordination, and transition. The course also provides students with guest instructors who themselves are parents of young children and young children with disabilities. Field experiences provided in this course include a semester-long family project (students become involved in the day-to-day lives of a family); observations and volunteer work at the Family Service Center (a full-services school project in the local school district); and attendance at local parent support meetings.
Assessment in Early Childhood Special Education	Although the course title appears traditional, this course provides students with a contemporary view of assessment using many aspects of current early childhood philosophies (e.g., authentic assessment; portfolio-based assessments; curriculum-based evaluation; nonbiased assessment). In addition, the course provides students with a field-based experience in conducting a complete transdisciplinary play-based assessment as outlined in Linder (1993). Evaluation reports and recommendations for intervention are presented to peers and invited family members. (continued)

Table 5.2 continued

Course	Description
Multicultural Issues in Early Childhood Special Education	Although the unified program's philosophy and conceptual framework are based on infusing multicultural content into every course in the curriculum, this course provides more focus on issues related to many aspects of diversity (e.g., culture, language, sexual orientation, religion, poverty, geography). The course also provides unified students with the ESOL (English for Speakers of Other Languages) endorsement required by a state consent decree. Strategies for teaching young children who are limited English-proficient speakers are covered in this course.
Education Programs for Infants/Toddlers	This course provides students with the knowledge and skills necessary to work with children from birth to age 3. Its emphasis is on PL 99–457, Part H, programs and state maternal/infant early intervention programs such as First Start and Early Start. It also introduces students to hospital/medical (e.g., NICU) and homebound service delivery programs. The course has been team-taught with a unified faculty member and a faculty member in the Department of Pediatrics at UF. Guest lectures by neonatologists, social workers, and human services providers are included.
Children with Severe/Multiple Disabilities	Although issues of disabilities are infused throughout the courses in the unified program, students gain specific knowledge of working with young children who evidence more significant disabilities and require extensive supports for inclusion in early childhood programs. Further, this course introduces students to medical aspects of disabilities and specific health-care issues in schools (e.g., HIV, hepatitis; universal health-care precautions, safety, ADA accessibility, medications, students with complex health-care needs).
Creativity in the Early Childhood Curriculum	Most of the students in a traditional early childhood or elementary education program are required to take individual courses in art, music, and physical education. The unified philosophy, however, supports integrated curriculum. This course is designed to develop students' appreciation for creativity as an important outcome for developmentally appropriate practice. Students learn how to promote children's creativity through art, music, movement, drama, and problem-solving experiences. Students apply their knowledge of curriculum adaptation as they develop creative activities to include children with and without disabilities.
Early Childhood Curriculum and Early Childhood Special Education Curriculum	In these two courses students experience a team-taught block of content. The courses provide students with content in the development and implementation of individualized education programs for children with and without disabilities, including developmentally appropriate curriculum, methods, intervention strategies, and environmental arrangements.

(continued)

Table 5.2 continued

Course	Description
Internship	Students are placed in exemplary programs for their student internship. Classrooms in the local school district that have integrated young children with disabilities successfully into the general early childhood classroom are used as internship sites for 15 weeks. In some cases, when inclusive placements are not available, students spend half of their internship (7 1/2 weeks) in an early childhood setting and the other half in an early childhood special education setting. As more schools provide full inclusion for students with disabilities, preservice students, we hope, will have full-time internship experiences in those settings.
Transdisciplinary Teaming	This course focuses on collaboration and consultation in inclusive educational settings and is taken in a 2-week intensive block prior to beginning the internship experience. Roles of related service personnel and development of skills in collaboration and communication with teachers, parents, peers, and specialists working with young children are emphasized. Also, students are introduced to the concepts of "teacher as leader" and are provided skills for becoming change agents in schools.
Master's Action Research	While in their internship, students will reflect upon what they are learning about teaching and select a problem upon which to focus their classroom action research project the following semester. This course helps students identify questions about their own teaching, develop skills in the use of action research methods, implement a plan of action in a classroom setting, and share findings and implications of the inquiry through writing, discussion, and oral presentation. The course currently is a requirement for all PROTEACH students.

early childhood and special education pedagogy in the internship experience as well as application of action research in the early childhood classroom.

The core of the Unified Early Childhood Program consists of courses that provide the bases for recommended practices in both early childhood and early childhood special education. Given the complexity of the needs of young children and their families, contemporary aspects of teaching young children had to be infused into certain core courses. Revisions and adaptions of courses in the unified program are ongoing as the fields of early childhood education and special education advance.

Issues in Unification

Institutionalization of the Unified Early Childhood Program has been an ongoing process involving collaboration, negotiation, and political acumen. Implementing each step of the process required extraordinary effort and time from administrators, colleagues within the respective departments, and each unified faculty member. Several issues that emerged during the unification process and contributed to early success of the program are described next.

Faculty Resources and Responsibilities

The most critical resource we had in developing a Unified Early Childhood Program was its *faculty*. The team of six faculty members has been built gradually as the program progressed. This gradual growth in program faculty has afforded some advantages. It has allowed the original faculty members to be selective in adding new faculty members whose talents match evolving needs of the program and who are committed to the idea of unification. Furthermore, new faculty members have had the opportunity to make substantial contributions to ongoing design of the program. This has helped to build a sense of ownership and commitment among all members of the unified faculty.

In 1991, when the unification process began, only three faculty members were involved in the program: one tenured full professor in Special Education, one visiting assistant professor in Special Education, and a newly hired tenure-track assistant professor in Instruction and Curriculum. That year, the dean of the college committed two tenure-track lines in each department to support future implementation of the program: one faculty line in Early Childhood Education and one faculty line in Early Childhood Special Education. The EC position was filled at approximately the same time that the OSERS grant was funded and the first cohort of unified early childhood students began the program. The ECSE position, which was filled temporarily by the visiting faculty member who participated in designing the program and directing the OSERS project, was filled eventually by a tenure line faculty position in the fall of 1993. OSERS will fund this grant manager position until July of 1997.

In the fall of 1995, one more faculty member was hired for the unified program. This new assistant professor was housed in the Department of Educational Foundations (EF) and was responsible for teaching the unified educational foundation courses (e.g., The Young Child, Social Foundations in EC, and Testing and Measurements). Now entering its fourth year, the unified faculty consists of three faculty members housed in SE, two in I & C, one housed in EF, and a graduate assistant (supported by grant funds). The five tenure-line faculty members will remain even when grant funds are no longer available; the sixth is supported by grant funds as well. Figure 5.1 illustrates the unified faculty and the specific areas of expertise of each member.

As the program developed, faculty roles expanded. Currently, all six unified faculty members meet 2 hours every week to discuss student progress, field experiences and placements, teaching methods and specific course content, portfolio assessment and program evaluation, professional development, and overall mechanics of running the program. Unified faculty members also have expanded their faculty roles in the area of team teaching. These team-teaching arrangements have demanded extensive exchanges of ideas and deep examination of philosophical and theoretical beliefs among the faculty members. For example, the faculty members involved in team teaching have had to carefully dismantle old course syllabi, examine and adopt textbooks that integrate EC and ECSE content, and jointly create new, integrated course experiences for students. It is anticipated that the team-teaching format will continue to be beneficial for faculty and the program.

In addition, a number of hours have been spent at faculty meetings discussing the best ways to teach students how to integrate multiple perspectives such as constructivism and behaviorism. The conversations have been informal; however, ongoing examination of our beliefs can be enhanced through day-long retreats and working brown-bag lunch seminars.

Additional faculty roles required in undertaking the development of a unified program include:

— overseeing collection, analysis, and interpretation of data relevant to program development and student outcomes
   writing annual reports and grant continuations
— overseeing grant budgets including student fellowships, travel, and personnel
— politicking at state, university, college, and departmental levels
— disseminating information about the program and its development through conference presentations and professional publications
— counseling and advising students
— collaborating with administrators and teachers in area schools and agencies.

These tasks are essential to the program's success and demand a substantial amount of faculty time and energy. Time devoted to attend to such needs is a factor that requires careful consideration from individuals seeking to develop a unified program. "Early career" faculty seeking tenure and promotion must devote a lot of energy and commitment to research and publication activities. Although unified faculty members put extended time and energy into program development, they have been able to dovetail their research and publication efforts with the unified program efforts. The combination of junior and senior faculty was important in developing the unified program at UF. Although the program is insti-

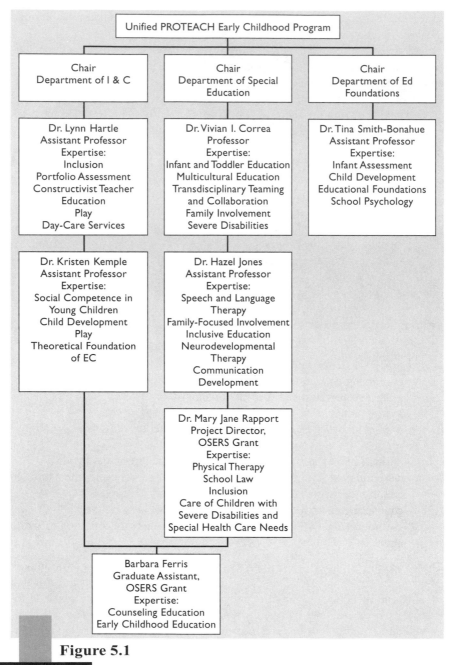

Figure 5.1

Unified PROTEACH Early Childhood Personnel and Areas of Expertise

tutionalized permanently, the "early career" faculty continue to need additional support toward achieving tenure and promotion. Clearly, a system of recognition and merit for service toward program development is necessary.

Resistance and Cross-Departmental Interactions

The cross-departmental nature of the unified program has presented challenges concerning which department receives full-time equivalent (FTE) credit for courses taken by unified students. For the most part, a balance of FTE-generated hours has been achieved across departments. Currently, students receive the undergraduate degree from the SE department and the master's degree from the I & C department. On occasion, however, faculty assignments and loads have presented problems. For example, one of the unified faculty members supervising unified students' internships (offered in the I & C department) was a special education faculty member. The faculty member was required to have a temporary joint appointment in Instruction and Curriculum and Special Education for that semester. In the future, this situation probably will be handled in a similar fashion. Furthermore, no mechanism is in place for course assignments that involve team-teaching a 3-credit-hour course. Splitting two faculty members' assignment to a 1.5-FTE percentage does not really allow the faculty member coverage for the amount of work generated in a co-teaching arrangement, and solutions to this problem have not yet been forthcoming. Unified faculty members and the chairs of both departments currently are discussing the possibility of alternating the course's home between Special Education and Instruction and Curriculum from year to year while maintaining the team-teaching arrangement. FTE issues such as these should be anticipated by others engaging in cross-departmental program building. Solutions will vary, of course, with the rules, regulations, and policies of individual institutions.

Another issue that emerged from cross-departmental collaboration was the importance of respecting diverse philosophical orientations. As mentioned earlier, faculty members from I & C were suspicious of integrating special education content into the early childhood program. They had concerns about the program becoming "behavioral" and not "constructivist." They also were alarmed that academic content courses such as art, music, and physical education were being integrated into one course in creativity. Similarly, SE faculty were concerned that the unified program would not provide preservice teachers with individualized teaching strategies for difficult-to-teach students. Their concern related to what seemed to be the absence of behavior management and discipline, direct instruction, and diagnostic assessment.

Interestingly, within the unified early childhood faculty itself, little if any dissonance is present regarding the merging of special education and early childhood philosophies. The unity and respect for multiple views and the common goal of educating diverse young children seems to come from the core belief in developmentally appropriate practices. The national push to teach young children in nondirective approaches integrating learning through play has had a significant impact on early childhood special education practices since the 1980s. The ECSE faculty at UF already had begun to integrate these less behavioral approaches in its teaching of ECSE courses. Furthermore, the 5 years during which the program was developed provided the opportunity for unified faculty to develop the common language and culture necessary to unify the two fields. The process of unification requires extensive discussion among faculty members from differing backgrounds. The unified early childhood faculty has had ample time to develop the sense of community, trust, common goals, and partnership necessary for a program of this nature to be implemented.

In addition, we have found it beneficial to have unified faculty members at all departmental and college meetings. Unified faculty members serve on key committees in the college and, therefore, assure that the college is responsive to the new program.

Field Experiences and Placements

A challenge that faculty faced from the beginning of the Unified Early Childhood Program pertained to field placements. Only a few classrooms in the surrounding public school districts provided inclusive educational settings for young children with and without disabilities. Placements for practicum and internships often have been in segregated preschool programs for children with disabilities, Head Start programs, traditional kindergarten, first-, second-, and third-grade classrooms, and noninclusive day-care centers. We understood early in program development that inclusive field placement sites would have to be developed so students could gain full benefit from the unified program. Getting the program up and running was our first priority. In the summer of 1995, this first step was taken to begin the process of professional development. With some financial support from the dean, unified faculty members designed and implemented a 2-day intensive workshop on developing inclusive classrooms and unification in teacher education. More than 10 local early childhood and early childhood special education teachers attended.

Collaboration with cooperating teachers must continue for successful program implementation. Ongoing summer workshops and faculty-cooperating teacher partnerships are expected to continue the professional development efforts.

Other Emerging Issues

After over 5 years of initiating and implementing a Unified Early Childhood Program, much has been learned. The three issues raised above—faculty resources, resistance and cross-departmental interactions, and field placements—

are most significant and have provided us with great opportunities to learn about unification. Some additional lessons that have been learned in the process are as follows.

- A collegewide infrastructure is needed to support unification, including ways to assign team-teaching arrangements and FTE hour generation.
- Political astuteness and an understanding of the micropolitics of universities, colleges, and departments is critical to move proactively through systems change.
- State certification that supports unification is beneficial; however, unified programs in states that do not have integrated certificates must be more creative about achieving unified outcomes for preservice students within a segregated certification structure. Certification structures should not stand in the way of reform.
- External grant support and funding for pilot-testing a unified program is highly advantageous. The use of project personnel and incentives for recruiting students through stipends has facilitated program implementation. Grant-supported fellowships assisted in recruiting students during the earliest years of the program. Now established, the program will sustain itself through the attainment of certification and successful employment of the graduates.
- Time for professional development of faculty must be built into the unification process.
- Informal mechanisms for communicating with faculty and creating a work environment that promotes "social" and "collegial" relationships is advantageous.

Future of the Program

The future success of the program will require further collaboration and professional development with teachers in the local school districts, continued support by the college to recruit, advise, and retain unified early childhood preservice students, and continued professional development on the part of unified faculty that promotes lifelong learning. The unified faculty has established long-range plans that include grant writing, program evaluation and research, national dissemination through presentation at conferences, and professional writing. Grant-writing activities will continue in:

— obtaining external student financial support
— augmenting program resources with additional faculty and graduate assistants

— securing resources for enhancing professional development activities
— expanding the idea of unification to the doctoral preparation level.

Furthermore, the faculty presently is developing a standardized procedure for collecting data on the progress of students in the program. A large part of the evaluation method being implemented will involve portfolio assessment. In the fall of 1995, data collection was initiated with a survey of students prior to beginning the program and small-group portfolio meetings with faculty and students. Faculty members have been assigned to advise three to four students and will meet with students at the end of each semester to discuss their portfolios and reflect on their experiences. These portfolio meetings are being tape-recorded, and transcriptions of the meetings will be analyzed over the course of the 3-year program.

Faculty members already have had multiple opportunities to present the unified model at state and national professional meetings. The faculty members have planned various writing projects to assist further in disseminating the program over the coming years.

Currently, the COE is engaged in the complete reform and restructuring of PROTEACH, using the concept of unification across special education and elementary education. PROTEACH II, as it has been termed, includes many aspects of the Unified Early Childhood Program, including a strong commitment to inclusive education, reflective teaching, inquiry learning, cohort training, and collaboration. Unified faculty members are participating on the key committees designed to develop the unified elementary and special education program. Furthermore, as changes are made in the PROTEACH II teacher education program, the unified early childhood faculty will have to continue to adjust and accommodate to some of the changes that will ensue.

The energy required to reform departments, colleges, universities, and state departments of education can be formidable, though changes in the system typically are slow. As university faculties elsewhere begin to integrate early childhood and early childhood special education programs, they will have to anticipate the time and energy commitment required to create reform and systems change. A collaborative and evolving program such as the unified program discussed in this chapter requires a multiplicity of phase-in procedures, extensive and creative curriculum reform, and awareness of the process of cross-departmental collaboration. The unified faculty at UF has come to understand the process and is moving forward in implementing a teacher education program that prepares teachers with the skills needed to teach all young children in the 21st century and beyond.

References

Association of Teacher Educators, Division of Early Childhood, and National Association of Education for Young Children. (1994). *Position statement: Personnel standards for early education and early intervention.* Reston, VA: DEC/CEC.

Burton, C. B., Hains, A. H., Hanline, M. F., McLean, M., & McCormick, K. (1992). Early childhood intervention and education: The urgency of professional unification. *Topics in Early Childhood Special Education, 11,* 53–69.

Center for the Study of Social Policy and the Annie E. Casey Foundation. (1993). State ranks low in children's well-being. *Gainesville Sun,* March 29, 1993.

Florida Department of Education (FDOE). (1991). *Early childhood certification standards and competencies.* Tallahassee: Author.

Hodgkinson, H. (1991). Reform versus reality. *Phi Delta Kappan, 73,* 9–16.

Kagan, S. L. (1989). *United we stand: Collaboration in organizations.* New York: Human Sciences Press.

Kemple, K. M., Hartle, L. C., Correa, V. I., & Fox, L. (1994). Preparing teachers for inclusive education: The development of a unified teacher education program in early childhood and early childhood special education. *Teacher Education and Special Education, 17,* 38–51.

Linder, T. (1993). *Transdisciplinary play-based assessment: A functional approach to working with young children.* Baltimore: Paul H. Brookes.

Miller, P. S. (1992). Segregated programs of teacher education in early childhood: Immoral and inefficient practice. *Topics in Early Childhood Special Education, 11,* 39–52.

National Association for Educators of Young Children. (1995). *Guidelines for preparation of early childhood professionals: Associate, baccalaureate, and advanced levels.* Washington, DC: Author.

National Association of State Boards of Education. (1988). *Right from the start: The report of the NASBE Task Force on Early Childhood Education.* Alexandria, VA: NASBE.

National Commission on Children. (1991). *Beyond rhetoric: A new American agenda for children and families.* Washington, DC: Author.

Note

1. In 1985 the College of Education at the University of Florida implemented the 5-year PROTEACH teacher education model. This program enables students to obtain both bachelor's and master's degrees during their professional preparation. Students enter the college in their junior year after having met 60 hours of preprofessional and general education requirements. The internship (student teaching) is completed during the fifth, or graduate, year of the PROTEACH program. Students pursuing a degree in teacher education and a teaching certificate in Florida are committed to completing their teacher education program according to this model. Degrees conferred by the Departments of Special Education and Instruction and Curriculum (elementary and secondary), including the Unified Early Childhood Program, fall under the requirements of PROTEACH. PROTEACH programs and advanced graduate programs are approved by the Florida Department of Education (FDOE) and the National Council for Accreditation of Teacher Education (NCATE).

The Multiple Abilities Program at the University of Alabama: Preparing Teachers to Meet All Students' Needs

Madeleine Gregg, Edwin S. Ellis, Alexander Casareno,
Barbara Rountree, Carol Schlichter, and Phyllis Mayfield

In the fall of 1994, the University of Alabama began a new, innovative teacher education program designed to merge general education with special education in both coursework and fieldwork. The Multiple Abilities Program (MAP) is a five-semester course of study that provides preservice teachers with knowledge of and practice in using strategies and teaching methods associated with general and special education. The goal of MAP is to enable teachers to accommodate the wide range of learning styles and developmental readiness for instruction found in all the learners in a given classroom. Specifically, MAP is preparing educators who will hold Multiple Abilities Certification, K–6. In the State of Alabama, this certification is equivalent to holding three certificates: Early Childhood, K–2; Elementary, 1–6; and Mild Learning and Behavior Disorders, K–6. The emphasis in MAP coursework and field placements is on developing the expertise necessary to meet the needs of individual children, regardless of the type of classroom placement or label they have been assigned.

MAPping Out History

The University of Alabama is located in Tuscaloosa, about 60 miles southwest of Birmingham. Tuscaloosa's population is about 50,000 when the college students are away. It is a typical college town with a beautiful and well-defined campus. It is the main campus of the University of Alabama system and has 11 colleges including the College of Education. Most of the 20,000 students who attend the university are residents of Alabama, although significant numbers are drawn from Georgia, Florida, Tennessee, Louisiana, and Mississippi, in that order.

The College of Education at the University of Alabama has 88 full-time faculty members, 57 of whom teach in the area of Teacher Education and 31 of whom teach in the area of Professional Studies. More than 2,300 students are enrolled in the college—about 1,650 undergraduates and about 660 graduate students. Between 150 and 225 students are placed in internships each semester, and more than 2,000 other clinical experiences are required of pre-internship students each semester.

MAP exists because the right people were in the right place at the right time. Ideas and events at the national, regional, and local levels combined to place the College of Education in a unique position to develop this new and innovative teacher education program. At the national level, powerful theories about learning as socially constructed and about teaching as reflective decision making had become the focus of countless research studies and professional meetings. The Holmes Group's report, *Tomorrow's Schools of Education,* was preparing the way for new teacher preparation programs that would include substantial field experiences in professional development schools (Holmes Group, 1995). The Council for Exceptional Children (CEC) passed a resolution supporting the inclusion of children with a broad range of exceptionalities in general education classrooms (Council for Exceptional Children, 1993). Like many others around the country, professors from Alabama were participating in the scholarly debates and research regarding these critical issues.

At the regional level, in the fall of 1991, the dean of the College of Education attended the annual meeting of the State of Alabama Superintendents' Advisory Group. This group exists to provide input to deans across the state about how teacher preparation programs can be improved to better service the public schools. Alabama's dean heard the expressions of dismay at the speed with which new teachers were referring children to special education. According to the superintendents, newly hired teachers had to be better prepared to make interventions in their own classrooms to meet the needs of children. Although the superintendents were speaking in general terms, the dean at the University of Alabama wanted the teacher preparation programs there to maintain their reputation for excellence. He asked the faculty to propose changes in the elementary and secondary programs that would address the superintendents' concerns.

At the local level, in the fall of 1991, the College of Education faced another extensive round of budget cuts. Since 1989 the college had lost nearly half a million dollars in permanent funds. In the face of continuing cutbacks, the entire college clearly would have to be reorganized. During the spring semester of 1992, a tentative reorganization plan was generated by the dean and his staff, revised by the Faculty Council, and voted on by the entire faculty of the college.

During the 1992–93 school year, as part of the preparation for, and initial stages of, reorganization of the college, the dean created six task forces consisting of all the professors in the college. Among these groups was the Task Force on Regular/Special Education. This group was charged with making "recommendations regarding preparation programs that more fully capitalize on faculty expertise and assist prospective teachers to develop appropriate attitudes and expertise in instructional strategies that (a) meet the needs of a wide range of students, (b) are child-centered rather than label-centered or program-centered, and (c) are collaborative in nature" (University of Alabama, 1993). By the end of the year, the task force recommended, among other things, that the area of teacher education develop programs of study that would lead to dual certification in early childhood education and in elementary education and mild learning/behavior disabilities. The faculty endorsed this recommendation in May 1993.

As a result of these simultaneous activities, the stage was set for the College of Education to create new and innovative teacher education programs. A small group of faculty members from special education and general education accepted the challenge to design a dual-certification elementary/special education program. During its meetings in the spring of 1993, the group roughed out a radically different kind of teacher preparation program, the Multiple Abilities Program (MAP).

MAPping Out the Curriculum Planning Process

MAP curriculum planning began in earnest during the summer of 1993 with the collaboration of a group of experienced elementary teachers, special education teachers, and university faculty members from both special education and elementary/early childhood education (Ellis, Rountree, & Larkin, 1995). Teachers were recruited by open invitation to help plan the program because the university faculty was committed to creating a program in which practitioners and university professors would be co-equal members of a team. Both would take responsibility for the preparation of MAP students.

Participants met in two groups, one for special education and one for general education. Each group was provided with competencies written by various professional organizations to establish standards in the profession (i.e., Council for Exceptional Children, Council for Learning Disabilities, National Association of Elementary School Principals, National Association of Educators of Young Children, State of Alabama Rules and Standards). The competencies were detached from their original documents so participants would not know if a specific competency was intended for general or for special education teachers.

The teams then independently analyzed and separated the competencies into three groups: (a) competencies exclusive to general educators (that is, special educators would not be expected to have attained these competencies), (b) competencies exclusive to special educators (that is, general educators would not be expected to have attained these competencies), and (c) competencies that both groups of educators would be expected to have attained. The findings of the two groups were essentially identical: there was very little that an elementary teacher should know that an elementary special education teacher should not also know (and vice versa).

In the second phase of curriculum planning, general and special education participants worked together as one large team. Their task was to create a master list of competencies that would reflect the knowledge base of an educator who would be qualified to teach students in both general and special education settings. The many standards from the various professional organizations were combined to form one long list from which redundancies were eliminated. Consensus was reached eventually to produce a single set of competencies. The new set of competencies was not much longer than the set required for single certification either as a general elementary school K–6 teacher or as an elementary 1–6 special education teacher.

Late in the summer of 1993, the third phase of the initial curriculum planning took place. A team of university faculty representing both special education and elementary/early childhood general education analyzed the goals and objectives found in existing course syllabi from the elementary/early childhood general education and elementary special education for students with mild disabilities programs. The purpose of this analysis was to determine the amount of overlap in the existing programs. A startling amount of overlap was found, which convinced the team that a dual-certification program was feasible. Furthermore, few competencies emerged that were not already part of the set created by the curriculum planners in phase two.

In the final phase of initial curriculum planning, competencies for the MAP program were established by integrating the master set of competencies identified by the teams of teachers and the set gleaned from the course syllabi. This list thus reflected the opinions of professional education organizations, experienced public school general and special education teachers, and the university faculty. Without regard for their origin (whether from a special education course or a general education course or from a special education or general education professional organization), the competencies were sorted into categories using a semantic mapping procedure. Four categories of competencies emerged: professionalism, the learner, facilitating learning, and communication/collaboration. MAP courses were built around the competencies in the four categories (see Figure 6.1).

In the fall of 1993, the five faculty members who had taken the lead in planning MAP invited wider collaboration in the project. Eight additional faculty members agreed to join this existing team of core professors as collaborative faculty. Their role was to provide assistance as the curriculum continued to be developed and to teach to MAP students competencies within their area of expertise. Thus, two concentric circles of professors worked in MAP: the core faculty, taking responsibility for day-to-day instruction, program administration, and mentoring of students; and the collaborative faculty, having less intense participation in MAP.

Also in the fall of 1993, the core faculty submitted to the State of Alabama Department of Education a proposal for this new experimental teacher education program. The response was enthusiastic, and provisional approval was granted. On April 7, 1994, the State Department of Education approved a Class B Multiple Abilities Certification, K–6—a new certification in Alabama.

Perhaps the most positive evidence that MAP would get off the ground eventually came from the enormous interest shown in the project by people in a position to fund this experiment. Support from the College of Education was critical. Two faculty members were assigned to MAP at a half-time level; three others were assigned at quarter time. In addition, the college provided summer salaries, a graduate teaching assistant, and generous support in terms of telephone and supplies.

In the fall of 1993, the MAP team applied for, and was awarded, a 2-year, $100,000 grant from the Kellogg Foundation. And in the fall of 1994, two junior faculty members who had become part of the university MAP core team were awarded a $90,000 Career Development grant from the Joseph P. Kennedy, Jr. Foundation. This also was a 2-year grant; it provided course buyouts for the two junior faculty members, enabling them to be assigned to MAP full-time.

These positive steps were welcome. The interest in MAP from people outside the university was gratifying and did much to provide the necessary energy and desire to continue the arduous process of getting MAP off the ground. The total amount of time, energy, and hope invested in the project cannot be easily estimated. Other forces, however, were hindering the development of MAP. Many faculty colleagues were not supportive of the project. Some did not approve of MAP because they philosophically distrusted the merging of general and special education; some because of their doubts that MAP's integrated curriculum would allow students to develop the required minimum competencies; and some because they perceived the entire project as having originated in the dean's of-

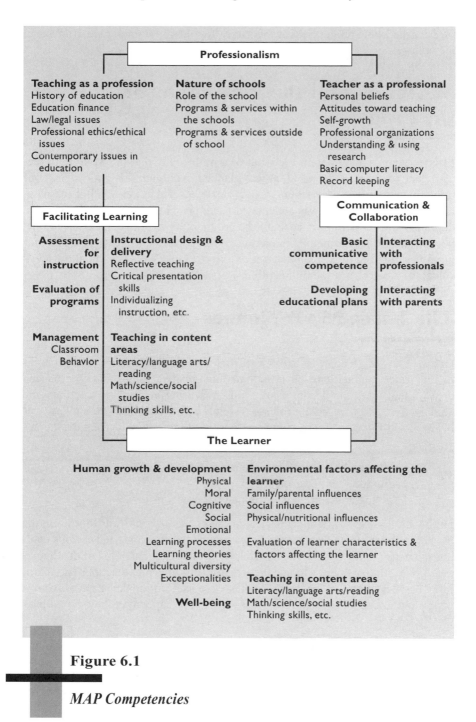

Figure 6.1

MAP Competencies

fice and the whole process was suspect as a "top-down" attempt to micromanage the college.

MAPping Out the Philosophy of the Program

MAP structures and content grew out of a philosophy that the MAP core faculty came to share as the program was planned. Although this philosophy continues to evolve as MAP encounters new situations and as new challenges arise, much of the philosophy was articulated early on. The idea that "less is more/ depth is more" was important to all the core faculty members (Sizer, 1985). It became the guiding principle in making all MAP curricular decisions. The program thus focused on a small number of powerful ideas and tried to allow MAP students to experience them in depth.

The Three MAP Themes

One idea sets MAP apart from other teacher education programs: A small number of themes can facilitate the development of understanding about how to teach in ways that meet the needs of all children. During a series of meetings, the collaborative and core MAP professors slowly articulated ideas about what was believed and valued about teaching and learning. From these ideas, three themes emerged:

1. Understanding child development and diversity
2. Facilitating empowerment
3. Utilizing authentic instruction and assessment

During the first semester a primary concern of the program was to present the themes to the students through field experiences, coursework, and various reading and paper-writing assignments. Slowly, as their understanding of the themes developed, students began to use them as tools to interpret teaching and learning. They began to see how these themes were useful to make sense of what is happening in schools and to recognize what is not happening, but should happen, in schools.

Understanding Child Development and Diversity

Understanding child development and diversity was the most accessible theme to the MAP students, and it emerged immediately as a concern for them as they visited local schools. The MAP students clearly saw diversity in children, including that resulting from disabilities and developmental differences, as well as from language, culture, class, race, and gender.

In the first semester, one set of field experiences designed to teach diversity placed MAP students at the Child Development Center on the university campus for 4 observation periods. The focus initially was on infant development, followed by the toddler, 3-year-old, and 4-year-old development of "normal" children. Each visit was guided by a worksheet that directed the students to focus on one child and make observations of his or her physical, social, emotional, and intellectual levels of development. During a weekly debriefing of the experience, a professor from the human development program came to the MAP classroom, provided added information about a stage of development, and addressed MAP student questions and concerns.

The students next visited RISE, the Rural Infant Stimulation Environment program that provides early intervention for children at risk in west Alabama. Here MAP students were able to observe developmentally delayed children and contrast what they saw with the development they had observed in the children who were developing normally. The 3- and 4-year-old programs at RISE practice "reverse mainstreaming," inviting several nonhandicapped youngsters to attend RISE as a nursery school, which added another dimension to the observations of the MAP students.

As diversity issues related to the multicultural character of classrooms today were woven into the studies of children's literature and social studies teaching methods, "teachable moments" arose. Confronting their attitudes about race became an important part of the weekly journal entries of many MAP students.

Facilitating Empowerment

During the first semester, MAP students also were helped to reflect on the second theme, facilitating empowerment, particularly on how elementary school students and teachers are empowered or disempowered through classroom structures and management. During their month-long field placement, students looked at a number of empowerment issues: how gender relates to which students raise their hands but do not get called on; how proactive management of student movement from place to place, both within their classroom and within the larger school space, prevents many discipline problems; the use of time-out in classrooms; and the extent to which various management programs in use in city and country schools empower children and teachers.

Empowerment came to be an important issue for MAP students, perhaps primarily because of their stage of development. As young adults, most of them were in the process of separating from family and establishing themselves as individuals. Issues related to empowerment in elementary schools often were transformed into broader issues with which the MAP students were struggling. MAP professors encouraged the students' personal identification with empowerment in the belief that they would need to understand the dynamics of empowerment personally before they could teach in ways consistent with the MAP philosophy.

Because of the radical difference between MAP and the typical teacher education program, the faculty anticipated some difficulty when the MAP students would begin teaching differently than their mentor teachers in the schools. The faculty wanted the students to understand empowerment so they would be able to use it as a tool in their own professional lives, as well as in their own classrooms.

Utilizing Authentic Instruction and Assessment

The third theme, utilizing authentic instruction and assessment, provided MAP students with ways to reflect on and evaluate how the pedagogical strategies they saw in practice related to their emerging understanding of the needs of certain children. Authentic instruction in MAP is presented in ways that offer students opportunities to personally construct knowledge and that engage students intellectually by stressing students' personal sense-making. MAP students began to understand the power of linking instruction to students' intuitive knowledge base (Iran-Nejad, 1994). Issues related to authentic assessment included requiring multiple pieces of information about progress in learning, evaluating students' products according to various criteria, and valuing children's thinking about interrelationships among ideas rather than valuing student acquisition of an amount of unrelated information.

One curricular activity designed to accomplish this goal required MAP students to keep track of all instructional activities during one day of school and categorize them as being authentic or nonauthentic. Students then wrote about their justifications for the decisions they had made. They thereby were made aware of how infrequently authentic instruction and assessment occur in classrooms.

The "Big Picture" Idea

A second idea that guided all of the MAP experiences at the university and in field placements was "the big picture" idea: *School success is a function of the interaction between the student and the environment* (see Figure 6.2). MAP students needed to learn the various factors that mediate this interaction, as well as how to provide meaningful instruction. In their field experiences, MAP students began to recognize the various ways in which these factors could be viewed. In their coursework, they learned how the field of education came to know about this interaction through research.

Figure 6.2 shows how the learner can be viewed from a variety of perspectives. The traditional perspectives that have long guided teacher education—such as physical, social, cognitive, moral, and affective development—were woven constantly into MAP coursework. So, too, were nontraditional perspectives such as the "multiple intelligences" perspective (Gardner, 1983).

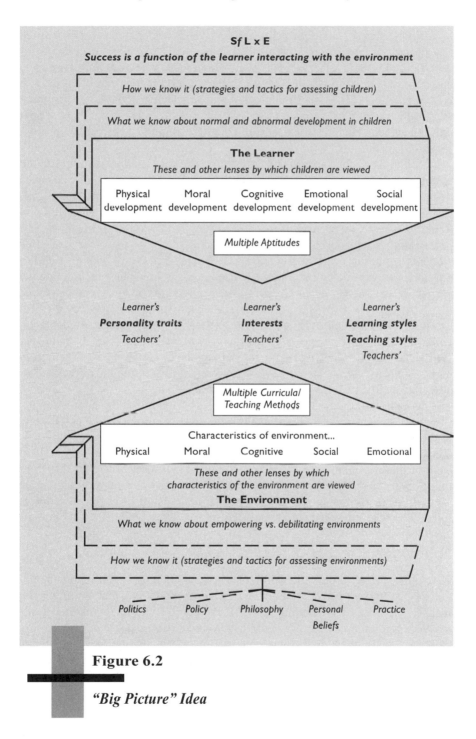

Figure 6.2

"Big Picture" Idea

Perhaps just as important as the perspectives by which the learner is viewed are the various lenses used to focus the perspective. MAP class discussions focused on telescopic, macroscopic, microscopic, and kaleidoscopic lenses—to name a few—through which reality can be viewed. Among these lenses, two were privileged: (a) the macroscopic, holistic perspective about how everything fits together and is interrelated in school, and (b) the microscopic lens of specific knowledge about physical, social, cognitive, moral, and affective development.

During the second semester, MAP students began to understand how to tell where a child might fit on a continuum of enhanced development to arrested development. At the same time, they were developing the knowledge and skills associated with assessing children using the different tools associated with particular perspectives or lenses.

In tandem with developing an understanding of how to view learners, MAP students needed to begin to recognize the various factors influencing a child's environment, especially the school environment, and how these factors interact with the learner. MAP students learned that the environment, too, could be viewed from many perspectives and with different lenses. Paralleling the way the program set up opportunities to learn about the learner, MAP helped students develop both a holistic perspective of the environment and knowledge about specific dimensions of the environment. Students learned how to assess environments along an "empowering-to-debilitating" continuum using the different tools associated with given environmental assessment strategies.

Some of the reasons that school success is a function of the interaction between the student and the environment were invisible to our students. We refer to these reasons as the "P factors": the roles of politics, policy, philosophy, personal beliefs, and practice. Woven into the entire MAP curriculum was study of each of these in relation to (a) the environment and the learner, (b) decisions made about facilitating learning, and (c) how the environment and learner are viewed. These factors were examined both from a historical perspective and in light of current issues such as school reform.

Reflective Process

Given that the two program-shaping ideas presented thus far (the three themes and the big picture idea) did not reflect much of the schooling that our preservice teachers received before coming to MAP, the core faculty knew that becoming teachers who embrace the MAP philosophy would be a difficult task for our students. The third MAP-shaping idea was to build in an ongoing, consistently reflective process that would give students the chance to critically examine their own experience of being learners in situations that were the opposite of authentic, empowering, and respectful of diversity. A reflective mindset in the preservice teachers was fostered in MAP by requiring the students to write extended weekly journal entries. In their journal entries, MAP students discussed their past and present experiences and what they were coming to understand about teaching and learning through them. The core faculty responded to the journals and pressed students to question the assumptions, pedagogies, and philosophies they were observing (Casareno et al., 1995).

Because one of the primary goals of MAP is for future teachers to become thoroughly at home in using technology as a professional tool, MAP students sent their journal entries to the faculty on electronic mail (e-mail). This not only provided a permanent record of the journal entries, but it also allowed the faculty to respond with their comments on e-mail. Through journal-writing experiences, the idea that teachers must be reflective decision makers became a central aspect of MAP. By making the MAP students accustomed to constantly reflecting on their own and others' practice, MAP professors hoped that the students would continue to critically examine their teaching even after they finished the program.

MAPping Out the Structures of the Program

Several MAP structures are highly visible reminders that MAP is an innovative program. Several of these are discussed in the following pages.

1. MAP students move through the program as a cohort. This has both positive and negative consequences. On the positive side, the students have really bonded. They know each other's strengths and weaknesses; they support each other in times of crisis; they learn a lot from each other. On the negative side, the dynamics of a cohort can make the emotional atmosphere of MAP resemble a roller coaster. A few disaffected students can disproportionately influence the entire group when a problem arises.

2. MAP students do not take any of the existing University of Alabama teacher education courses in classroom management, mathematics or social studies methods, testing and measurement, or educational psychology, for example. Instead, all of their coursework integrates the content found in the separate classes. This feature of the MAP design allows MAP faculty to weave the teaching of material that normally would be addressed in one semester over a period of five semesters. For many students, one semester of decontextualized instruction in a course permits only shallow development of understanding. When given five semesters to build understanding of a topic, however, instruction can be tailored to the students' changing levels of understanding resulting from their experiences working with children and growth in their professional knowledge

base. Thus, MAP professors embrace a constructivist stance toward teaching and learning. The development of totally new courses also allowed us to integrate technology into all of our assignments and into many of the students' learning experiences.

In addition to e-mail, MAP students learned word processing, and how to use spread sheet, database, and multimedia programs. Familiarity with and use of software within classroom instruction has been stressed.

3. Students spend 50 percent of their time in field placements interacting with real teachers and real students in real school settings. MAP field placements are in early childhood classes (kindergarten through grade 2), elementary classes (grades 3–6), or special education classes (resource room or inclusion experience). Most of the classrooms where field experiences take place belong to the teachers who were part of the effort to design MAP. The teachers in these classrooms are assigned one MAP student to mentor (more will be explained later about teacher mentors). With much guidance and help, MAP students gradually begin to assume more and more responsibility for planning and delivering instruction as they progress through their field placements.

The first-semester placement is a month-long experience designed to help the students appreciate the complexity of a school as an institution. Through observation and interview, MAP students learn firsthand the various jobs that exist in schools, from the principal to the guidance counselor, to the janitor, to the cafeteria worker, to the nurse, to the special educator, to the speech therapist, to the classroom aide. MAP students also visit a variety of public and private schools that showcase "best practice" in technology use or constructivist teaching of mathematics or science instruction.

In the second semester, students are assigned 2 days a week for 8 weeks[1] to a classroom where they gradually begin to contribute to the teaching of literacy, social studies, and science. This field experience gives them the opportunity to try out lessons they have planned. In the second semester, the teacher mentor does not leave the room while the MAP students are teaching and the MAP students are not responsible for groups of students larger than five at a time.

The third semester's field experience occurs in a 3-week summer enrichment program that exists to provide an internship for master's-level students seeking certification to teach gifted and talented children. Each master's-level intern is assigned two MAP student interns to assist in classroom instruction. Most of the children who attend the program are already identified as gifted and talented. Planning the instruction for these highly able students in the summer enrichment program challenges MAP students to base their teaching on the children's needs rather than on the demands of a state-required curriculum.

The fourth and fifth semester are the official "student teaching" internships for MAP students. During one semester the students are placed in special education settings, and during the next semester they teach in regular classrooms.

Lower- and upper-grade placements also are balanced against each other. During these 7-week internships, MAP students are responsible for gradually assuming all responsibility for instruction and assessment of students for a minimum of 10 consecutive days.

4. In the traditional approach, a theoretical foundation of understanding is constructed first, eventually leading to practice. In MAP, the approach is generally the reverse. Typical teacher preparation programs place theoretical coursework, such as in educational psychology or child development, early in the sequence of courses, and schedule methods courses and their related field components just prior to the student teaching internship. In contrast, MAP has an early and continuing emphasis on developing basic competencies in instructional methods, primarily through field placements, in which MAP students gradually learn more and more about what and how to teach (Cognition and Technology Group at Vanderbilt, 1990). The experiences from field placements thus become the basis for understanding theoretical concepts and for making decisions about educational strategies and methods. In each subsequent semester, MAP students receive progressively more exposure to theoretical underpinnings. This is another example of the constructivist approach to instruction in MAP.

5. MAP introduces students to the benefits of taking advantage of the need for ongoing professional development. MAP students attend at least two national or state professional conferences (e.g., literacy, math, special education) every semester. There, as they meet and hear the concerns of practitioners, they are socialized to assume a stance of continuous professional growth and development.

6. Mentoring relationships are an important part of MAP. Each core faculty member is named as university mentor to five or six students each semester. During that semester the professor responds to the students' journals, tutors individual students, listens to their problems, visits them in the field placements, and generally acts in a mentoring capacity by providing information, by keeping track of paperwork, and by making decisions about how to modify program expectations to meet the needs of MAP students as learners. The university mentors try hard to walk the talk; we are preparing preservice teachers to respond to and adapt and accommodate individual differences, and as much as possible the faculty do the same.

Students also are assigned to a teacher mentor each semester. Unlike the traditional role played by cooperating teachers with whom students do internships, teacher mentors in MAP have a great deal to say about what content is addressed in the university setting. Teacher mentors teach many aspects of preservice education that are traditionally part of the university experience of preservice teachers. For example, lesson and unit planning happens primarily in the field, as does learning about professionalism (e.g., appropriate language and dress, accountability, the ethical treatment of children). Teacher mentors play an essential role in MAP. They are in the best position to determine the particular academic needs of the MAP student entrusted to their care.

Each university mentor makes contact each week with the mentor teachers of the MAP students for whom they are mentor. These meetings keep the lines of communication open between the two mentors and provide ongoing information about content that has to be addressed in the university setting. Teacher mentors also coordinate field placement experiences for the MAP students. Often, these experiences take place in their own classrooms, but when an experience is needed that is not available in a mentor's own classroom, the mentor arranges with a colleague in his or her school for the MAP students to have it. Teacher mentors thus are responsible along with the university mentors for MAP students' learning and progress.

MAP also provides parent mentors for the MAP students. To date, these mentoring relationships have been of short duration. The mentors are parents of children whose specific academic needs are being met through special education. The mentors meet with MAP students at evening sessions several times each semester. The goal of inviting parents to share their experiences with MAP students is to help MAP students become committed to the idea that each child they teach is a special, much-loved son or daughter. During the evening sessions, small groups of MAP students and parents of exceptional children discuss a set of questions designed to help the MAP students see school life from the parents' perspectives. Sometimes a short reading is given to them to reflect on together. After an hour in the small-group setting, the whole group reconvenes to share significant insights. At present, we are trying to identify enough parent mentors to assign one to each MAP student for the entire five semesters of the program. The development of the parent strand of MAP represents an exciting direction for the program.

7. MAP has its own secured classroom space that no other classes in the university use routinely. This means we can display works in progress and not have to worry that they will be treated with a lack of respect. For example, we can leave partially completed charts and other kinds of sense-making efforts on the walls and not have to be concerned that others will be judging them as finished products. The walls of the classroom thus can function as a kind of working memory for the class. In addition, because we can leave books and other personal curriculum materials for MAP students' use without worrying about losing our belongings, the range of materials with which MAP students can work is expanded.

In summary, MAP has a qualitatively different feel to it than typical elementary teacher education programs. The cohort and mentoring structures mediate the quality of interactions among the people associated with MAP. The emphasis on methods first and theory later, the allocation of 50 percent of the time in field experience, and the fact that MAP students do not take any of the regular university coursework also contribute to this feeling. The physical reminder afforded by the MAP classroom space, which allows us to have a "home" at the university, is another qualitative difference. Furthermore, the continual exposure of MAP students to professionals who care enough about teaching to attend national- and state-level professional meetings creates a norm that striving for excellence is fundamental to MAP.

MAPping Out the Curriculum

The central goal of MAP is for students to learn how authentic teaching and learning are mediated by cognitive abilities, learning styles, physical and social development, and cultural, ethnic, and socioeconomic diversity. In keeping with our philosophy of "less is more/depth is more," MAP students' time at the university is structured as a series of multifaceted experiences designed to facilitate the development of knowledge of and skill in state-required competencies. Early in the program, the MAP curriculum was structured around processes that used information from student observations and collections of data about instruction, student learning, curriculum, and other essential topics. MAP students write thematic essays, case studies, and units of instruction using the information they personally collect, as well as information from reading books and articles and from presentations by the university faculty.

Because MAP curriculum experiences are so richly layered, many of them are able to be unpacked by different professors to help develop different kinds of understandings. For example, one professor had MAP students generate a set of social studies learning activities that would accommodate certain kinds of student needs in certain ways. MAP students each were assigned a topic and were asked to design instruction for their topic by creating authentic learning activities that would offer all elementary school students an opportunity to explore it. The goal for MAP students was to design, and then implement, instructional sequences that would enable all students in their classrooms to have learned the topic by the end of the unit.

Across the set of activities generated for the topic are some that provide students who already have knowledge of the topic a chance to deepen it. Other activities introduce the topic to students who know little or nothing about it. The written products that result from the activities also vary according to ability level, ranging from lists of words through organized visual displays of information to drafts of essays that have been revised and rewritten several times. Some activities are done independently, and some are part of cooperative learning groups. Some require fine-motor control, and others do not.

One MAP professor wanted her students to understand how this variety of activities was their major means of accommodating differences in cognitive ability, learning style, level of physical and social development, and cultural, ethnic, and socioeconomic diversity. Another professor then used the activities to show the MAP students how to analyze the ways in which modifications of learning activity affect the cognitive processing of children. A third professor used the activities to teach MAP students how to create and use evaluation rubrics.

These lessons occurred over a period of 2 months, during which time the MAP students constantly refined their learning activities in response to what they were learning about social studies content, cognitive processing of information, and authentic assessment. In the end, they had a ready-to-use resource for their future teaching, as well as the knowledge of state-required competencies.

MAPping Out Assessment of Student Progress

Throughout the program, evaluation of MAP students' acquisition of teaching and communication skills has taken place using three primary formats: (a) real-time evaluation, (b) permanent product evaluation, and (c) analysis of reflective journals.

Real-Time Evaluation

Several kinds of opportunities for real-time evaluation provide valuable feedback to MAP students, mentor teachers, and university mentors about the students' developing teaching skills. Informal observations of MAP students' interactions with elementary students, other professionals, or parents are followed immediately by debriefings, or conversations that ensure appropriate feedback to MAP students.

Co-teaching lessons with their mentors allow a professor and a MAP student to take turns teaching elementary students. The mentor models techniques that are appropriate for the elementary students receiving the instruction and that target the MAP student's zone of proximal development (Vygotsky, 1978) with regard to the instructional methodology being demonstrated. Co-planning lessons give mentors the opportunity to tailor instruction in lesson planning to the needs of the MAP student and allow the mentor to evaluate the student's depth of thinking and understanding.

Product Evaluation

MAP students produce a number of products by which they are evaluated, including video recordings of their teaching; photographs of, or actual, learning centers; lesson and unit plans; and assessment portfolios with tests and product rubrics developed by the MAP students. These products reflect the developing sophistication of MAP students' expertise.

Product evaluation typically involves two dimensions: (a) an evaluation of the product itself, and (b) an evaluation of a student's assessment of the product. For example, each student makes a videotape of teaching a 15-minute lesson to four students, one of whom is labeled as having learning disabilities. Each videotaped lesson is followed by a videotaping of the MAP student as he or she explains the intent of the lesson and reflects on how well the lesson went. The MAP students discuss the nature of their instruction and assessment of elementary student learning, as well as their understanding of the characteristics of the learners they have instructed in the light of the three themes (authenticity, empowerment, and diversity).

The teaching shown on the tapes is evaluated using a specially developed rubric. University mentors meet with MAP students individually and provide feedback about their teaching. Often the mentor and the student watch specific portions of the video recording together and then discuss what they have seen. The information about the student then is used to design subsequent learning experiences for the student.

At the end of the first semester, students view their videotaped lessons again and then record an end-of-semester critique of their teaching. This reflection is based on the additional knowledge they have acquired about learners and facilitating learning during that semester. Thus, over the five semesters of MAP, these teaching recordings and student self-critiques produce a clear history of the developing sophistication of the emerging teacher. Similar evaluation and feedback mechanisms have been used for other products.

Reflective Journals

Like the video recordings of MAP students' reflections, reflective journals provide important data about MAP students' beliefs and understanding of the MAP themes: authentic instruction and assessment, development and diversity among children, and empowerment. The journals also provide important information about what students are motivated to learn at the time they are written—an important piece of information in MAP's constructivist approach to teacher preparation.

MAPping Our Experience of Collaboration

Mostly, our experience of collaboration has meant spending a great deal of time together. In the summer of 1994, the university mentors, graduate students, and the collaborative faculty sat together for days and sketched out the curricular ideas that would guide the program. We created a five-semester timeline of ideas that were theoretical, yet practical. We grappled with issues about how many hours the students would spend out in the field during each semester, how much time we would have at the university for our teaching, the point in the program at which it made sense to introduce specific competencies, and when we would expect students to have developed certain levels of expertise in certain competencies.

In addition to the initial weeks of meeting daily from 8–5, our experience of collaboration has meant spending what has occasionally seemed an inordinate amount of time planning each week during the semester. Four-hour planning meetings have been scheduled each week, in which we do not plan lessons as much as juxtapose concepts, content, time, and methods. We also talk about our understanding of students' needs, perceptions, and difficulties that have emerged from our reading of the reflective journal entries. We attempt to solve the problems that arise in the interface between MAP as a new program and the University of Alabama as an old institution or from our personal roles within the institution.

As we walked the talk, we learned to compact the curriculum. We prioritized and made drastic changes in our program and constantly struggled to be sure we were teaching students instead of content. We became very much more educational generalists, incorporating all aspects of teacher preparation into our portions of MAP's instructional time, even as we were becoming MAP specialists. Although this has been incredibly time-consuming, we have managed to get through the ordeal of inventing and launching a new program by helping each other out, and we have found the experience good.

In addition, all of us—core faculty, teacher mentors, and collaborative faculty—have grown in our knowledge of teaching methods, of content, of how the University of Alabama and the local school systems function as systems, of human relations, of the basic connections between theory and practice, and of the power of reflection. As we have pushed our students to be reflective, our own commitment to being reflective has been strengthened.

It has not all been sweetness and light. At times we have not liked one another. At times we could not speak to each other directly because of what someone said or did not say or wrote in an e-mail message. At any one moment in time, though, no more than one person was in deep despair about how MAP was going; the other four were there to provide perspective.

Two emerging trends have helped us. First, as our experience of MAP has evolved, we have come to better understand the dynamics of our interrelationships. Second, as evidence of our students' competence has begun to accumulate, the moments of absolute doubt by any one of us have disappeared. We still get tired, and we still are working hard, but the payoff is already manifesting itself, and we are content with what we have accomplished so far.

MAPping the Future of the Program

MAP already has had an impact on other programs at the University of Alabama, both directly and indirectly. One direct impact has been the creation of a new administrative unit within the College of Education: the Interdisciplinary Unit. Especially designed for programs like MAP,[2] the interdisciplinary unit will facilitate dialogue among programs about assignment of faculty to courses and service within and across programs.

One of the most difficult problems for MAP faculty has been that we have been required to give the same amount of service to the programs for which we originally were hired at the university (in elementary or special education) as we gave before taking on MAP. Thus, we attend faculty meetings, serve as advisors to large numbers of students, read comprehensive exams at the master's and doctoral levels, and help with doctoral screening. We also participate in evaluating applicants to the Teacher Education Program, which is required of all students who will receive certification, no matter what program they choose, and which is a long, involved process. For example, in the fall 1995 semester, the elementary education program gave to one professor, who is assigned full-time to MAP, 22 writing samples to evaluate and 40 interviews (15 minutes each) to conduct.

Many issues remain to be worked out, but the general principle is that professors who teach one course in a program will be responsible to give one-fourth of the service level of professors who teach full-time in that program.

MAP also has impacted the university directly by beginning to develop plans for both master's-level and secondary multiple abilities programs, for which many requests have been made. Clearly, because of the subject-specific nature of secondary programs, the model used in the elementary program will not transfer. MAP faculty members are collaborating with secondary education professors and looking at various models to determine how a Secondary MAP might best be done.

The largest indirect impact probably has been the heightened awareness in the College of Education faculty of issues associated with team teaching, compacting curricula, and the inclusion of children with exceptionalities in the regular classroom. Professors are giving serious consideration to how to modify existing programs to incorporate some of the goals of MAP.

We have been requested to move MAP from experimental to permanent status, which suggests that, in the view of the University of Alabama, MAP is a viable, stable program. Although MAP is extremely time-consuming for the participating faculty at present because we are still inventing the program, we have every hope that the second and third cohorts of MAP students will require no more faculty time for teaching and preparation than other teacher preparation programs. We have learned many things to improve the next cohort's experience of MAP:

1. It is better for students to spend 3 days a week out in the schools for a shorter period each semester than to spend 2 days out all semester.
2. We know more about how to compact curriculum.
3. We know more about how to integrate rather than simply merge curricular projects.
4. Students need "pay-back" time closer to the extra event they attend rather than at the end of the semester.

MAP has proven to be a successful collaboration between special and general education. The first students seem to compare favorably with interns from other programs. They are similar to typical intern teachers in terms of lesson planning, classroom management, and presentation of content. They are quite different in their sensitivity to children's needs, in their use of most constructivist teaching approaches, and in their willingness and ability to modify instruction. As one MAP student said recently, "Since being involved in MAP, my eyes have been opened to the needs of children. Teaching is about more than books, paper, and pencils."

References

Casareno, A., Gregg, M., Ellis, E. S., Rountree, B., Schlichter, C., Heineke, S., Colvert, G., & Larkin, M. (1995). Learning through reflection: The development of constructivist thinking in MAP. *Canadian Journal of Special Education, 10*(2), 32–66.

Cognition and Technology Group at Vanderbilt. (1990). Anchored instruction and its relationship to situated cognition. *Educational Researcher, 19*(5), 2–10.

Council for Exceptional Children. (1993). *CEC policy on inclusive schools and community settings.* Reston, VA: Author.

Downs, R. (1985). The representation of space: Its development in children and in cartography. In R. Cohen (Ed.), *The development of spatial cognition* (pp. 323–345). Hillsdale, NJ: Lawrence Erlbaum Associates.

Ellis, E., Rountree, B., & Larkin, M. (1995). General and special education master teacher perceptions of elementary school inclusion teacher competencies. *Alabama Council for Exceptional Children Journal, 12*(1), 3–16.

Gardner, H. (1983). *Frames of mind.* New York: Basic Books.

Gregg, M. (1994). Learning geographic reasoning: Mapping the course. (Doctoral dissertation, University of Pittsburgh, 1994). *Dissertation Abstracts International, 54*(07), 2688A.

Holmes Group. (1995). *Tomorrow's schools of education.* East Lansing, MI: Author.

Iran-Nejad, A. (1994). The global coherence context in educational practice: A comparison of piecemeal and whole-theme approaches to learning and teaching. *Research in the Schools, 1*(1), 53–76.

Palincsar, A., & Brown, A. (1984). Reciprocal teaching of comprehension-fostering and comprehension-monitoring activities. *Cognition and Instruction, 1*(2), 117–175.

Sizer, T. (1985). *Horace's compromise: The dilemma of the American high school.* Boston: Houghton Mifflin.

University of Alabama, College of Education. (1993). *College of Education plan.* Tuscaloosa, AL: Author.

Vygotsky, L. S. (1978). *Mind in society: The development of higher psychological processes* (M. Cole, V. John-Steiner, S. Schribner, & E. Souberman, Eds. and Trans.). Cambridge, MA: MIT Press.

Notes

1. In our judgment, the 2-day-per-week format was not successful. Students were not able to bond with their classes and they did not do as much teaching as we had hoped they would do. For the second cohort of students, the second-semester placement will be for 4 days a week for 4 weeks.
2. Since MAP was started, another new program has been launched: Education for Young Children with Diverse Abilities. Sometimes referred to as "little MAP," this program prepares early childhood educators with the knowledge and skills needed to facilitate learning and development of *all* young children, birth through 5 years of age. In addition, the Teaching English as a Second Language Program has become part of the unit.

Teacher Education Reform Within the Special Education Program at the University of Cincinnati: An Ongoing Journey

Regina Sapona, Jerry Etienne, Anne Bauer, Ann E. Fordon, Lawrence J. Johnson, Martha Hendricks-Lee, and Nelson C. Vincent

Our journey—to redesign our teacher education program in special education—began in 1985 with internal events (new faculty members, changes in department head) and external events (changes in our profession) resulting in a critical period of self-examination. After we began this process, the College of Education at the University of Cincinnati accepted an invitation to become a member of the Holmes Group.[1] Membership in the Holmes Group committed all teacher education programs in the College of Education to a comprehensive reform agenda, with a central focus on urban education.

In previous years the college's connections with schools and teachers, and among ourselves as teacher educators, depended primarily on personal relationships initiated and sustained by faculty, and not on institutional and programmatic agreements. We now had an opportunity to pursue program reform efforts within a wider context (the entire College of Education) and to have an impact on teacher education programs beyond special education.

As we reviewed artifacts for this chapter (documents prepared for college administration, state certification review, NCATE reviews, and minutes from program meetings), we observed several phenomena that were key to changes in our program: learning to talk with one another, leaving the safety of our own group, and developing a special education core. As we shifted the focus of our teacher education efforts, we were able to articulate our program more carefully and work with other teacher education programs within the college as well as develop new relationships with teachers in the Professional Practice Schools (also known as Professional Development Schools). These changes were facilitated and supported by a collegewide reform effort now referred to as the Cincinnati Initiative for Teacher Education.

In this chapter then, we describe two aspects of interrelated changes in teacher education. We share various aspects of our journey through the reform process, while describing the influences of collegewide program reform and changes within teacher education on our thinking. Because the reform continues, we report on our work to date, the challenges we confronted, and our next steps.

The Special Education Program Context for Reform

A major challenge for the special education faculty was how to prepare teachers and other educational personnel to meet the needs of all children in the next millennium. Our practice had been successful with children in self-contained, isolated settings but would not meet diverse children's needs in settings such as general education classrooms. The faculty was charged to identify a vision within and across special education certification areas, and for services to children across the developmental contexts.

Prior to 1985 the Special Education Program consisted of 12 full-time faculty members, two part-time faculty members who shared appointments with other colleges in the university, and one faculty member who had a full-time appointment at the Cincinnati Center for Developmental Disorders teaching the equivalent of one course per quarter for special education. The Special Education Program was housed in the Department of Early Childhood and Special Education. Programs of study associated with Ohio certification areas were independent of each other and of other teacher education programs in the college: two undergraduate teacher education programs in the areas of multiple disabilities and developmental disabilities (the Ohio category for mild mental retardation) and eight graduate programs in the areas of hearing impairment, specific learning disabilities, emotional/behavioral disorders, developmental disabilities, multiple disabilities, speech and language pathology, audiology, and administration and supervision in special education. A program in Early Childhood Special Education that had been attempted in 1975 subsequently was inactive and was just reemerging in 1985.

Graduate students enrolled as master's degree students, or as post-baccalaureate students in the certification areas mentioned above, or as post-baccalaureate students seeking a validation or endorsement in Early Childhood Special Education. Each certification or validation area had separate methods courses and field experiences, with little collaboration among faculty members within special education. In addition to these programs, special education's contribution to the education of general education students was through two courses: an introductory course on individuals with disabilities and one course on mainstreaming.

During fall quarter 1985, a core group of faculty members in the Special Education Program volunteered to serve as members of a program development committee. This group developed a faculty survey to identify the goals of the existing programs and the issues related to these goals. A focused follow-up survey was distributed, and this was used to develop a concept paper describing a framework for the program to use as a guide for future work.

By fall 1986, faculty members had reached consensus on the framework and a plan to develop a special education methodology core that would serve all special education teacher education programs. Also in this concept paper we identified a core of knowledge and experiences we believed to be unique to special education. This core was intended for all graduate students in special education (not only those interested in pursuing certification) and would be shared across all disability areas. In addition, we expressed interest in beginning formal collaborative activities with faculty members in elementary and secondary education programs and strengthening the existing collaboration with the early childhood education program.

Our conceptual model, to be used for future program development, referred to:

— the *dynamics of the learner,* indicating a strong developmental perspective;
— the *dynamics of the profession,* referring to pedagogical knowledge; and
— the *dynamics of the field,* indicating an emphasis on the public school-aged population identified as having disabilities.

This model was used to generate new programs of study based on a unified special education core of knowledge and also was used in response to a state certification program review that took place in February of 1987.

The Collegewide Context for Reform

At about the same time that we shared our model publicly, the College of Education Holmes Planning Task Force presented a design process to guide collegewide reform efforts. The strategy was to build consensus around principles that would guide planning. In so doing, faculty members would learn to work together rather than to begin this process by debating educational theory, practices, or curricula. For the design process the task force borrowed heavily from an experiment in architecture at the University of Oregon. Frustrated that their master plans for campus building and development became obsolete before it was enacted, the University of Oregon, led by architect Christopher Alexander, developed an alternative process that was sensitive to changing conditions and responsive to the needs and experiences of the people who used the facility (Alexander, Silverstein, Shlomo, Ishikawa, & Abrams, 1975). The task force revised the initial principles to guide change within the College of Education at the University of Cincinnati (1987). The six planning principles that emerged are as follows:

1. *The principle of patterns:* All design and implementation will be guided by communally developed and adopted teaching and learning frameworks called "patterns." Collegewide deliberations will determine a set of patterns to embody the missions, goals, and primary means by which teachers would be educated in the College of Education at the University of Cincinnati. These central patterns will frame all curricula and pedagogy and become criteria by which program effectiveness will be judged.

2. *The principle of organic order and change:* Planning and implementation will be guided by a process that allows the whole to emerge gradually from local acts. Rather than imposing a master plan on the college, the nature of teacher education at the University of Cincinnati will emerge progressively and responsively from the design work of faculty and students in local program areas.

3. *The principle of local decision making:* Decisions about what to do and how to do it will be initiated and made by members of the community who are most affected. Not only will design work be focused locally, but decision making about program form and content will be localized in the faculty, students, and school collaborators who are closest to the work of educating teachers.

4. *The principle of individual program growth:* The design undertaken in each evaluation/implementation period will be weighted overwhelmingly toward local program areas. All programs will not be expected to change in the same ways at the same pace. Growth and change will be

weighted most heavily toward local projects rather than toward collegewide initiatives. This process is expected to provide the freedom for faculty to explore alternative ways of defining programs and program responsibility.

5. *The principle of evaluation:* The well-being of the whole will be protected by a biennial evaluation detailing which program area activities are working and which are not, based on the patterns adopted by the community. The focus of the evaluation work will be to provide an opportunity for local participants to examine the effectiveness of program activities and experiences and the extent to which they are aligned with program and college goals.

6. *The principle of coordination:* The deliberate emergence of organic order in the whole will be assured by an open process that assesses current program status and regulates proposed program changes. A process open to the college and university communities will be established to coordinate the local work of educational programs according to the core set of patterns and to provide a means by which patterns may be modified or added.

Even though all of the principles must be present for the process to succeed, the principle of local decision making was paramount. "Local" first was defined by programs—for example, the Elementary Education Local Group and the Secondary Education Local Group. Later, as more areas in the college made contributions to teacher education, other local groups, such as the Educational Studies Local Group and the Student Support Services Local Group, emerged. The Special Education Program had worked for a year on redesigning programs when the collegewide reform activities started and, fortuitously, the principle of local decision making guaranteed that our efforts would continue in ways that respected the primacy of local programs.

The principle of the patterns is a complicated and unique approach to ensuring consistency and flexibility across programs. To safeguard against merely repackaging existing teacher education programs, the college asked a basic question: How might we best describe the knowledge and skill of the experienced practitioner? Rather than responding to this question with a list of isolated features, the structure and function of the pattern language provided us with a means to envision what our programs could be. Language has an explicit framework with individual components that are interactive and generative. Whereas Christopher Alexander's architectural pattern language is one of design (Alexander, Ishikawa, & Silverstein, 1977), a pattern language for teaching is one of both design and performance.

As a planning principle, the pattern language concept allowed us to deliberate in a nonthreatening way on the theoretical and practical matters of teaching and learning. Everyone was encouraged to submit ideas for patterns. Just as a language develops with new experiences, the pattern language has grown and changed. The current (1992) version, *A Pattern Language for Teaching* has 89 patterns, organized into three levels.

1. College Core Patterns, with 10 patterns (for example: multicultural focus, individual diversity, and urban mission) that embody our most important values; these should infuse everything we do.
2. Outcome Patterns, addressing outcome patterns in three areas: Professional Ways of Knowing (such as knowledge of content, knowledge of self), Professional Ways of Doing (such as planning instruction, discussions, collaboration), and Professional Ways of Being (such as commitment to each student, personal development orientation).
3. Professional Study Patterns, addressing outcome patterns in two main areas—Professional Study Patterns and Professional Practice Patterns—both of which are subdivided into Knowledge-Related Activities and Knowledge-Related Structures.

Each pattern follows the same general format: a rationale (based on the nature of teaching practice, professional needs, theory and research, and college goals); a prescriptive statement (which acts as a general guideline for pattern enactment in each of the teacher education programs); a list of essential pattern indicators (describing specific activities that would provide evidence for the existence of the pattern-in-use); and a statement of the pattern's relationship to other patterns in the language (patterns connect in network-like fashion to represent complex activities). For example, the pattern Knowledge of Contexts begins with a rationale for using a constructivist approach:

> The contextual basis for learning, understanding, and practice should be a central theme in each teacher education program. Students should study various contexts, their general characteristics, and their manifestation in particular teaching situations. Practical experience should be afforded in a variety of contextual configurations.

This statement is followed by a listing of essential pattern indicators (such as "case studies of contextual configurations influence local classrooms; working with teachers successful in urban contexts" and the relationship to other patterns (for example, Multicultural Focus, Urban Mission).

The pattern language has been accepted as part of our NCATE knowledge base. Each newly developed course in the redesigned programs arises out of a selection of patterns. Rather than using syllabi to represent our courses, we use portfolios in which all outcomes, readings, activities, assignments, and evaluation techniques are connected explicitly to the pattern language. When course portfolios are submitted for initial approval, they typically include information distributed to students, such as expectations for specific assignments, readings, and possible agendas for class meetings. Portfolios also include information on how that particular course or experience fits within an overall program of study and how the course content is integrated across other courses or experiences.

As courses are offered in future years or by different faculty, the initial course portfolio is modified or adjusted based on feedback from students and teachers in the Professional Practice Schools. Consequently, we are assured that every teacher education program meets the collegewide vision and that each program has the freedom to address values, skills, and dispositions in ways that the respective program faculty sees fit.

Reform Efforts Within Special Education

The use of the pattern language and design principles provided the context within the College of Education to support local groups as they tackled the challenge of program reform. Two events seemed to contribute to the development of a special education core and areas of emphasis. Through use of the pattern language, Special Education Program faculty members learned to talk with one another about our beliefs. As we discussed our ideas with faculty members outside our program, we began to clarify our beliefs. The special education faculty also developed a sense of community as we shared our frustrations and successful discussions with faculty members outside our program. This allowed us to become more comfortable with confronting the tough questions and decisions our program faculty needed to make.

Learning to Talk with One Another

After years of maintaining separate programs of study, how do faculty members begin a dialogue about core beliefs? As mentioned earlier, the program faculty developed the concept paper describing core knowledge and experiences we believed to be unique to special education. Still, we had still been unable to agree on adopting a core of coursework for all graduate students entering our master's in education program. This may have occurred because of lack of time and commitment to examining shared beliefs. Four faculty members in the program who worked with graduate students piloted integrated coursework, but others within the program were unwilling to surrender control and maintained separate courses. Faculty members who were engaged in teaching both graduate and undergraduate programs did not have the time to experiment with their programs of study.

One model being proposed worked well at the graduate level because most graduate faculty members had developed shared beliefs about teaching and learning through their piloting efforts. Similar modifications to the undergraduate programs were much more difficult because of dissimilar beliefs, strong feelings of ownership of specific courses, and heavy instructional responsibilities that did not allow time to develop programmatic changes. Further, because the certification areas of developmental disabilities and multiple disabilities were offered at both levels, changing only the graduate preparation program would have been awkward.

Despite the constraints, faculty members in special education began to learn about each other's visions and the changes that had to occur in special education to accomplish those visions. The first step was to learn to talk with one another, and our vehicle for beginning these discussions was the pattern language.

The problems of ownership of specific courses and varying commitment to the development of a shared vision seemed overwhelming. In keeping with the principle of local decision making within our collegewide design process, special education faculty members had become members of the Special Education Local Group. The faculty participated in bimonthly special education program meetings to discuss the day-to-day operations of our program (e.g., admissions, scholarship awards, class orders, graduation lists) and bimonthly Special Education Local Group meetings to engage in dialogue to redesign our program using the pattern language. The Local Group meetings were facilitated by a member of the Educational Administration Program. This faculty member helped set agendas and ensured participation and engagement by all special education program faculty members.

Using the pattern language freed us from the jargon unique to the field of special education and provided us with a shared language, both within our program and across other programs and departments. The pattern language was unfamiliar and new for most faculty members. We were engaged in examining particular patterns to make our own meanings explicit to one another when a key event occurred in November 1988, related to the pattern of respect for diversity. Our department head requested that each faculty member bring a one-page response, interpretation, or definition of the respect for diversity pattern to the next local group meeting. For some of us, sharing our most basic beliefs was particularly difficult. Over the course of several intense discussions, we learned about one another's views and participated in conversations that led eventually to refinement and redefinition of the shared philosophy of our program.

Our previously published philosophy had not required us to examine critically how we were preparing teachers with respect to diversity of all learners and, more specifically, individuals with disabilities. This philosophy had become comfortable, and it no longer challenged us. The recognition that we were not challenging ourselves to ask new questions about meeting individual needs led to development of the guiding principles given below:

- Individuals with disabilities should be viewed as learners who demonstrate variations in development. This implies that teachers need to understand typical development as well as the impact of various conditions

on learning, and to recognize that all individuals have a right to participate in the community of learners.

■ Special education graduates must be prepared for the future. We anticipate that special education and general education teachers will be expected to fulfill a variety of roles and positions in educational settings
and agencies that are very different from current roles. Teachers also
will be expected to collaborate routinely with one another in the years
ahead. The forms of this collaboration and the types of roles teachers
assume will, by necessity, be fluid and will be developed over time to
meet the needs of a wide variety of learners.

■ The program will be committed to the inclusion of all learners (inclusive education) in educational settings. This orientation will emphasize
excellence in teaching, integrated programs, and an exploration of alternative program delivery systems (in contrast to the current separation of
special and general education students and categorical programming).

These new principles required us to make dramatic changes to our program.
Based on our belief that special education teachers need to have an understanding of typical development and experience with typical learners, on January 6,
1989, the Special Education Local Group voted to discontinue undergraduate
certification programs in special education and eliminated two program options
at the undergraduate level (Ohio certification in developmental disabilities and
multiple disabilities). A major factor in reaching this decision was the increased
demand for special educators to work in general education settings, requiring
an understanding of both general and special education. As the undergraduate
major was phased out, the special education faculty became more involved in
working collaboratively with faculties in the early childhood, elementary, secondary education, and educational foundations programs to ensure that all
preservice students would be better prepared to meet the needs of all learners.

Leaving the Safety of Our Own Group

Deciding on our own destinations for this journey was difficult enough, let alone
discovering the multiple ways we could travel and work together. Our journey
also was influenced by expeditions with colleagues outside our program. These
sometimes turned into side trips, just as rigorous and stressful as the journeys
within our own group, with relative strangers that taught us many things about
one another.

As the special education faculty continued its own reform work, the Holmes
Planning Task Force raised issues that cut across all programs. Through that
task force, committees were created to address various issues: Professional Practice
School Committee, General and Educational Studies Committee, and Admissions and Advising Committee. In those committees special education faculty
members regularly represented our concerns about educating teachers to work

with all learners including those with disabilities. For example, our contributions to the Educational Studies Committee, which later became a local group, led to development of a course entitled Individual Diversity, now part of all undergraduate teacher education programs with the college.

After articulating our vision and guiding principles in 1989, special education faculty members volunteered to serve as representatives to other local groups. As representatives, we contributed to development of the teacher education programs in early childhood, elementary and secondary education. Our intent was to help integrate ideas related to special-needs learners into those programs of study rather than to view topics associated with special education as add-ons. For example, course portfolios developed for the secondary education program include topics such as "accommodations for individuals with diverse needs." We also had faculty representatives on a local group that emerged later—the Student Support Services Local Group. This group designed experiences to enable all preservice teachers to work collaboratively in teams (with school psychologists, counselors, nurses, work-study coordinators, administrators, and personnel from nonschool agencies) to meet the needs, not just the "labels," of all learners in schools.

Special education faculty members met with varying degrees of success in attempting to participate in the conversations taking place in the other local groups. During the early stages of development, the Holmes Task Force held large-group meetings, referred to as Friday Forums, to which all teacher education faculty members were invited. These meetings centered on issues such as resolving internal programmatic concerns, working with the arts and science faculty, developing relationships with public school faculties, refining the process of teacher preparation, and working with Professional Practice Schools.

Often, dialogues among faculty members across programs illustrated our differing beliefs about learning and teaching. We were pleased by the many shared beliefs that emerged as we worked together. Some tenured faculty members expressed their amazement that conversations with colleagues across programs were occurring; other more recently hired faculty members were excited about the possibilities these conversations would yield. In these large-group discussions there were no balkanized program boundaries. We were all learning how to use the pattern language to design our programs; it gave us a common place to begin dialogue, and through its use we were learning how to share ideas across programs.

During an April 1989 meeting of the Special Education and Elementary Education local groups, some long-time faculty members commented that this was the first time in over 20 years that open and collaborative discussions had taken place across program areas. Examples from the minutes of this meeting illustrate this collaboration: "potential courses special education can offer," "help in course development," "work together on ways to adapt instruction to a range of learner needs," "conduct seminars in special education concerns," "serve as members of a teaching team," and "participate in various internship experiences . . . during fourth and fifth years as members of faculty cohorts."

As faculties across local groups engaged in discussions around the pattern language, we all began to develop our ideas for reform more clearly. As we left the safety of our own local group to serve as representatives to other local groups, we met with success and also encountered obstacles and dilemmas, which we shared informally and during our regularly scheduled local group meetings. Thus, two processes occurred simultaneously:

1. Discussions across local groups helped special education faculty clarify our ideas.
2. Discussions within our own local group led to the development of a sense of community and trust in one another.

The emergence of trust and comfort in sharing ideas was necessary to development of a cohesive special education core. We also needed to be very clear about our shared beliefs as we became aware of our potential to influence or participate in the education of all teachers in the college—general and special education alike.

A Program Shift: Developing a Special Education Core and Areas of Emphasis

Despite the participation of special education faculty members as collaborative partners in general teacher education reform issues, we each were still associated with a categorical preparation program. Faculty members taught classes, advised, and supervised teacher education students separately in the identified Ohio areas of developmental handicaps, multiple handicaps, hearing impairment, specific learning disabilities, severe behavior handicaps, speech and language pathology, audiology, and administration and supervision in special education. Clearly, we had to move away from this categorical orientation and move forward to developing a common core of courses that all special education students would take, whether they were interested in certification or were pursuing a master's degree without certification.

Developing a Special Education Core

Most of our special education programs offered separate courses (e.g., methodology courses, field experiences), and faculty members associated with different disability categories seemed to share few philosophical beliefs. This situation arose during a period of some 10 years in which the special education program faculty rarely met more than once a year. The absence of frequent communication led to fragmenting of the program into individual efforts. The years from 1985 to 1989 were utilized to reestablish lines of communication and to build trust across all programs within special education. We thought that building relationships across programs lines would be extremely difficult unless we trusted one another.

The special education faculty revisited the conceptual model and competencies developed in 1985 that describe the dynamics of the learner, professional knowledge, research, communication/consultation, and assessment. Much of the discussion centered on the need to build a common field of knowledge that would provide the basics for meeting the needs of all learners. We debated how far this commonality existed, if at all, and with whom it existed. We negotiated the content areas and reviewed publications that supported or detracted from the notion of a common field of knowledge.

During this time we developed an initial version of our graduate program in special education that included several course sequences. This was published first in January 1989 when we proposed to the Holmes Task Force how our program might look under the Holmes Initiative Program guidelines. A review of this first document indicated that we had retained categorical programs of study. An external review team highlighted the faculty's overall efforts to date to ensure that all students would receive quality education across all the programs involved in teacher preparation. The review team also mentioned that the faculty needed to address the "separateness" within special education—that is, the separate programs of study. The reviewers also seemed to believe that this separateness was a 'work in progress' and that this could be resolved at a later date.

Not until October 1991 did we revisit the strategy we had utilized originally as we discussed the pattern of respect for diversity. All special education faculty members were asked to develop a one-page description of "shared content" or knowledge that was common to all our programs of study. Until this time we had been afraid to ask this question about shared beliefs, as we had become comfortable with distinct programs based on various conceptions of teaching and learning; we were literally afraid of the conflicts that might arise if we were to confront our differences. We had developed enough trust in the course of this multi-year process, however, to move the program development to the next level.

A small group of faculty members reviewed the ideas about "shared content" that everyone submitted and then grouped these into pattern language categories: professional ways of knowing, professional ways of being, professional ways of doing. We shared our work with special education faculty members, who then made modifications and finally achieved a consensus about what shared content had been produced. By November 13, 1991, we had drafted these ideas into a series of thematic statements. With minor revisions, the following themes were endorsed by all faculty members in special education:

- ■ Knowledge of human growth and development including learning theories and principles, and of variations in development, is essential in supporting the learning process.

■ Recognition of the role of communication/language development and cognitive development in its broadest sense provides insight into the learner's behavior, interaction, and learning.

■ Acknowledging and valuing the individual diversity, culture, ethnicity, and gender of each learner contributes to the development of all individuals involved.

■ An understanding of our history (where we have been) and where we are currently (in terms of addressing individual diversity) supports the process of ongoing development (where we are going) so we will be prepared in the future to meet learners' needs.

■ Knowledge of political, research, legal, professional, community, and ethical contexts in which services for learners who vary from their peers are developed, implemented, and evaluated is necessary/essential.

■ The special educator is a lifelong collaborative co-learner who communicates with colleagues, parents, community members, other professionals, and learners through the perspective (or from the viewpoint) of understanding families, cultural and ethnic perspectives, and community influences.

■ The special educator supports each individual's learning and development through an ongoing process of assessment, generating curricula specific to the information that emerges, and evaluating not to judge the learner but, rather, the process in which the learner and teacher have been engaged.

■ Advocacy for learners, families, and teachers directs [drives] our interactions within the field.

■ Teaching is research; it is ongoing RE-searching and reflection to discover how to best facilitate learning for each student and community of learners.

■ Teachers should assume an inclusionary, proactive stance in facilitating the development of all learners with whom they interact.

■ Teachers are questioners who, conjointly with parents, colleagues, community members, and learners, strive continuously to engage in professional best practices and seek effective and innovative alternatives in addressing issues and concerns.

■ As professionals, we are engaged in modeling and supporting our students in behaving as ethical and responsible individuals, with a strong sense of social justice and an interest in contributing to others' well-being.

These themes were developed into four core seminars: Human Development and Diversity of the Challenging Learner, Educator as a Collaborative Co-Learner, Teaching as Reflective Practice, and Designing Learning Environments for the Challenging Learner. Because we had no interest in duplicating the emphasis on human development in the College of Education master's degree core, only four core seminars central to special education were necessary. Work groups drafted course portfolios for these four core seminars.

To introduce our thematic statements, our program documents include references to a major long-term disciplinary trend that has guided our program development and implementation efforts. We believe all children develop within a series of nested contexts (Bronfenbrenner, 1977; Kurdek, 1981). This recognition of the diverse developmental contexts of all learners is reflected in the following theoretical beliefs:

- All development occurs within a personal context, which is unique for each individual. The personal context is a complex interaction of interpersonal, community, and societal relationships.
- Development is transactional; each response has an impact on the subsequent responses of the individuals in the context in which they are interacting.
- Children learn from a variety of "teachers."
- Children vary in their developmental rates and learning styles, in their ways of accessing the environment, and in their interactions and communication with others.

In addition to developing themes and a common vision, the faculty also agreed later on the development of a three-quarter methodology sequence beginning with the core seminar entitled Designing Responsive Learning Environments for the Challenging Learner. This sequence is intended to present information and engage graduate students in inquiry in general areas of literacy development. Students enroll concurrently in professional seminars associated with specific disability areas. If the topics in the methodology sequence involve the design and implementation of Writer's Workshop, for example, the discussion in the professional seminar might include specific considerations or modifications needed when implementing a workshop format with learners identified as having learning disabilities or behavior disorders. Because certifications in Ohio have a range of kindergarten through grade 12, students interested in early childhood special education enroll in their own methodology sequence and professional seminars.

Developing Areas of Emphasis

As we worked on the Special Education Program Core, we also had to make decisions about which certifications we would offer and which we would not because of limitations in resources. Eventually we settled on areas restricted to school-age learners who had been identified as having a disability (with associated certifications).

After integrating our programs of study and eliminating the two undergraduate teacher certification areas, the Special Education Local Group developed one master's degree program with various program-of-study options. Four of the five options, or areas of concentration, lead to teaching certificates (in Developmental Handicaps, Hearing Impairment, Multiple Handicaps, Several Behavior Handicaps, Specific Disabilities) or a validation (Early Childhood Special Education), added onto an initial teaching certificate. Students interested in working on a specific teaching certificate or validation work with an advisor to select an area of concentration that most lends itself to earning the teaching certification, or validation most representative of their area of interest. The specific areas of concentration associated with specific certification or validation program options are:

1. *Classroom Structures and Behavior Management:* selected by graduate students seeking Ohio certification in Severe Behavior Handicaps and Specific Learning Disabilities

2. *Educational Alternatives for Individuals with Significant Challenges to Learning:* selected by graduate students pursuing Ohio certification in Developmental and Multiple Handicaps

3. *Language and Communication:* selected by graduate students pursuing Ohio certification in Hearing Impairment

4. *Working with Young Children and Families:* selected by graduate students pursuing Ohio validation in Early Childhood Special Education.

A fifth program-of-study option was developed to meet the needs of individuals pursuing a master's degree only (those who are not interested in seeking a teaching certificate or validation). This *individually designed area of concentration* is designed with guidance by, and approval of, a faculty committee.

Feedback from the Field and Other Groups

As we worked through the design process for the Special Education Program Core and program structures, we sought feedback from teachers in the field and other professionals. We received support and funding from the college to hold two large group meetings: a teacher consultation meeting (January 1992) and an administrators/supervisors meeting (March 1992). The Teacher Education Council, a group of faculty members from across the college, administrators, and representatives from the public schools, reviewed an April 1992 program version to look for evidence of pattern language and to examine how well the Special Education Program met the tenets of the Cincinnati Initiative for Teacher Education—a name change from the Holmes Initiative to indicate progress and ownership of the new preparation programs.

Many program documents were developed as we underwent review from other groups within the college, the university, and external agencies such as the Council for Exceptional Children and NCATE. With each new audience we tried to specify how we were going to actualize the feeling of responsibility we had for educating all learners. Various reviews described our program as forward thinking and as having a strong thematic and theoretical basis.

Special Education Contributions to Collegewide Undergraduate Teacher Education

Though the Special Education Program phased out its two undergraduate teacher education programs, faculty members believed that all education majors should be prepared to work with learners who have special needs. This led to a strong commitment to the education of undergraduates in the early childhood education, elementary education, and secondary education programs. Our influence and participation in these general education programs currently takes two forms: direct participation in providing instruction and ongoing work with Professional Practice Schools.

Providing Instruction to Undergraduates at Various Levels

The Special Education Program faculty's goal was to become a presence in all levels of undergraduate teacher education, starting with the very first experience students have in the College of Education. One of the first patterns to be identified in the pattern language was Linking Seminar. Linking Seminars were designed as one-credit-hour education courses offered in the students' first and second years. Linking Seminar was designed to explore the relationship between the teacher and the school, and the students and the community, in regard to present and future goals and objectives.

A seminar designed to help undergraduates link their Arts and Science degree majors and their initial work as students preparing to become teachers allowed college faculty to build consensus about the requirements for the Arts and Sciences degree. The Linking Seminar guaranteed that students would interact with College of Education faculty, and that they still would be "our" students, even though most of their early years in the program were spent in the College of Arts and Sciences. Special Education Program faculty members have designed and taught Linking Seminars for 4 years, and they continue to add their voices and influence to the topics presented in this seminar.

The Special Education Program faculty also participated in developing a series of coordinated seminars that occur in the third, fourth, and fifth years of the Cincinnati Initiative undergraduate preparation programs. A local group referred to as Educational Studies was created to address three areas: learning and development, human diversity, and culture and schooling. Faculty members in special education and educational foundations formed cohorts to design and implement six coordinated seminars: human learning, individual development, individual diversity, language and communication, assessment and evaluation, and social inequalities and schooling, as well as Linking Seminars. The Coordinated Seminars, so named because they were to be coordinated with other components of an undergraduate preparation program, were intended to provide information on specific content areas such as language and communication or development.

For example, elementary education undergraduate students enrolled in the Language and Communication seminar were expected to also enroll in coursework in literacy learning and the study of children's literature in addition to their work as interns in a Professional Practice School. Ideally, the faculties associated with those courses and experiences would work together to provide an integrated experience (developing shared assignments, for example).

Some of these seminars are in the first year of implementation. Others have been offered the past 4 years. Coordination among faculty and across various programs has been a new experience for many faculty members.

During the fifth year of study, special education faculty members participate in a seminar known as Student Support Services. This seminar is integrated with the fifth year internships and was developed by the Student Support Services Local Group. It is designed to provide content knowledge in topics such as referral for additional support, referral for possible identification of disability, and knowledge of the array of services required by law and by need in order for a child with a disability to function within a group of peers. Students also are exposed to the range of factors that impinge upon quality education for all students.

Working with Professional Practice Schools

The special education faculty has made significant contributions to the development of new ways of working with the public schools. Although individual faculty members had developed strong relationships with specific teachers in local school districts, the college—in partnership with the Cincinnati Public Schools and the Cincinnati Federation of Teachers— worked together to create a system of Professional Practice Schools. Professional Practice Schools have three interrelated goals (American Federation of Teachers, 1988):

1. To support student success.
2. To provide professional education and professional induction programs for teacher education students and for beginning and experienced teachers.
3. To support systematic inquiry directed toward the improvement of practice.

The Cincinnati Public Schools are well known for their innovations, including those in the area of professional development of teachers. Teachers and administrators in Cincinnati have created a career ladder, as well as a peer evaluation and assistance program. These recent achievements in collaboration helped to ease the functioning of a joint planning committee consisting of five members each from the school district, the union, and the university. The joint planning committee created guidelines for design and asked individual schools for proposals to become Professional Practice Schools. Schools were selected, and a pilot program was started.

The relationship with the Professional Practice Schools was clarified in 1992. The responsibilities of the team of professional practitioners were expanded to include a full partnership between the university and the public school faculties. This partnership was solidified through a series of meetings that began in 1993 and has continued since then. Teams of faculty members in the Professional Practice Schools worked collaboratively with campus-based faculty members to design innovative ways of working together.

Pilot efforts in the 1994–95 academic year with special education graduate students serving as interns in two Professional Practice Schools were highly successful. Special education graduate students now are working as interns who assume half-time teaching responsibilities in six Professional Practice Schools. Campus-based special education faculty members serve as liaisons to the schools through their participation as members of teams that mentor interns. In addition, special education faculty and school faculty members work together regularly to gain insight into educating all children, to assist the schools in educational change activities, to encourage the school faculty to become more inclusive in its practices, to engage in professional development activities, to model teaching practices and, most important, to learn from faculty members who are implementing theory and providing the daily guidance necessary for our special education interns to become quality teachers. This sharing of expertise is modeled in a setting where respect and effort are expected and evident from both groups of faculty in each of the teams.

Future Challenges: Where Do We Go from Here?

As we examine the artifacts and reflect on our journey to date, we are amazed at how far we have come and how much we have learned about one another. The journey has been rugged, with detours and many new traveling companions. We are revising and fine-tuning our program constantly as well as learning to communicate better where we want to go and how to get there. We are examining emerging concerns: development of the pattern of faculty cohort, changes in state certification requirements, fidelity to program themes, linkages to Professional Practice Schools, and program evaluation.

We currently are immersed in our third year of implementation for the Special Education Cincinnati Initiative for Teacher Education program. The other local groups in the college are offering for the first time fifth-year courses and internships in the Professional Practice Schools. Though the challenges we face are not as dramatic as our initial need to integrate our programs, they are critical to the ongoing success of our redesign efforts.

Working Together: Fine-Tuning the Pattern of Faculty Cohort

One challenge faced during pilot efforts was the linking of internship requirements with coursework requirements. Communication has been a constant challenge, and we have targeted this for specific attention. Special education faculty members currently are meeting regularly with teachers who serve as mentors to our interns in the Professional Practice Schools as well as representatives from other local groups. We are trying to define what is meant by the pattern of Faculty Cohort and how we can implement a team approach to mentoring interns. Special Education Program faculty members are assigned as liaisons to specific Professional Practice Schools and have tailored their roles to the specific needs of their school, ranging from helping teachers initiate discussions on inclusionary practices to providing support for interns who work in inclusionary settings. This cohort also attempts to ensure the integration of course requirements with internship responsibilities in the Professional Practice Schools.

Certification Issues

Our basic program of study was designed for individuals who enter our graduate program with a teaching certification. Our challenge now is to develop program modifications needed for graduate students who enter our program with backgrounds other than in teacher education. This is particularly important given the likelihood of changes in state certification requirements.

Initial Certification Requirements

In the past a number of highly qualified graduate students have completed our program without a prior background in education—for example, social workers and students with degrees in psychology, economics, or journalism. Given that one of our guiding principles has been "experience and background in general education," and given that changes in state certification standards will require special education teachers to have a general education certificate, certification programs that provide initial certificates in early childhood, elementary, and secondary clearly will best allow talented graduate students from diverse backgrounds to prepare to enter special education. We are in the initial stages of discussion of a blended teacher preparation program for graduate students who would like to enter the field of special education from backgrounds other than general education.

We are, in essence, redefining the culture of teacher preparation and redefining the population from which teachers are being prepared at the University of Cincinnati. We are asking the early childhood, elementary, and secondary education programs to accept the responsibility for teaching all children, including those with variations (whether identified as having a disability or not) and to share coursework with students in special education. This is a major paradigm shift that will require time to actualize.

Changes in State Certification Requirements

Changes in state certification programs will continue to impact on our work. Though we acknowledge that we believe we are preparing teachers for a wider audience than the State of Ohio, we are a major state university. Consequently, we must ensure that our graduates fulfill state licensure standards. This regulatory provision requires continuous reexamination of how our experiences are implemented and how we set priorities for program reform. Although the pattern language, the philosophical positions taken by the faculty, the relationships with other programs and with the Professional Practice Schools provide us with a well grounded starting point for continuous program reform, we do anticipate that ongoing program modifications also will be based on our response to new state requirements.

We will continue to revise our program as we improve working with one another both within the college and in the Professional Practice Schools. Although we may have to modify the delivery of experiences to preservice students, we believe the program can sustain the delivery of high quality teacher preparation to all students.

Fidelity to Program Themes

Fidelity to our themes is a constant source of concern. Some faculty members are reluctant travelers on our journey, for a variety of reasons. Our intent was that the themes would be infused throughout all courses, yet we realize we must not infringe upon any individual faculty member's academic freedom. Revisiting or reaffirming our themes, co-teaching, and team teaching should provide strategies for maintaining our fidelity without using coercive or subversive methods. Faculty development is a key to the issue of fidelity. This has been achieved by building understanding and consensus in all discussions during meetings and as we share information about our successes and challenges in working with other faculty across the college and in the Professional Practice Schools.

We also need to look at innovative means of providing faculty with the time and resources to explore different ways of preparing teachers. We need to find the means of providing 'real' rewards for these efforts. For example, this past year the division head offered relief from one class per year for each faculty member who was a member of a school planning committee in the Professional Practice Schools. This was a major breakthrough because it provided tangible evidence that the effort is considered important. The College of Education's Research and Development Office also has awarded small grants that allow faculty members to study their own teaching with the goal of improving our own practice.

Linkages to Professional Practice Schools

Establishing linkages to Professional Practice Schools requires time for those of us at the college and for those in the schools to learn about one another. Some of us are serving as liaisons to schools in which we have little familiarity with the local neighborhood communities. Some of the Professional Practice School teachers who assist us with our efforts to integrate internship and course requirements have had little experience in serving as partners in the teacher preparation process. We are engaged in discussions leading to the development of a common philosophy and the development of inclusionary practices in the schools. We have worked and continue to work to restructure our relationships to dispel myths of "ivory towerism" from the university and "a lack of concern for theory" in the schools. Equal responsibility and equal involvement are the intended reality.

Redefining the culture of teacher preparation requires immense dedication and investment of time. We find ourselves working against the tendency to become jaded and the associated danger of losing sight of our vision. This applies to both faculties, those in the Special Education Program and those in Professional Practice Schools. Both institutions are limited in the numbers of faculty members available and resources. Over the next few years the faculty cohorts will work to resolve some of these problems by sharing coursework, mentoring, program development, and professional development. If our experiences with program reform hold true, this model of sharing should provide the richness of outcomes necessary to soften the burdens of time and effort inherent in program reform.

Evaluation

The special education faculty has adopted a 4-pronged approach to assist us in evaluating our program reform efforts.

1. We evaluate individual courses through student evaluations completed anonymously at the end of each quarter.

2. We have established a cohort group consisting of school-based and campus-based faculty to examine each course syllabus to determine how well the individual courses are integrated into a program of study.
3. We ask graduate student interns and Professional Practice School faculty members who serve as mentors to evaluate the degree of fit between campus coursework requirements and the demands of the internship.
4. We survey all our graduates yearly to determine whether the knowledge and skills developed in the program actually prepare them for a career as a teacher of children with disabilities. This survey is sent to graduates one year after they have completed the program.

In addition to these efforts, we have developed a complex cycle of feedback and feed-forward as an important part of our continuous evaluation efforts. For example, prior to the start of spring quarter 1996, mentor teachers and campus faculty will meet to share course requirements and discuss internship responsibilities such as writing IEPs. Possibly, campus-based faculty will modify course requirements to provide clearer coordination across the courses and a better fit to the internship requirements. Various groups, especially the mentor teachers, provide information about the program's impact on Professional Practice Schools—that is, impact in terms of the professional development of teachers and impact on learners in the school settings. Program and school coordinators also meet bimonthly to problem-solve other cross-program issues as they emerge.

The Teacher Education Council, composed of education, arts and sciences, and school representatives, ensures program fidelity to the pattern language and consistency in program and course delivery despite changes in the faculty. Each course is submitted to three cycles of review before it is taught All courses have a portfolio housing student work, student and faculty evaluations, and a narrative including rationales and a participant list of the course's evolution.

We now are moving into an outcome evaluation phase. Several faculty members have undertaken studies of our efforts to date, and most recently the college provided $10,000 to support groups of faculty conducting research on their teaching practices. This money facilitated the development and implementation of 10 studies. The college also is supporting a forum in which the findings from these projects will be shared. Our future challenge is to find ways to systematize and sustain our evaluation efforts.

Closing Thoughts

Now that we are seasoned travelers, we sometimes look back to where we have been, where we are now, and where we are going. Though our program still has many challenges to meet, we sometimes reflect on the beginning of our journey and feel proud of our accomplishments. When we began the process of redesign and reform, we did not anticipate accurately the time and energy needed, nor did we anticipate the many positive outcomes of our work. Some experiences have modified our initial expectations, and we realize that much work is yet to be done before our ideals, derived from our guiding principles, will be realized. We also believe that our program reform efforts could not have happened without the parallel collegewide reform. The design principles and the use of the pattern language gave the Special Education Program faculty guidance and support for the dramatic changes we made in our program.

How has our day-to-day work as Special Education Program faculty members changed as a result of our reform efforts? In the past, our courses typically were taught in isolation from one another and were associated with specific disabilities. We served as supervisors of students in many field placements that often were new to us. We provided instruction to elementary and secondary education students through two courses offered in isolation from the rest of their programs of study.

Now, Special Education Program faculty members work together to provide an integrated program of study. University faculty and Professional Practice School teachers work as part of a cohort that examines course assignments and internship settings to monitor how those assignments support the interns' teaching situations. Special education faculty members serve as liaisons to one or two Professional Practice Schools. We work as members of teams to provide mentoring for special education interns. The teams also try to initiate or support ongoing reform in the Professional Practice Schools leading to inclusionary practices. We provide seminars to elementary, secondary, and early childhood students and work with their faculty members to ensure that the seminars we provide are integrated and coordinated with other coursework in the 5-year undergraduate program.

We have a better idea about our destination now, though we always are interested in information about other people's journeys through program reform efforts that might provide us with interesting side trips or detours. We now know how to communicate better about our eventual destination and to talk with others we encounter on our journey. We are more comfortable with the detours that result from new ideas, from new administrative structures, and from new traveling companions. We continue to embark on these explorations into uncharted territory. For many of us, this has become both exciting and rewarding.

References

Alexander, C., Ishikawa, S., & Silverstein, M., (1977). *A pattern language.* New York: Oxford University Press.

Alexander, C., Silverstein, M., Shlomo, A., Ishikawa, S., & Abrams, D. (1975). *The Oregon experiment.* New York: Oxford University Press.

American Federation of Teachers (1988). *Professional practice schools: Building a model.* Washington, DC: AFT.

Bronfenbrenner, U. (1977). Toward an experimental ecology of human development. *American Psychologist, 32,* 513–531.

Holmes Group (1990). *Tomorrow's schools: Principles for the design of professional development schools.* E. Lansing, MI: The Holmes Group.

Holmes Group (1985). *Tomorrow's schools of education.* E. Lansing, MI: The Holmes Group.

Holmes Group (1995). *Tomorrow's schools of education: A report of the Holmes Group.* East Lansing, MI: Holmes Group.

Kurdek, L. A. (1981). An integrative perspective on children's divorce adjustment. *American Psychologist, 36,* 856–866.

National Commission on Excellence in Education. (1983). *A nation at risk: The imperative for educational reform.* Washington, DC: U.S. Government Printing Office.

National Science Foundation. (1983). *Educating Americans for the 21st century: A report to the American people and the national science board.* Washington, DC: Author.

Shulman, L. (1995). *What is your vision for the field of educational research and for AERA in the twenty-first century?* Panel discussion at annual meeting of American Educational Research Association, San Francisco, April 19.

Teitel, L. (1994). Can school-university partnerships lead to the simultaneous renewal of schools and teacher education? *Journal of Teacher Education, 45*(4), 245–252.

University of Cincinnati, College of Education, Holmes Planning Task Force. *Progress report,* Oct. 22, 1987.

Wong, M. J., & Osguthorpe, R. T. (1993). Continuing domination of the four-year teacher education program: A national survey. *Journal of Teacher Education, 44*(1), 64–70.

Yinger, R. J. (1992). *A pattern language for reading.* University of Cincinnati: Author.

Note

1. The Holmes Group has 250 members (approximately one-fifth of the teacher preparation programs in the United States) who are working to improve education by designing a new curriculum; developing a university faculty that works well in public schools; recruiting and retaining a more diverse student body; creating professional development schools (new locations for all educational partners' work); and building networks at the local, state, and national levels (Holmes Group, 1995, pp. 2–3). The degree of success these institutions have achieved is difficult to determine because serious reform work entails changing the organizational cultures of two or more institutions. Gains made can disappear with changes in personnel and funding.

   Ten years after the most recent wave of calls for education reform (such as *A Nation at Risk* in 1983; *Action for Excellence* in 1983; *America's Competitive* in 1983; *Educating Americans for the 21st Century* in 1983; and *Educational Reform* in 1983), Wong and Osguthorpe (1993) published a survey revealing the continued domination of 4-year, undergraduate teacher education programs. Researchers are cautious at best in predicting the endurance of professional development schools (Teitel, 1994; Shulman, 1995).

Fusing Special
Education-Elementary
Education with Bilingual/
Cross-Cultural Emphases at
California State University
San Marcos

A. Sandy Parsons, Lillian Vega-Castaneda, and Toni Hood

Calilifornia State University San Marcos, chartered in 1989, was the first
new public university to be launched in 25 years. This newness provided an unprecedented opportunity to develop and construct teacher
education programs for the 21st century. CSU San Marcos (CSUSM) is the 20th
campus of the California State University System. Located in the northern part
of San Diego County, it joined a distinguished community of institutions of
higher education including the University of California at San Diego, University of San Diego, and San Diego State University. This new campus met a great
need in the region, and the student body has grown quickly from several hun-
dred in 1990 to 2,768 full-time enrollees (FTEs) in the 1995–96 academic year.

Collaborative efforts of the CSUSM faculty to develop an innovative teacher
preparation program addresses these main areas: (a) special education and issues of exceptionality, (b) bilingual and multilingual education and issues confronting children who speak a first language other than English, and (c) elementary
K–8 general education and the core curriculum. The result is a developmental

model for fusing special education, bilingual/multilingual education, and general education theory and practice into a seamless teacher preparation program.

The University and the College of Education

The mission statement of CSU San Marcos clearly states the university's commitment to multicultural education, global awareness, collaboration, and preparation of professionals for the 21st century. The graduation requirements are higher than most other campuses and require 2 years of foreign language; courses with emphasis on critical-thinking skills; race, class, and gender issues; a computer competency requirement; and collaborative team efforts throughout coursework. During commencement of 1994, the student speaker from the College of Business stated, "Welcome to our last group project, graduation!"

The university currently is composed of three colleges: Arts and Sciences, Business, and Education. Many of the credential candidates applying to the College of Education at CSU San Marcos are graduates of the College of Arts and Sciences in Liberal Studies. The College of Education at CSUSM has a diverse faculty committed to excellence in teacher preparation designed around a shared mission. The mission statement of the College of Education (see Figure 8.1) was written by the faculty of the college as a group. This mission includes emphasis on multiple ways of knowing, the premise that all children can learn and succeed, collaboration between faculty and candidates, the value of ideas and individuals, and the celebration of education in a diverse and interconnected world. The college is nondepartmentalized, with a blending of pedagogy and practice across disciplines. Faculty members team-teach and share in the delivery of courses across content areas. In addition, nondepartmentalization prevents concerns of awarding FTEs from team-taught courses to particular discipline departments.

The university and college emphases on issues of diversity have contributed to the milieu created in the CSUSM College of Education. One of the most unique and valuable commitments on the part of the COE has been dedication to diversity exemplified by requiring the new California State Cross Cultural Language and Academic Development (CLAD) or the new Bilingual Cross Cultural Language and Academic Development (B/CLAD) credential of all our graduates as part of the base program. Consequently, every credential program we design infuses the new B/CLAD competencies into the pedagogy and curriculum in teacher education. This ensures that all candidates graduate with preparation in addressing the needs of the ethnolinguistically diverse groups of learners in California schools today.

The mission of the College of Education at California State University San Marcos is threefold:

1. To foster continuous advancement of student learning in elementary, middle, and secondary schools in our immediate service region;
2. To contribute to improvement of instruction in the university;
3. To advance teaching and teacher education at the state and national levels.

The primary means of pursuing this mission are:

1. Preparation of newly credentialed professional educators who are reflective practitioners with the commitment and ability to assure that all students learn to use their minds well;
2. Provision of advanced learning experiences for inservice professional educators;
3. Conduct of educational research and scholarship planned in collaboration with K–12 educators;
4. Provision of service to the education community, which is closely integrated with our teaching and research programs;
5. Participation in university programs aimed at instructional improvement and research on teaching.

The college faculty is committed to modeling excellent instruction and engaging in scholarly activities, which have application to contemporary problems of schooling.

Figure 8.1.

College of Education Mission Statement

Specifically, candidates possessing the required standard in Spanish and English language and literacy enroll in the Bilingual Crosscultural Language and Academic Emphasis component (B/CLAD). The CLAD emphasis prepares English-speaking candidates to deliver instruction to second-language learners through English Language Development (ELD) and Specially Designed Academic Instruction in English (SDAIE). The B/CLAD Emphasis prepares bilingual English/Spanish preservice teachers to deliver instruction in Spanish, ELD, and SDAIE.

The first program in the CSU San Marcos College of Education was the multiple subjects credential (elementary education). Then, in 1992, this program was redesigned to infuse the new State of California emphasis in cross-cultural education, the Cross Cultural Language and Academic Development Credential (CLAD) emphasis (bilingual students earn the Bilingual CLAD [B/CLAD]; others earn the CLAD). Two years later, the middle-level B/CLAD program was brought on line.

The theme of COE program development efforts, from its inception, has been collaboration across disciplines, and a firm belief in the dignity and ability of all children in the diverse group of learners encountered in today's schools. These concepts are summarized best in this excerpt from the Concurrent Credential Program Proposal document presented to the California Commission on Teacher Credentialing in Spring of 1993 (College of Education, 1993). This program document is an adaptation of the original Multiple Subjects Bilingual Cross Cultural Language and Academic Development (B/CLAD) program document prepared by the faculty of the College of Education in 1992–93 (College of Education Faculty, 1992):

> These are essential elements of school restructuring in the 1990s. All schools must focus continuously on student learning, and all education (including teacher education) must be based on two fundamental premises:
>
> 1. All students can learn, not only rote facts but to reason and use their minds well, and teachers are the primary agents for this learning; and
> 2. in order to meet the considerable challenge of assuring that all students learn, teachers must be lifelong learners themselves, professionally empowered and skilled at building and participating in powerful learning communities at the school level. (p. 4)

The document states further:

> These are the two fundamental themes of the CSU San Marcos teacher education programs. While the...above present a case for school restructuring nationwide, nowhere is the need for such positive change more readily apparent than in California. We are keenly aware of the fact that ours is one of the most diverse populations of any state, and that many social and economic trends which reach the national consciousness have actually started in California several years earlier.
>
> In California, we have an opportunity to teach the rest of the nation how to address issues of social and economic justice through public education, while modeling the multicultural society of the future. Inherent in the notion of multiculturalism is the notion that the milieu of disability is yet another parameter of a multicultural society. The teacher education programs we present here are intended to do no less than make a significant contribution to the long-range solution of the many social and economic problems facing California, by producing teachers who: (a) believe in the ability of each and every student to be a happy, productive adult member of society, and (b) act on that belief each and every day of their teaching careers. (p. 4)

The College of Education faculty conducted needs assessments in 1991–92 to obtain information on personnel needs and interests in the area. Special education emerged clearly as an area of critical need. Many emergency and waiver certificates have been assigned in California because of the critical shortages of credentialed special education teachers. Even though California has moved to "untie" regular and special education certification in its new standards for certification (that is, one no longer must earn the complete elementary education credential before adding special education endorsement), CSUSM made the decision early in the planning process to build a unified program preparing candidates for full credentials in general education, special education, and cross-cultural education. In 1994, the Concurrent Credential Program in general, special, and cross-cultural education was brought on line. This new program is entitled the Concurrent Credential Program, as students study and earn credentials in three pedagogical and practical areas of certification concurrently: elementary education, special education (learning handicapped), and cross-cultural education (B/CLAD).

Theoretical Frameworks Grounding the Preparation Program

The Concurrent Credential Program is grounded firmly in the literature on inclusive education. The term "supported included instruction" (Parsons, 1994a) indicates the philosophy of preparation of candidates to address the needs of all children in the schools, not just special groups, while mainstreamed to the extent they can succeed with related and support services. Candidates are prepared in the pedagogy and skills of collaborative consultation with general educators, and in the notion of co-teaching in the general education classroom. The program philosophy prepares them with the idea that, though the goal is for all children to succeed in the mainstream, individuals will need varying levels of support over time until they can sustain successful full inclusion. Equity of access, authentic and nonbiased assessment, and adapting instruction to meet needs of all children are the hallmarks of their preparation.

Most teacher preparation programs are offered totally on college and university campuses; only student teaching and practicum work take place in the schools. Traditionally, the interaction between schools and universities has been characterized by the location of research sites for faculty (Johnson & Pugach, 1992). For personnel preparation programs for teachers to become actively involved in restructuring and reform, new styles of interaction and methods for IHE and K–12 collaboration must be developed (Barth, 1990). This process must be examined carefully in regard to several old and tarnished tenets such as:

(a) the education of teachers takes place on the university campuses; (b) one university professor serves as primary instructor of each course, the content is determined by published texts or the personal perspective of a professor or by department philosophy; and (c) the program consists of a series of segmented courses. (Paul & Roselli, 1995, p. 196).

The design, implementation, and ongoing evaluation of teacher education programs at CSU San Marcos leave these old tenets and assumptions far behind. For example, the program committed from the start to be site-based in the public schools. The planning committee, which includes university and public school personnel, has been proactive in inclusive teaming in the inception, design, and implementation of the Concurrent Program. Courses were designed to integrate content from many disciplines, and delivered through a variety of approaches to instruction, including large- and small-group instruction, role plays, scenarios from day-to-day teaching, field work, puzzles, student presentations, thematic units, individual assessment, videos, and media presentations.

The titles of the courses in the curriculum reflect integration of content, skills, and pedagogy. Shared foundations and theory predominate, rather than the elitist view that "good pedagogical skills for children with disabilities are the property of special education teachers and distinct from good academic teaching" (Paul & Roselli, 1995, p. 203). University faculty members across the disciplines team-teach, and K–12 educators are an essential part of the teaching team across the areas.

This program addresses the need for reconstruction of education, based upon the need for a much greater fusion of general and special education (Goodlad, 1993). Teachers in this new genre of reinvented preparation programs and entering restructured schools must be prepared and empowered to function in a merged setting. As categories of service delivery fade and related service delivery blends with general education responsibility, all teachers will focus more on the education environment and provision of good teaching to all children. As the focus shifts from seeking to identify the problem as indigenous to the individual, and toward ecological factors that facilitate success, general education teachers should realize new empowerment in their current skills of excellence in teaching. The saying "good teaching is good teaching" levels the playing field as all educators team to bring the best services to the child and family, irrespective of program title.

Fusion of Bilingual and Special Education Preparation

Early conversations between the special education and bilingual faculties, along with a review of the relevant literature, showed a natural connection between bilingual and special education. The two fields share some common theoretical contexts, similar pedagogical practices, and similar use of acronyms, program practices, and labels. Similarity between these fields is great, although they have important distinctions as well.

1. *Early bilingual programs were characterized by pull-out instruction, usually for teaching English as a Second Language (ESL).* By the mid 1970s, bilingual education realized that pull-out instruction was not the best instructional practice for Limited English-Proficient (LEP) children. Often, students missed critical content area lessons. By extension, in the 1970s special education "service" took the form of pull-out instruction by the resource teacher. As in the case of ESL pull-out, students often missed critical lessons that were occurring in class. Clearly, the model of inclusion presented in the Concurrent Program challenges these past practices.

2. *Teaching the LEP child to become proficient in English at a fast rate, usually 3 years.* The 3-year schedule reflected the funding cycle provided by the federal government and did not bear any relevance to teaching or learning. This arbitrary 3-year exit of LEP students from bilingual to English-only classrooms translated to academic failure to many children. By extension, an inference can be drawn that special education practices have sought to provide individual intervention with a prompt exit from resource services to facilitate full inclusion.

3. *Bilingual education utilizes a variety of labels with regard to children and programmatic practice.* For example, once children are identified as speaking a language other than English as their first language, they are assessed for oral, written, and content fluency in English. Once assessed, they are categorized either as Limited English Proficient (LEP) or Fluent English Proficient (FEP). Parents of the LEP students must give their written permission to allow their children to receive specialized services. By extension, special education programs have created similar situations, in which identified students are placed in classes, often isolated from the rest of the school building and children. This notion of isolationism also is evidenced in past bilingual practice, in which bilingual and ESL classrooms were placed in temporary building space—trailers, the last corridor, and so on. The parallels in composition and delivery of services are clear.

4. *Bilingual classroom teachers are called upon to provide specialized instruction in class, consisting of primary and second language and literacy instruction.* The bilingual teacher is responsible for teaching the LEP child to read and write in his or her primary language, to speak in English, and eventually to make the transition from Spanish to English reading. Bilingual teachers also are expected to assess their students (ongoing) with regard to proficiency in English and the L1 (primary language), as well as content area performance. In this way, the bilingual classroom teacher acts as a specialist in his or her own

classroom. Finally, for LEP children to be reclassified and moved to a general program of instruction, a variety of assessments must be made (including academic performance, language, and literacy in the L1 (primary langauge) and L2 (second language), and recommendation by a Student Study Team). Similarly, students in special education programs must meet specific criteria, including assessment, input from the school psychologist, and the Student Study Team.

The challenges posed to bilingual and special educators are many, expanding the requirements for a general classroom teacher considerably.

Bilingual/Cross Cultural Program Foundations

In 1991 the B/CLAD/CLAD standards were designed and introduced by the California Commission on Teacher Credentialing (CTC), largely in response to the growing diversity in the California Public Schools. For example, the number of children of Limited English Proficiency has grown to well over one million, with more than 100 languages represented in this population. In designing the B/CLAD/CLAD programs, the faculty of CSUSM, along with educators in our service area, elected to design a program that would prepare all credential candidates with the necessary competencies related to the education of all children in a variety of contexts: English Only, Bilingual, Multilingual, and, by extension, Special Education.

The program emphasizes preparation of preservice teachers to address the needs of English speakers and children who speak other languages. The program emphasizes cultural diversity, first- and second-language acquisition principles and pedagogy, curriculum and instruction based on recent research in the areas of first- and second-language acquisition, effective English language development instruction, and effective instruction in general as well as bilingual and multiple-language settings (Garcia, 1994; Minicucci & Olsen, 1992; Ramirez, 1990; Tikunoff et al., 1991).

The B/CLAD/CLAD also emphasizes issues surrounding language, literacy, and learning contexts. Further, issues of sociocultural communication and interaction serve as an undergirding theoretical base (Carrasco, 1978; Cazden, Maldonado-Guzman, & Carrasco, 1984; Delgado-Gaitan, 1988; Erickson, Cazden, Carrasco, & Maldonado-Guzman, 1983; Mehan, 1979; Moll, 1978; Philips, 1983; Trueba, 1987).

Concurrent students are introduced simultaneously to the critical competencies of the Multiple Subjects, B/CLAD/CLAD, and Special Education programs. The B/CLAD/CLAD competencies are introduced in Education 364, the prerequisite, Cultural Diversity in Schooling. This course gives students a theoretical awareness of culture as a way of "front-loading" them with information that will be further built and emphasized in the remaining coursework. Through course readings, individual, small-group and whole-group activities, students are challenged to consider various notions of culture in the hope that they will take this understanding into their observation/student teaching experience and, ultimately, their own classrooms. Culture is thus viewed in these ways:

■ Multiple and alternative ways of knowing and showing what one knows.
■ Building a multidimensional understanding of culture (language and curriculum) including: macro/micro, emic/etic, visible/invisible, immigrant, bilingual, poverty, ethnicity, exceptionality, linguistic, school/classroom, and community, home/school perspectives.

As evidenced from this list, the faculty challenges students to consider a culture that moves beyond the obvious, or stereotypical perspectives—for example, with regard to holidays, customs, national dress. Students are encouraged to consider their individual cultural context and relate it to the children they will find in the schools. Regarding culture, we ask that our students look both holistically and in focused ways, moving from an understanding of the culture of a given classroom to the culture of linguistic difference, or the culture of exceptionality or, specifically, the physically challenged.

Meshing Multiple Subjects, B/CLAD, with Special Education Specialist: Learning Handicapped Program

The Concurrent Program enfolded its curricula into the Multiple Subjects Curriculum, which already had incorporated the B/CLAD/CLAD competencies. Collectively, the meshing of elementary, CLAD and B/CLAD, and special education pedagogy and practice undergirds all aspects of the curricula and instruction. The fusion of competencies, literature bases, and practices capitalizes on the rich and overlapping histories of program development in each field. Our aim is to offer a program and courses that move beyond the obvious notions of culture and exceptionality—and we challenge our students to do the same. One specific course does not constitute the cultural or exceptionality component. Cultural diversity and exceptionality are at the heart of the program, and these competencies are infused across the curricula and also in the foundations courses.

Thus, Concurrent students are introduced to a composite of critical competencies from the elementary, bilingual, and special education curricula. These competencies are introduced in several core/foundations classes and are reinforced and expanded on in the field and in other courses. In sum, critical competencies include theory and practice in general elementary (mainstream), B/CLAD, and special education contexts. For example, with regard to B/CLAD/CLAD, students are introduced to delivery of academic content through specially designed academic instruction in English; or, in the Language and Literacy course, students are introduced to whole-language principles for all children, including EO, bilingual, multilingual, and special education contexts. Thus, students are involved in a series of situations:

1. Theory and practice in whole-language curricula and instruction.
2. Application of first- and second-language acquisition principles.
3. Application of special education concerns.

In this respect, faculty work hard to challenge the students and provide them with a variety of possible scenarios that could well surface in a California school setting.

Specially Designed Academic Instruction in English (SDAIE)

A hallmark feature of the B/CLAD/CLAD emphasis is its focus on successful curricular and instructional approaches for the education of linguistically and culturally diverse students. Topics related to effective delivery of academic content are at the heart of the program and are reflected clearly in the Concurrent Program. For example, candidates experience culturally diverse schools prior to and during the program. They are assigned to observe and participate in culturally diverse schools and classrooms in all three field experiences. Students prepare lessons based on a model of inclusion, one that further enhances the LEP and special education students' access to the content core curricula.

Content core curricula are enhanced further and made accessible to LEP students through the SDAIE approach, characterized by:

— integration of first- and second-language acquisition theory, which emphasizes language and literacy learning in a natural context
— deemphasis on overt error correction and discrete skills instruction
— emphasis on meaning rather than rote memorization of facts, rules for grammar, and direct recall
— cooperative grouping
— use of visuals and manipulatives
— use of advance organizers
— flexible grouping (e.g., homogeneous/heterogeneous)
— provision for building prerequisite skills (e.g., vocabulary) (Castaneda, 1994).

Several environmental features characterize effective instruction for LEP children. Students require an environment that is risk-free, one in which they are allowed to make mistakes in written and spoken language, one in which "mistakes" are acceptable (Castaneda, 1991). This emphasis on environmental context is reflected in the notion of creating a context in which the "affect" is lowered (Krashen, 1981). This stress on a risk-free environment is supported further in the Concurrent Program.

The Concurrent Program prepares candidates for work with ethnolinguistically diverse children in EO, bilingual, multilingual, and special education contexts.

Throughout their coursework, candidates prepare lessons specially targeted at addressing general and specific needs. Candidates prepare and deliver lessons utilizing ELD/SDAIE for heterogeneous mixes of students with special attention to issues of exceptionality. The overall goal is to prepare candidates in various theories and practice that emphasize a socially inclusive, holistic model of education. In sum, candidates are challenged to:

— build knowledge and gather information regarding the design and delivery of learning and instruction in specific social and learning contexts
— create learning environments that are specifically situated to a given class
— take into account daily how children learn and show what they know in a variety of ways
— critically analyze curricula and instruction and the relationship to the social organization of teaching and learning.

Development and Design of the Program

Internal and external forces facilitated the development of this unique program. Externally, there was a great need for certified special education personnel across California. A highly diverse state, the southern region is densely populated with a high incidence of primarily Spanish-speaking youngsters. In addition, the schools are multicultural settings with great ethnolinguistic diversity within pupil population. As many as 91–100 different languages are spoken across the school, districts, and counties of California.

Internally, the COE provided the basis through the newly developed multiple subjects credential with infused CLAD (Cross Cultural Language and Academic Development) competencies. The special education planning and advisory committee made the decision to enfold the state's competencies for special education teachers into this existing curriculum, which then would be team-taught by faculty from all three disciplines. The community desired a special education preparation program that would meet the needs in today's schools. The faculties to develop and implement this innovative program were available and eager to work together.

Field Research

The design of this program is based upon the results of local field-based research (Parsons, 1994b). The first task of program development incorporated site-based interviews of directors of special education. Through these interviews several consistent themes emerged. Without exception each director stated that knowledge of general education curriculum frameworks is the first qualification they desire in teachers, and collaboration and consultation skills for supporting inclusion is the second.

In addition to these two essential skills, they want teachers who are trained in broad bases of skills to address the needs of learners with mild-to-moderate disabilities across the board, and the ability to work with culturally and linguistically diverse populations. They expect their teachers to know and understand early developmental patterns and effects of disability on development and learning. They expect candidates to have a firm grasp of assessment principles and nonbiased diagnosis, assessment, and translation of results into curriculum planning with adaptations. Computer literacy, with the ability to use adaptive devices as well as infuse technology into the curriculum, also is desired. The following list crystallizes the directors' expectations for newly graduated special educators of the future:

- Knowledge of general education curriculum frameworks
- Collaboration between general and special educators
- Cross-cultural education and adapted instruction for second-language learners
- Consultation with general education teachers for supported inclusion of youngsters with special learning needs
- Knowledge of typical and atypical patterns of development and learning abilities
- Nonbiased assessment, curriculum planning, and adaptation of instruction and materials
- Linkages with institutions of higher education for lifelong learning and continuing education

Stages of Development and Human Aspects of the Program

In the COE of CSUSM, all programs are developed in conjunction with members of the local education community. This program was designed over a year-long period of intense collaboration among representatives of general education, special education, and cross-cultural bilingual education. Parents, teachers, district consultants, San Diego County Office of Education consultants, directors of special education, and faculty from the COE participated side by side (see Author's Note). The mix resulted in the design of an innovative program. All agreed that we wanted a unique program that would draw outstanding candidates to prepare to meet the needs of the heterogeneous group of children in today's classrooms.

A dynamic design process was implemented that had four major stages of work (Parsons, 1994a):

1. Brainstorming traits of the program graduate based upon the COE mission statement and the personnel needs of California.
2. Delineation of program goals and characteristics.
3. Subcommittee working group on designing the configuration of the program in concert with the State of California credential program guidelines.
4. Designing the coursework, field work, and titles of the courses.

This process may seem to be the inverse of most program development efforts, which list the courses first, then flesh them out. The discipline barriers in typical colleges of education, however, do not exist at San Marcos. Faculty representatives from all three component disciplines drafted nondepartmentalized courses entitled Integrated Programs.

At the first planning meetings, the four major themes for the initial brainstorm consisted of:

1. Response to the CSU San Marcos mission statement and its implications for Special Education.
2. Training needs of North San Diego County, the region, and the State of California in special education.
3. Competencies for teachers: "What should this teacher 'look' like?"
4. Preparation program configurations.

The College of Education faculty did not provide any *a priori* sets or constraints on the process or the expected program outcomes. During the first meetings participants worked in small groups with easel charts to brainstorm the characteristics of the special education teacher they would like to see. The results showed great congruity of responses by the participants, even across the four topical areas.

The second meeting was dedicated to delineating the program goals and characteristics. The large-group work was readily accomplished, as participants quickly reached consensus about the specific goals and characteristics of the program. In this second phase of planning, a smaller working subcommittee of teachers and faculty then began the laborious task of designing a program that would respond to the California program guidelines and standards and also prepare the teachers of our design.

At this stage we still were considering the development of a special education program. COE faculty and K–12 faculty, however, reached consensus on the shape of the program early in the subcommittee planning and agreed to write a fused curriculum without redundancy or overlap. This preparation program would cover the competencies included in the two credentials (elementary education and special education: learning handicapped) with the new California B/CLAD emphases.

During the fourth and final phase of planning, the committee of the whole was briefed on the configuration of the concurrent preparation program. The advisory committee embraced the vision of a seamless preparation program, and committee approval facilitated further work.

The working subcommittee then met to delineate further the specific goals and objectives of the coursework. The committee drafted as few categorically defined courses as possible. Most of the courses are entitled "Integrated Programs" to reflect the fusion of pedagogy and skills across the three disciplines. Of the 48 credits hours, only three courses include "special education" in their titles: Advanced Practicum in Special Education, Technology and Communication for Special Populations, and Approaches to Instruction and Assessment in Special Education.

Goals and Feature Components of the Concurrent Teacher Education Program

The goals and program characteristics that follow have been designed in relation to initial teacher preparation programs at CSU San Marcos and apply to all teacher education programs in the college. The stated goals and characteristics form a public statement of intention that allows potential candidates to choose our teacher education program with confidence, a statement which has been subject to public scrutiny and debate. Second, they guide the faculty in designing curriculum and instructional delivery systems that will foster their attainment.

The goals stated in the program document are reflected in the following information regarding the elements and aspects of the Concurrent Program. The major program features can be condensed into the following descriptors.

Fused General Education Special Education with Cross-Cultural Emphasis Preparation Curriculum

The Concurrent Credential Program is completely fused (see Figure 8.2) and is the first credential program in the state of California covering all three disciplines in one program. Coursework is integrated and team-taught by faculty from all three disciplines, and courses are entitled "Integrated Programs."

Cohort Model of Preparation

Candidates pursue coursework in cohorts of 25. The program of study spans 12 months: summer session, fall semester, winter session, and spring semester. These cohort groups take all of their classes together and are expected to form a learning community in which everyone is a teacher and everyone is a learner. Each cohort is assigned a faculty mentor. Graduating candidates earn two clear credentials (general and special education) with an emphasis in B/CLAD.

The endeavor is intense and rigorous. The pedagogy is integrated and taught with parsimony; little overlap or repetition is present. B/CLAD students are in-

Concurrent Multiple Subjects/B/CLAD with Special Education Specialist Credential: Learning Handicapped

Prerequisites:

EDUC 364	The Role of Cultural Diversity in Schooling {Core B/CLAD course (3)}	3
EDUC 501	Mainstream Instruction for Children with Special Learning Needs {Core LH Course (3)}	3
EDUC 350	Early Field Experience	3
		Total (9)

Program Courses:

Summer Session I

EDMX 526A	Learning and Instruction in Integrated Programs {Core LH course (1) with field experience}	2
EDMX 531	Approaches to Instruction & Assessment in Special Education* {Core LH course (3) with field experience}	3
EDMX 540A	Language & Literacy Ed in Integrated Programs* {Core LH course (1)}	3
		Total (8)

Semester I

EDMX 540B	Language & Literacy Ed in Integrated Programs {Core B/CLAD course (1)}	2
EDML 552	Theories & Methods of Bilingual/ Multicultural Ed {Core B/CLAD course (3)}	3
EDMX 526B	Learning & Instruction in Integrated Programs* {Core B/CLAD course (1)}	3
EDMX 532A	Technology and Communication for Special Populations {Core LH course (2)}	2
EDMX 561	Field Experience 1*: Observation/Participation & Beginning Integrated Student Teaching in Elementary Schools (with seminar) {Core B/CLAD course (1)}, {Core LH course (1)}	6
EDMX 533	Consultation and Program Development {Core LH Course (2)}	2
		Total (18)
		(continued)

Figure 8.2

Concurrent Program Curriculum

Figure 8.2 continued

Winter Session

EDMX 563	Advanced Practicum in Special Education {Core LH Course (4)}	4
		Total (4)

Semester II

EDMX 543	Mathematics Education in Integrated Programs* {Core LH course (1)}	4
EDMX 547	Social Studies/Science Education in Integrated Programs* {Core LH course (1)}	5
EDMX 532B	Technology & Communication for Special Pop.* {Core LH course (2)}	2
EDMX 562	Field Experience II*: Observation/Participation & Advanced Integrated Student Teaching in Elementary Schools {Core B/CLAD course (1) }, {Core LH course (1)}	7
		Total (18)

B/CLAD Course:	For B/CLAD credential candidates only:	
EDML 553	Pedagogy in the Primary Language* Fall Semester	2
EDML 554	Pedagogy in the Primary Language* Spring Semester {Core B/CLAD course only (3)}	1
		Total (3)

Totals:	Special Ed Core	(22)	{including 3 prerequisite and 6 field)
	Field Experience	(17)	{including 13 MS, 4 EX, plus field work in 526 & 531*}
	CLAD Core	(10)	{including 3 prerequisite and 2 field}
	B/CLAD	(3)	
	TOTAL:	CLAD/EDMX	(48)
		B/CLAD/EDMX	(51)

*Requires participation and observation in both regular & special education classrooms.

Note: Candidates end with Multiple Subjects B/CLAD and Special Education Specialist Credential: Learning Handicapped Clear (if CPR and one unit of Health Ed are cleared).

tegrated into all the cohorts across the College of Education; thus, a "B/CLAD-only" model is nonexistent. This provides a way of integrating for inclusion, modeling for our students what we hope will be modeled in their future classrooms and schools.

Our students benefit from this integration model in that all students are exposed to bilingual issues (ongoing) although they may be English-only speakers. This is viewed as a strength of the program in that one does not have to speak the target language to understand the importance and role of primary language, literacy, and content instruction.

Multi-Site-Based Instruction

The courses and practical experiences are delivered at various sites. One of the most important characteristics of this credential is location on K–8 campuses for course delivery. Home sites are located, and students take their courses onsite in elementary buildings in districts that have joined a consortium with CSUSM. Candidates benefit from guest lecturers and experts from the districts who otherwise would not be able to leave the building to lecture off-campus. Faculty members with California credentials may substitute for master teachers so that these teachers can teach the candidates. In addition, several sessions of the technology class can be held in school labs with building lab coordinators to learn how they set up their programs and rotate youngsters in and out of lab.

Collaborative Consultation Model

Candidates are prepared in the skills of consultative collaboration. Coursework includes scenarios requiring active listening, conflict resolution, shared problem solving, and effective skills in working with parents, fellow faculty, related service personnel, assistants, and administration. Attending IEP meetings and Student Assistance Teams or Student Study Team meetings is required. Candidates perform observations for assessment, administer psychoeducational assessment instruments, and write ecological case studies and assessment case reports.

Family Systems

Knowledge of family systems is one area of expertise that special education often has neglected in preparation programs. Often, this is assumed to be the domain of the social worker, school counselor, or school psychologist. Fortunately, this content is embedded in courses easily. Students learn about the family as a system, the impact of individuals on that constellation, support services, parent conferences, home visits, and interagency support services. The ecological case study assigned during the summer session requires home visits and parent interviews. Students comment on how valuable this assignment is for them.

Nonbiased Assessment

Candidates are prepared in the process of nondiscriminatory assessment. This is requisite to serving the diverse population of today's schools. The focus of the preparation is on nonbiased approaches to assessment. Rather than centering on the instruments themselves, preparation for assessment, administration, interpretation, and use of results provides the focus and pedagogy of the course. Through funding secured through a California Lottery Grant for Education, an intrainstitutional competition, assessment batteries, instruments, and protocols were acquired for teaching the assessment course (Parsons, 1995b).

Adapted Instruction for Teaching All Children

Throughout the coursework the curriculum infuses strategies for learners with disabilities and for second-language learners. In this way, methods are not taught in isolated and fragmented fashion. This program highlights the parallels and similarities between adaptations made for children with learning disabilities and second-language learners who require sheltered instruction. The idea that "good teaching is good teaching" is stressed, too. Adaptations made for "special learners" also improve instruction and support learning for all children.

Computer Literacy and Adapted Technology

The Concurrent curriculum includes a course on adaptive technology and communications for special education. This course meets the requirements for clearing the California probationary credential. Candidates become confident users of educational technology, application, and utility software for their own productivity, and evaluators of educational software for pupils. In addition, use of adaptive and assistive devices and special-access software are taught. The design of technology plans within a grant application format is required.

Field Experiences Across the Duration of the Program

In addition to these program features, field experiences occur across the duration of the Concurrent program. Candidates pursue their coursework condensed into the first half of each semester in fall and spring semesters, with part-time observation and participation in their master teacher's classroom during that time. Courses are scheduled to allow at least two mornings a week in their classrooms to acquire 35–45 hours of observation and participation before entering full-time student teaching. The last half of each semester is devoted to full-time student teaching. Fall semester consists of 8 weeks of courses and 6 weeks of full-time elementary education student teaching. Upon successful completion of beginning student teaching, spring semester consists of 9 weeks of courses with part-time observation and participation, and 7 weeks of full-time student teaching (Parsons, 1995a). These experiences include the following.

Ecological Case Study

During the first summer session, candidates are assigned to schools (summer-school session or year-round schools) to observe, study, interview, and report on a child. The report must be comprehensive of the home, school, and community environments.

The First Day of School

At the beginning of fall semester, all candidates are assigned to a site to participate in the often hectic pace and events of the first day of the school year. Traditional-year school sites receive the student teachers as volunteers on this first day. Efforts are made to place the student teachers with their master teachers for that semester.

High School Special Education Experience

As the specialist credential embedded within the Concurrent program licenses teachers for service in K–12 special education, all candidates spend part of their observation and participation during the fall semester in a high school special education setting. This provides exposure to service delivery at the high school level.

Observation and Participation, Spring and Fall Semesters

During the weeks of the condensed college coursework, candidates spend 6 hours each week in instruction in the rooms of their master teachers. Activities involve becoming familiar with the routines, getting to know the children, and planning materials and activities. Thematic unit plans are made in conjunction with the plans of their master teacher.

Beginning Integrated Student Teaching

Students pursue their full-time beginning student teaching in K–8 classrooms in schools with diverse populations. Candidates are required to address the needs of all children including second-language learners and those with special learning needs in the elementary school classroom.

Advanced Special Education Practicum

In between beginning and advanced integrated student teaching, candidates who have successfully completed beginning student teaching pursue the advanced special education practicum in a special education classroom. Candidates are required to support youngsters in the mainstream, consult with general education teachers, and do an in-depth formal assessment and case study on an individual child.

Advanced Integrated Student Teaching

Students pursue their full-time advanced student teaching in K–8 classrooms in schools with diverse populations. Candidates are required to address the needs of all children, including second-language learners and those with special learning needs, in the elementary school classroom. During their last 2 weeks of full-time advanced student teaching, they take full responsibility for the classroom.

The advanced practicum in special education occurs between the two elementary education student teaching experiences. Candidates pursue the first 2 weeks of advanced practicum in special education before leaving for the winter holidays in December, and complete the last 4 weeks during the winter session (4-week period between fall and spring semesters). If a student teacher has had difficulty in beginning student teaching in integrated programs (elementary education), the candidate will be required to complete advanced student teaching in integrated programs and postpone advanced practicum in special education until successfully completing beginning and advanced integrated student teaching. This allows for individualizing programs of study (Parsons, 1995c).

K–12 Linkages and CSU San Marcos

Another aspect of the CSU system as a whole involves K–12 and institutions of higher education (IHE) linkages. In September of 1991, the chair of the Committee on Educational Policy of the CSU Board of Trustees formulated a committee to study the relationship of the CSU to K–12 schools. This special focus was stimulated by state and national educational reform efforts (CSU Board, 1992). This initiative promoted K–12 linkages with the CSU campuses in efforts to collaborate in educational reform. As stated by the dean, Dr. Steve Lilly, "We truly believe that a collaborative effort will change both professional development of teachers and the programs through which we prepare beginning teachers" (Lilly, 1992, p. 54). He further noted that colleges must work toward systems in which faculty members can receive workload credit for activities in K–12 settings because it is as important as the workload conducted on campus in teacher preparation (Lilly, 1992, p. 54).

CSU San Marcos has been particularly proactive in this emphasis through development of consortia between the COE and neighboring districts in North San Diego County. In addition, a highly innovative program, the Distinguished Teacher in Residence Program (DTiR), has been developed and implemented. We were fortunate to have a DTiR in special education during the year of program development and the first year of implementation. A resource specialist from a local district provides an overview of this program and her insights into the program development effort.

Distinguished Teacher-in-Residence Program

The idea for the Distinguished Teacher in Residence Program (DTiR) came about when local superintendents expressed to the College of Education their desire to build a collaborative relationship between their school districts and the university's teacher preparation program. Formal agreements between local participating school districts and CSUSM include specific goals to establish and maintain a close connection between teacher education and exemplary school practices. The DTiR program is one tangible example of this connection.

The DTiR consortium agreement also provides assigned-time opportunities for CSUSM faculty to work with participating school districts on collaborative projects to ensure that teachers in local schools stay well grounded in current concepts of teacher roles, instructional pedagogy, and effective school/effective teacher qualities.

DTiRs are chosen by the College of Education to render full-time services as instructional faculty for a term of 2 years. They remain employees of their respective districts, and are on loan to the university for this 2-year period. General duties of the DTiRs include:

— teaching courses appropriate to their areas of specialization, interest, and experience
— advising and supervising preservice student teachers in a variety of teacher credential programs
— holding committee assignments in the College of Education
— team-teaching, guest lecturing, conducting research, collaboratively and independently
— presenting at local, state, and national professional conferences
— facilitating student teacher seminars.

The DTiR program also provides opportunities for advancement and expansion of professionalism in the subtle, yet significant ways not articulated specifically in the program description or interview process. Distinguished Teachers are encouraged to continue a professional relationship with the university long after their official assignment has ended. Emeritus DTiR ventures have included site-based student teacher supervision, teaching evening- and summer-session classes, and collaborative conference presentations.

DTiRs often are counseled and encouraged by college faculty to consider higher education teaching as a future career option, while being valued and validated at every juncture for their dedication to teaching children in the schools. Frequent conversations and student evaluations indicate that DTiRs have been held in high esteem by faculty and students alike.

At the end of the 2-year assignment, the hope is that DTiRs will return to their school districts with refreshed, reassessed perspectives on educating children. Their teaching skills will be honed, their enthusiasm rekindled, and their professional engines finely retuned.

Distinguished Teachers in Residence Emeritus indicate that the experience is uniquely satisfying and rewarding. The 2-year term provides the opportunity to advance their teaching skills far beyond their expectations, and it has provided a significant dose of theoretical renewal that few teachers are fortunate enough to attain during their already busy and demanding K–12 school careers.

Site-Based Program Delivery

The CSU San Marcos College of Education has been proactive in establishing of consortia with LEAs in the area. Through these local school districts, many of the college's cohorts pursue their coursework onsite at local elementary and middle school campuses. The Concurrent Credential Program forged an alliance with the Carlsbad Unified School District, a small coastal district with a highly diverse population of youngsters. The Barrio Carlsbad Community schools were selected because of their rich Latino culture and history. The schools are impacted heavily with enrollment from a densely populated attendance area. Children of families who have lived in Carlsbad for decades and children of newly immigrated families attend school together.

The Concurrent program has received much support from the Carlsbad Unified School District and the Barrio Carlsbad Association. The Carlsbad USD provided a portable classroom on its Pine School campus, where the preparation program courses can be delivered. On this campus is located the Centro de Informacion, a community-based branch of the Carlsbad City Library, rich in books in Spanish for the school district and the community. Families and school district children can visit the library, attend its functions, and read and check out books.

Our programs always attempt to place student teachers in schools that meet the requirements of diverse populations. As the Concurrent program doubled in size this year, the second cohort is located in the San Marcos Unified School District. The new inland cohort attended university classes held at Koob School in San Marcos in the classroom of the off-track third-grade teacher throughout the academic year of 1995–96. The school's attendance area is rich in cultural diversity, and the faculty has welcomed the students.

Concluding Thoughts: Reflection Upon Implementation

CSU San Marcos and the California Commission on Teacher Credentialing have adopted the Concurrent Credential Program as an approved credential program. The program currently is in its second year of implementation. The first year was well received, and requests for admission so increased that the COE faculty voted to double the number of cohorts admitted from one to two in academic year 1995–96. The first-year participants gave the program high marks, and several suggestions were implemented in this second year of the program. The conclusions presented below are organized according to the program features to which they are related.

Site-Based Program Delivery

During the first year all the courses were delivered onsite at a public elementary school in Carlsbad Unified School District. After program evaluation of the first year of implementation, student feedback indicated a desire to be on campus part of the time. Many of the candidates were immediate past graduates and wished to remain active in the campus culture, student activities, and student committees. Students also needed to use the open computer lab for personal productivity, and the library for research. Classes now are held on campus as well as onsite in the schools. We hold class sessions on campus 2 days per week, and in the schools 3 days a week. In this way, students still can play a role in campus life, access the library and computer labs, and maintain friendships with cohorts that meet on campus.

Field Experiences

Although carefully planned, the original sequence of extensive field experiences was revised fairly comprehensively for the second year of implementation. Program evaluation by program graduates, master teachers, and university supervisors provided information for data-based decisions in the revision of some aspects of the program.

High School Observation Experience

The high school observation provides an introduction to special education services at the 9–12 level, as the learning handicapped credential authorizes teachers to teach special education at the K–12 level. The first year, all candidates attend the first day of school at a traditional calendar campus to see the activities of first day—their only opportunity to do so as an observer. Then they spent 2 to 3 weeks with their master teachers for observation and participation. The candidates bonded immediately with their master teachers and children, and they then were reluctant to leave to do the high school observation.

Now the high school observation takes place at the beginning of the program, immediately after the first day of school experience in fall semester. Student teachers who are placed in year-round schools spend the 3 weeks with their master teacher in a high school special education setting observing. If there are fourth and fifth weeks, these are spent in their master teacher's building in a "sister" room for that grade level. In this way, we can use year-round schools without sacrificing student teaching time in the classroom. The students now have a better understanding of the sequence of the field placements and look forward to returning to their master teachers. The students were happier with this schedule this year.

Advanced Practicum in Special Education

During the first year of the program, the advanced practicum in special education was offered at the end of the 12-month program in June, for a period of 4 weeks. Feedback from student teachers and master teachers indicated a need to have this experience earlier in the year and for a longer time. Master teachers commented that it was too late in the school year for candidates to participate fully in assessment, IEP meetings, and other important educational events. The advanced practicum in special education now is offered in the middle of the program of study rather than at the end of the school year and has been expanded to 6 weeks.

Sequence of Field Experiences

The sequence of field experiences has varied from the first year of implementation and is documented in the Credential Handbook (Parsons, 1996). The new line-up provides flexibility in the progression of experiences based upon the candidate's performance. If all goes well, candidates now may progress through beginning student teaching, advanced practicum in special education, then finish with advanced student teaching in integrated programs. If evaluations indicate that a candidate needs more time in the general education classroom to hone and perfect basic skills before moving on to advanced practicum in special education, students will take advanced student teaching immediately after beginning student teaching. After successfully completing both, the student culminates the preparation program with advanced practicum in special education. This new design provides maximum flexibility and individualization of the program of study based upon candidate need.

Clear Credential the First Year Out

The sequence of courses leads to a clear credential in 12 months of full-time study. In the other preparation programs, candidates graduate with a preliminary credential, then have 5 years in which to clear their credential by taking a mainstreaming course and an educational technology course. These competencies have been built into the Concurrent credential. Students gain confidence through acquisition of computer literacy, adaptive equipment, and grant-writing skills for acquisition of these materials. Skills in use of adaptive hardware, specialized software, and bilingual software programs are highlighted. Our graduates, therefore, graduate with a clear California credential; this is popular with the students. Other cohorts now are interested in attending school during the long winter session to complete more work. Although the 48–51 credit-hour Concurrent program is intense and rigorous, the reward is two credentials with an emphasis on Innovation and Contemporary Practice.

Creating and implementing a preparation program that teaches cutting-edge pedagogy and practice is exciting. Nevertheless, the current system within the public schools (or individuals within that system) may not be ready in terms of changing to newly restructured paradigms. Student teachers are prepared to be sensitive to the demands of their setting, apply what they have learned to the extent their master teacher is comfortable, and wait until they have their own classroom to implement certain of the ideas and techniques they have been taught.

One area of limitation has been co-teaching in the general education class-room while student teaching in special education—evidently a relatively new idea for some teachers in both special and general education classrooms. Strict adherence to recommended practice in running student study teams and indi-vidualized education plan reevaluations and meetings also has been an issue. The zeal of "newness" often must be cushioned by the reality of today's busy world and limited resources. Though not a new or novel idea, the notion of home visits became problematic in some instances. If the special education master teachers did not do them, they did not want the student teachers to do them. A required component of their ecological case study during the summer session work, students enjoyed and learned the value of these experiences. Many will conduct them when in the field even if the opportunity was not provided during student teaching.

Preparation with the Cohort Model

While the cohorts develop a sense of unity and family, faculty members learn quickly that they can take on a life of their own. Most interesting, each cohort has its own unique chemistry, style, charisma, and gestalt. During the second year the program expanded to two cohorts. Each had its own unique flavor and approach to learning. Also, each developed a completely unique interactive style and community organization. Although both became cohesive, one was heavy in social activities (class cookbook, wear-a-hat day) and the other more into cooperative study and mutual support in academics. Both groups became close during the year. Faculty members learned to appreciate the unique chemistry of each group and adapt their teaching styles to meet the different audiences.

Development and Implementation of Fused Curricula

The notion of a seamless program of preparation covering the three areas of general, special, and bilingual education was somewhat novel. CSU San Marco was the first institution to infuse the B/CLAD competencies into a special education preparation program curriculum. At the same time, the traditional separatist approach to certification in general and special education of the California Commission on Teacher Credentialing (CTC) presented some hurdles in terms of writing the program document and going through the approval process. The CTC was helpful and supportive of this innovative program and, when presented for approval, the faculty received accolades for the forward-thinking approach to program design.

This curriculum is not an amalgam of separate and distinct courses in three disciplines; it is not additive. The resulting design and pedagogy provide an integrated approach to addressing the needs of all learners in the schools. The candidates are well received in the districts, and all but one or two were hired either before graduation or within 6 to 8 weeks thereafter. We expect the same success for the two groups going thorough the program this year.

References

Barth, R. S. (1990). *Improving schools from within.* San Francisco: Jossey-Bass.

Carrasco, R. (1981). *Expanded awareness of student performance: A case study in applied ethnographic monitoring in a bilingual classroom.* Unpublished qualifying paper, Harvard Graduate School of Education.

Castaneda, L. V. (1991). *Social organization of communication and interaction in exemplary SAIP classrooms and the nature of competent membership.* Paper presented at annual meeting of American Educational Research Association, Chicago.

Castaneda, L. V. (1994). Meeting the needs of language minority students in multiple language contexts. In A. Nava, H. Molina, B. Cabello, B. De La Torre, & L. Vega-Castaneda, *Educating Americans in a multicultural society* (pp. 13–18). New York: McGraw-Hill.

Cazden, C., Maldonado-Guzman, A. A., & Carrasco, R. L. (1984, October). *Harvard crosscultural ethnographic study of bilingual and mainstream classrooms.* Final report to Ford Foundation for Grant #800-0753.

CSU Board of Trustees Committee on Educational Polity. (1992). *Compiled papers from the open forum and special seminars: CSU's relationship with the schools.* Long Beach: California State University Board of Trustees.

College of Education Faculty. (1992). *College of Education, CSU San Marcos: Program proposal for multiple subjects with B/CLAD emphasis, 1992–93.* San Marcos, CA: CSU San Marcos COE.

College of Education Faculty. (1993). *College of Education, CSU San Marcos: Program proposal for multiple subjects with special education specialist: Learning handicapped credential with B/CLAD emphasis, 1993–94.* San Marcos, CA: CSU San Marcos COE.

Delgado-Gaitan, C. (1988). *Parental assistance on children's home literacy activities.* Unpublished manuscript.

Erickson, F., Cazden, C., Carrasco, R., & Maldonado-Guzman, A. (1983). *Social and cultural organization of interaction in classrooms of bilingual children.* Final Report for NIE, G-78-00-99.

Garcia, G. (1994). *Understanding and meeting the challenge of student cultural diversity.* Boston: Houghton Mifflin Co.

Goodlad, J. I. (1993). Access to knowledge. In J. I. Goodlad & T. C. Lovitt (Eds.), *Integrating general and special education* (pp. 4–22). New York: Charles E. Merrill.

Johnson, L. J., & Pugach, M. S. (1992). Continuing the dialogue: Embracing a more expansive understanding of collaborative relationships. In W. Stainback & S. Stainback (Eds.), *Controversial issues confronting special education* (pp. 215–222). Boston: Allyn & Bacon.

Krashen, S. D. (1981). Bilingual education and second language acquisition theory. In California State Department of Education: Division of Instructional Support and Bilingual Education, *Schooling and language minority students: A theoretical framework* (pp. 51–82). Los Angeles: California State University, Evaluation Dissemination and Assessment Center.

Lilly, K. S. (1992). Compiled papers from the open forum and special seminars: CSU's relationship to the schools. In *CSU Board of Trustee's Committee on Educational Policy* (p. 54). Long Beach, CA: California State University Board of Trustees.

Mehan, H. (1979). *Learning lessons: Social organization in the classroom.* Cambridge, MA: Harvard University Press.

Minicucci, C., & Olsen, L. (1992). *Program for secondary limited English proficient students: A California study.* Washington, DC: National Clearinghouse for Bilingual Education.

Moll, L. (1978). *Bilingual and cross-cultural referential communication.* Unpublished doctoral dissertation, University of California, Los Angeles.

Parsons, A. S. (1994a, November). *California spotlight model: The CSU San Marcos design of a dual credential teacher education program in regular and special education, with a cross-cultural emphasis.* Paper presented at annual meeting of Council for Exceptional Children: Teacher Education Division National Conference (TED), San Diego.

Parsons, A. S. (1994b). *Results of field research on directors of special education's expectations of new graduates in special education for today's schools.* Unpublished raw data.

Parsons, A. S. (1995a). *Concurrent credential program student teaching handbook: Multiple subjects B/CLAD emphasis with special education specialist in learning handicapped.* Unpublished manuscript, California State University, San Marcos.

Parsons, A. S. (1995b). *Non-discriminatory assessment for special and diverse populations.* California Lottery Funds grant application. California State University, San Marcos.

Parsons, A. S. (1995c). *Concurrent credential program student teaching handbook addendum: Advanced practicum in special education: Multiple subjects B/CLAD emphasis with special education specialist in learning handicapped.* Unpublished manuscript, California State University, San Marcos.

Paul, J. L., & Roselli, H. R. (1995). Integrating the parallel reforms in general and special education. In J. Paul, H. Roselli, & D. Evans (Eds.), *Integrating school restructuring and special education reform* (pp. 188–213). New York: Harcourt Brace College Publishers.

Philips, S. (1983). *The invisible culture: Communication in classroom and community on the Warm Springs Indian Reservation.* New York: Longman.

Ramirez, D. (1990). *Longitudinal study of structured English immersion strategy, early exit and late exit transitional bilingual education programs for language minority children.* (Contract No. 300-87-0156). Washington, DC: U.S. Department of Education, Office of Bilingual Education.

Tikunoff, W., Ward, B. A., van Broekhuizen, L. D., Romero, M., Castaneda, L. V., Lucas, T., & Katz, A. (1991). *A descriptive study of significant features of exemplary special alternative instructional programs: Final report for researchers.* Washington, DC: U.S. Department of Education, Office of Bilingual Education and Minority Languages Affairs.

Trueba, H. (1987). Organizing instruction in specific sociocultural contexts: Teaching Mexican youth to write English. In S. Goldman & H. Trueba (Eds.), *Becoming literate in English as a secondary language: Advances in research and theory.* Norwood, NJ: Ablex Corporation.

Authors' Note

The planning committee members worked tirelessly to develop this innovative program. Their critical thought, flexibility, and risk-taking shaped a novel and innovative seamless teacher preparation program. We thank Shell Cox (parent), Exceptional Family Resource Center; Julie Kincaid (general education), Alvin Dunn School; Beverly Barrett, Director of Special Education; Bobbie Smith, Special Education Consultant of San Marcos USD; Adrienne Moreland (Resource Teacher), Mt. Woodson School, Ramona USD; Rhonda Johnson, Coordinator of Special Education Consultants; Dr. Myrna Vallely, Director of Special Education, Vista USD; Dr. Lynette Robinson, Director of Pupil Personnel Services, Encinitas USD, Mrs. Rebecca Sapien-Melchor, ESL Specialist, San Diego County Office of Education; Mrs. Arlene Kagan, Consultant, North Coastal Consortium for Special Education; Mr. Doyle Knirk, Coordinator, North Inland Special Education Local Planning Agency; Mr. Bill Chiment, Director of Human Resources, Poway USD.

In addition, many thanks to the wonderfully collaborative faculty and staff of the college of Education at CSU San Marcos who served on this committee with the authors: Dr. Laurie Stowell (Language and Literacy), Dr. Janet McDaniel (Coordinator, Middle Level Program), Dr. Peggy Kelly (Math Education), Mrs. Nancy Proclivo (Credential Analyst), Ms. Donna McArdle (Support Staff to the Concurrent Credential Program), and last, but with great appreciation, Dr. Steve Lilly, Dean of the College of Education, CSU San Marcos.

The Carlsbad Unified School District and the San Marcos Unified School District have contributed greatly to the implementation and success of this curriculum. Without their assistance, the substance, spirit, and flavor of the program would never have been realized. Special thanks go to Mrs. Patty Arendt, Principal, Knob Hill School, San Marcos USD; Mrs. Nancy Woolsey, Coordinator of Special Education, and Mr. Steve Ahle, Principal, Pine and Jefferson Schools of Carlsbad Unified School District; Mrs. Ofelia Escobedo and Mrs. Connie Trejo, sisters and President and Secretary respectively of the Barrio Carlsbad Association. Much gratitude and many thanks to all.

From Individual and Ambiguous to Collaborative and Explicit: Reform in Urban Teacher Education at the University of Wisconsin-Milwaukee

Ann Higgins Hains, Chris Burton Maxwell, Linda Tiezzi, Mary Jett Simpson, Alison Ford, and Marleen C. Pugach

The collaborative, interdisciplinary reform efforts undertaken in early childhood, primary/middle level, and special education at the University of Wisconsin-Milwaukee have not been the result of specific administrative mandates or other top-down directives, although these efforts have had strong administrative support. Rather, they have emerged from the collective motivation of a group of faculty committed to realizing the full potential of the university's urban teacher education mission.

Using the working program title *Collaborative Teacher Education Program for Urban Communities,* we developed a framework for reforming the early childhood, primary/middle, and special education programs based on substantial integration of special and "general" education. In our new programs early childhood certification is designed for students interested in working with children from birth through age 8 and will include an area of concentration for either birth to age 5 or ages 3–8. It merges and redefines what previously was part of a dual-certification program in early childhood and early childhood special education. The primary/middle years certification is designed for students interested in working with children from ages 6 to 14 and will include an area of concentration for either ages 6–10 or ages 10–14. Special education will be blended into the early childhood and primary/middle programs for all students; students interested in adding special education certification will do so by completing a fifth year, postbaccalaureate program.

Four broad aspects of the University of Wisconsin-Milwaukee (UWM) program restructuring efforts are described in this chapter: (a) the context for reform, (b) program philosophy and design configurations, (c) the processes of reform, and (d) future challenges. The essence of our work lies in the progress we have made in moving from individual, often private, beliefs about what is involved in preparing teachers for urban schools to collaboratively construct shared understandings. It likewise is rooted in a commitment to move beyond ambiguity and uneasiness in embracing an urban focus, replacing this with explicit and open articulation of the values that guide our definition of the urban mission.

The Context for Reform

Consistent with the national trend toward educational reform, our work has taken place in the context of an urban community committed to improving its public schools and is working actively toward that goal. This community context and the local institutional context were the setting for our efforts. We see these as interdependent aspects of our work.

The Broad Community Context for Change

The demographics of the University of Wisconsin-Milwaukee mandate a larger responsibility to the urban community. Serving a population of approximately 25,000 students, UWM is the only urban university within the University of Wisconsin System, which consists of 13 degree-granting institutions, 13 two-year centers, and UW-Extension. UWM is one of only two doctoral-granting universities in the system and awards the Ph.D. in Urban Education.

Located in the largest urban community in the state, we are challenged to prepare teachers to work with the now familiar characteristics of children and families in urban environments: racial diversity, cultural and linguistic diversity, economic poverty and its attendant stresses, and high dropout rates. Of the Milwaukee Public Schools' 102,560 students, 77 percent are students of color. The student characteristics stand in stark contrast to Milwaukee's teaching force, which, like other urban districts nationwide, is predominantly white (in the case of Milwaukee, 70 percent) ("Milwaukee Public Schools," 1995). Most School of Education undergraduates are white female commuter students who originate from suburbs and surrounding towns. Enrollment of students from underrepresented populations in the School of Education is approximately 17 percent, up from 9 percent during the past 5 years (Maxwell & Hains, 1996). Of the 85 education faculty members, 11 are culturally or linguistically diverse, and few of these individuals are instructors in the teacher education program.

Within the context of these complex and intense challenges, many groups in the community—families, service organizations, parts of local and state government, Milwaukee Public Schools, and the University of Wisconsin-Milwaukee School of Education—are committed to working to make schools more responsive to students' and families' needs, to construct stronger and more meaningful educational programs and experiences for students, and to develop collaborative networks to do so. Developing these collaborative networks is made even more challenging by rapid changes within the Milwaukee Public Schools. The past 6 years have seen three different superintendents. To address the mounting challenges for teaching and learning, a number of initiatives have been attempted such as ungraded classrooms, inclusive education, African American immersion schools, School-to-Work, and the closing and "reconstitution" of failing schools. In addition, political support for public education from the general citizenry has been in flux. An erosion of support is fueled by negative media coverage and Wisconsin's strong momentum for school choice. Historically, and throughout this period of rapid change, UWM has retained a longstanding and positive working relationship with the public schools.

The Institutional Context for Change

The UWM School of Education has five departments: Administrative Leadership, Curriculum and Instruction, Educational Policy and Community Studies, Educational Psychology, and Exceptional Education. All departments contribute to preparing teachers; however, the departments of Curriculum and Instruction and Exceptional Education are responsible primarily for teacher education programs. The Department of Curriculum and Instruction houses the early childhood, elementary, middle, and secondary education programs, as well as bilingual and English as a Second Language (ESL) preparation.

Like our counterparts in schools and colleges of education elsewhere, departments traditionally have operated with a high level of autonomy. Courses provided for the teacher education program by other departments are considered service courses to the departments of Curriculum and Instruction and Exceptional Education. In most cases these have been taught with little interaction among faculty members who teach them. Conventional mainstreaming courses traditionally were required for all elementary and secondary majors. Special education majors were required to complete a field experience in general education classrooms.

With the exception of a few individuals, the sense of ownership for the teacher education program outside these two departments has been predictably limited. This attitude has continued to prevail even though teacher education courses generate the largest number of student credit hours for the School of Education.

Much of our teacher education program evolved through the years from Wisconsin Department of Public Instruction mandates for requirements in teacher certification programs. Each time a mandate was received from the Department of Public Instruction, we responded by adding a course to the program. As needed, requests were made to departments outside Curriculum and Instruction and Exceptional Education to provide service courses to meet these mandates. Some changes also were made by individual faculty initiative. As a result, the program grew and changed piecemeal, without a strong framework within which changes could be considered.

First Efforts: Multiple Forums for Collaboration

Since 1988, several different efforts began to take place that moved faculty members from various teacher education programs toward a more collaborative model for our work. These three "forums for collaboration" sometimes operated independently and sometimes with interactions between them. In any case, the end result was faculty engaged in collaboration at an institution, like so many others, that did not have a history of doing so.

Center for Teacher Education

One attempt to cut across departmental boundaries was the Center for Teacher Education. As an alternative governance structure charged with reforming teacher education, the center brought together faculty across programs for several initiatives. One of these initiatives was to develop and implement urban Professional Development Schools (PDS) that were linked closely with teacher education programs (Pugach & Pasch, 1994). Through these efforts, we began to experiment on a small scale with developing elementary student experiences in the PDS sites and, in addition, began to block some of the methods classes together and teach some of them in PDS settings. In this way, we began to increase student experiences in urban schools by providing them in each semester of the current program and to modify methods classes to reflect more closely the realities of teaching in urban settings.

Faculty members who led PDS efforts came from both the Departments of Curriculum and Instruction and Exceptional Education. Cross-departmental teaching of new or revised courses, as well as some early efforts at faculty teaming, also were conducted as part of the center's activities. Through these efforts, we also began to explore how a research agenda could be embedded in our teacher education program work. Whether the center faculty was engaged in PDS work, program development, or research, the efforts were based on a collaborative model. We began to understand some of our common goals, philosophy, and intense concerns for improving our work in urban settings, and to envision the possibilities for change.

Collaborative Conversations About Early Childhood Programs

In 1989 the early childhood faculty from the Departments of Curriculum and Instruction, Educational Psychology, and Exceptional Education began ongoing conversations about program development. The discussion regarded the multiple types and contexts of interactions that early childhood educators and early childhood special educators have in providing comprehensive, seamless, community-based services to young children and their families. Issues of role, including what contributions early childhood educators and early childhood special educators make as generalists, as specialists, and as interdisciplinary team members, continued (ATE, DEC, NAEYC, 1995; Bredekamp & Willer, 1992; Odom & McLean, 1996).

While the students in early childhood special education received "unified" preparation (early childhood education and early childhood special education) for working with *all* children from birth to age 5 and their families, interdisciplinary collaboration with UWM faculty from disciplines outside of teacher education (e.g., nursing, social work, occupational therapy, speech therapy) was of concern. With young children the discipline differences tend to be one of focus rather than exclusive function (McCollum & Maude, 1994; McCollum & Stayton, 1996). A parallel concern was the knowledge that the underrepresentation of professionals who are culturally, ethnically, and linguistically diverse, economically disadvantaged, bilingual/bicultural, disabled, and male adversely influences the quality and availability of early childhood and early intervention services for a significant proportion of the urban population (cf. Chan, 1990; Christensen, 1992; Garcia, McLaughlin, Spodek, & Saracho, 1995; Lynch & Hanson, 1992).

To address both concerns, the faculty experimented in a variety of team-teaching arrangements with parents, faculty from other disciplines, and community professionals in a few targeted courses (e.g., Home-School Relations, Partnerships in Service Coordination, Family-Centered Assessment). Broader activities, such as developing collaborative grant proposals, attending state and national faculty institutes, and creating an early childhood research center on campus, expanded the network to include faculty from other disciplines (e.g., nursing, social work, speech pathology, psychology, architecture and urban planning, and health sciences). These interactions encouraged faculty members from multiple disciplines to step outside disciplinary boundaries and contribute to program reform.

Conversations About Special Education

A third set of conversations was beginning to take place with a specific focus on special education. This forum, which occurred primarily within the Department of Exceptional Education, but which had an active representative from Curriculum and Instruction, consisted of discussions and informal planning around a proposed dual-certification program in elementary education and special education. Faculty members participating in this effort brought their collaborative experiences from both the Center for Teacher Education and Early Childhood.

Further, the arrival of several new special education faculty members in the years around 1990 signaled a new set of expectations for what should constitute a high-quality program to prepare special education teachers. As planning moved ahead and intensified, progress was shared regularly but informally with various faculty members from Curriculum and Instruction. Ultimately, the conversations that were taking place within special education had major implications for how we would conceptualize the new program, the *Collaborative Teacher Education Program for Urban Communities.*

New Conceptions of Special Education

The original goal of "dual certification" was revisited many times as faculty discussed what the new program might look like. We would ask ourselves what we would hope to accomplish through a dual-certification program. In terms of basic intent, our response was always the same. Like many others, we want educators—special and general alike—to leave UWM with a high level of commitment to diversity, including learners with disabilities. More specifically, we believe our graduates should be committed to educating all children, be prepared to work in collaborative team structures, and have a reasonable level of expertise in adapting the curriculum and providing support for students with disabilities.

To accomplish this, we had to integrate our teacher education programs more fully. Just as we advocated for special educators to have a greater presence in the general curriculum experienced by students with disabilities, we saw the need for special education faculty to have a greater presence in the "general" teacher education program at UWM.

Throughout these deliberations and planning, we remained committed to a dual or unified teacher education approach. Determining which certifications to award our graduates, however, was a different matter. At the primary/middle school level, we became less enthusiastic about a new program leading to both special and general education licensure. We reminded ourselves that we were preparing beginning teachers within a 4-year program structure, which placed a serious constraint on our program space. We also gave considerable thought to the educator's role and asked ourselves: Are the roles of the special and general educator so interchangeable that, upon completion of our unified program, graduates could assume either role with no distinction? Or, through this unified approach, are we mostly hoping to prepare more collaborative, more accommodating, and more highly skilled general educators and, in turn, be in the position to expect more unique contributions from our special educators?

At least for now, we have concluded that our certification structure should be consistent with the latter scenario. We will collectively prepare UWM's general or urban educators to embrace all children, including those with disabilities, as full members of their classrooms. Our expectation and goal is that these teachers will be prepared to work within a collaborative structure that is likely to include a special educator who has different expertise.

Throughout our past deliberations and current practices, we all continue to be painfully aware of the need for all teachers to welcome all students into their classroom communities and be willing to make accommodations for them, and to expect this from our students. Especially in urban schools we are concerned fundamentally with preparing teachers who will not perpetuate the overrepresentation of minority students in the special education system. These goals represent high expectations for our students and a high level of knowledge about and commitment to the meaning of teaching diverse learners without penalizing them unduly with unnecessary labels and the low expectations that often accompany those labels. We believe the challenge of inclusive education is precisely to prepare teachers like these, and we intend to work hard to achieve success in the face of this challenge. At the same time, we have rejected explicitly a certification structure that prepares all teachers to be all things to all students, one that implies that no specialized knowledge is to be had by special educators and that everyone can do it all.

For those interested in assuming the role of special educator, which will require additional expertise, a fifth-year postbaccalaureate option is available. Therein, the special educator is expected to extend his or her expertise in a manner that strengthens the interdependency of the team, and not simply provide a body of decontextualized knowledge. In this scenario, teams would be able to depend on the special educator to bring expertise in accommodating the "more difficult to educate" student who has learning, developmental, or emotional/behavioral disabilities.

Our decision to reject a conventional dual-certification model is based on our belief that we need to redefine special education expertise at a much more sophisticated level and place a high value on the process of teaming. Our intention is that the general teachers we prepare will be able to work effectively with many students who now are placed unnecessarily under the auspices of special education, thus demanding a new set of skills for special educators themselves. Our belief in expertise does not signify a return to the traditional practice of special education; rather, we see it as a challenge to identify what this new expertise is and how it fits with new conceptions of teaching and learning on which our new program is based.

Similar conversations took place with respect to early childhood education. At the early childhood level, undergraduate students in the Department of Curriculum and Instruction receive prekindergarten to grade 3 certification (birth to age 8). In the Department of Exceptional Education, students receive dual certification in early childhood education (prekindergarten/kindergarten; birth to 5 years) and early childhood special education (birth to 5 years; noncategorical by disability). With the shift toward family-centered services and toward inclusion of young children with disabilities in "natural" environments (such as the home, family-based and center-based child-care settings, preschools, and community programs), we realized that our general early childhood students need to look more like the dual-certification special education students. They have to be committed to serving the full range of diversity in young children and their families. Judgments about one's ability to work with young children and families should not be based on labels or categories (e.g., at risk, high risk, developmental delay, atypical behavior, substance exposure), especially in urban environments where these labels and qualifications are based often on funding resources rather than children's needs.

Similarly, our special education students should reflect the shift in service delivery from that of providing primarily direct services to indirect service delivery (ATE, DEC, NAEYC, 1995). When direct services are provided, they likely are to be delivered within an inclusion model as a team member (e.g., team teacher). Increasingly, early childhood special educators serve in indirect service delivery roles as consultant, collaborator, parent educator, program administrator, interagency coordinator, or staff development specialist for family members, other professionals, and paraprofessionals (Bailey, 1989; Bricker, 1989; Bricker & Widerstrom, 1996).

Our discussions evolved around the following questions:

- ■ What should early childhood educators possess as knowledge and skills that includes content specific to young children, birth to age 8, both with and without disabilities, and their families?
- ■ Given the common core possessed by early childhood educators, what specialized knowledge and skills should early childhood special educators have?
- ■ What are the career ladder/lattice implications? What should we provide in preparing our undergraduate and graduate students?

The faculty agreed that the program would prepare entry-level early childhood classroom teachers (birth to age 8) who would develop their expertise according to their career goals. This perspective was essential because the faculty saw continuing education and graduate programs as critical to promoting depth in specializations, directed to an age group such as infancy and early intervention, a curriculum area such as social-emotional development, a special population such as children with hearing impairments, or an instructional methodology such as parent-child language interventions. The undergraduate program reform clearly could not stand alone.

Certification and licensure issues are unresolved tensions. We acknowledge that our new program will prepare students to work in the role of classroom teacher with children who have a wide range of abilities and special needs. Additional expertise is needed, however, for more specialized roles in direct services such as home-based early intervention for infants and toddlers with disabilities and their families and indirect services for children with more significant health, social welfare, and educational needs. Although we still are struggling with these issues, we are more comfortable with career ladder/lattice structures (Bredekamp & Willer, 1992) that would identify beginning teachers and advanced specialists with descriptors than we are with our present certification (e.g., inclusive early childhood teacher [beginning/advanced], early interventionist [beginning/advanced], language/literacy specialist [beginning/advanced], consultant specialist in disabilities [infant/preschool/primary and beginning/advanced]).

Reaching Consensus: Program Philosophy and Design

With these preliminary collaborative experiences behind us and in the face of the ongoing discussions about the relationship between special and general education, we were anxious to move ahead with specific program plans. In the fall of 1994, an existing task force on program revision was reconstituted as a critical mass of faculty members from early childhood, elementary, and special education who were ready to move on program reform. Our initial efforts had been directed toward creating a new departmental structure that would place many of the members of this critical mass in one new department focused on early childhood and elementary education and that may or may not have included exceptional education programs. The political battles that accompanied this effort seemed to be absorbing much of everyone's energy and time.

One day as we were meeting, we realized that the departmental barriers really were less of an obstacle than we had assumed, and we made the decision to go ahead directly with program reform. Although we probably did not realize it at the time, this was a momentous decision in many ways because it meant we were committed to finding ways to making the existing structure work for the program. Many of us had been working together across departments and programs in the various collaborative efforts described above, and we recognized that this collective experience had strengths that could support us in the hard work ahead and eventually could lead to the structural changes we were trying to achieve anyway. We reasoned that if our work was good enough and our resolve strong enough, we could make the case for the changes we believe were needed.

Freed from a narrow focus on institutional structure, we reorganized the leadership of the task force to include co-chairs, one from Exceptional Education and one from Curriculum and Instruction. In 1995–96, coinciding with the arrival of a new dean, the terminology associated with the task force was dropped and the informal title "working group" was used to identify those involved in the reform effort and their activities. With this accomplished and with program reform very much on our minds, we undertook the development of a set of core values.

Core Values

One of our major goals was to develop a program with conceptual and theoretical continuity. We agreed to begin our work with discussions of values, beliefs, and outcomes of an urban teacher education program. These discussions took place within the Department of Exceptional Education and among the critical mass of faculty in Early Childhood and Elementary Education. These conversations were intense and intellectually stimulating and centered on the following questions:

- What kind of people do we want our graduates to be?
- What intellectual, social, and moral dispositions do we want our graduates to have as persons, learners, and teachers?
- What attitudes, values, and beliefs about urban children, families, and communities do we want our graduates to have?
- What content knowledge do we want our graduates to have?
- What learning experiences on campus and in the urban community will support our students' learning experiences?
- What commitments, knowledge, and organization are necessary from our faculty and administration in the School of Education?
- What resources are needed to construct and implement an urban teacher education program?

Shared understandings gradually began to evolve from our dialogue, resulting in eight core values that provided the foundation for our *Collaborative Teacher Education Program for Urban Communities*. Achieving a high degree of consensus was not difficult, and although our discussions were intense, they were headed in the same direction. As we began this phase of the work, the special education faculty and the faculty in early childhood and primary/middle education generated separate sets of core values. When we brought these lists together, they were in near perfect agreement. These core values will function as constant major themes across the total program and will serve to guide formative and summative evaluation of our work. Not only will these values be represented consistently in course content; they also will be infused into the daily operation of the program and guide how we work together as faculty teams. These values are:

- Valuing the child as *the center* of teaching
- Valuing and promoting *equity* and the *inclusion* of diverse learners in the schools
- *Responsive, interactive teaching* based upon sound knowledge of content and pedagogical content
- *Collaboration* among teachers, support staff, paraprofessionals, families, community agencies, and school administration
- *Caring and commitment* to diverse student learners, to being advocates for children, to supporting the development of all children, to viewing diversity as an asset
- *Promoting reform* by being involved actively in the process of change and advocating for improved education
- *Reflection* as a professional stance, a focus on improving one's practice through various forms of inquiry over the course of one's career
- *Integration* across content areas, across levels of education, across developmental domains, and across field and academic experiences in the teacher education program.

Once our core values emerged, we concentrated on what our students needed to know so they could practice these values in urban settings. The core knowledge we identified to support these values is:

- Knowledge of child development and learning
- Knowledge of academic content
- State-of-the-art curriculum knowledge including an individually responsive curriculum and instructional technology
- State-of-the-art pedagogical content knowledge
- Classroom climate and management
- Assessment of learners
- Cultural foundations of education emphasizing the urban, social-family context.

Although we valued the local understanding we had constructed in identifying the core values and the knowledge base, we also looked to our state and national education communities to broaden and challenge our thinking about the underlying principles and knowledge base for our urban teacher education program. We examined the national teacher education reform agenda (Carnegie Task Force on Education and the Economy, 1986; Holmes Group, 1986) and the restructuring of higher education (Holmes Group, 1995; Johnson Foundation, 1993; Twigg, 1995). We also drew on the Interstate New Teacher Assessment and Support Consortium (INTASC) model standards (1992), the Restructuring Teacher Education and Licensure in Wisconsin report (Wisconsin Department of Public Instruction, 1995), and position statements and documents from a number of national organizations (e.g., the Association of Teacher Educators, Council for Exceptional Children: Division for Early Childhood and Teacher Education Division, National Association for the Education of Young Children, National Board for Professional Teaching Standards, National Council for Accreditation of Teacher Education, and National Council of Teachers of Mathematics). In many cases our reading of these documents verified what we had concluded already. In others it stretched our thinking and strengthened the outcomes. Once these core values and associated knowledge were established, we moved to the work of program design.

Design Features

Our task was to design two new, interrelated programs that had a serious commitment to preparing students for urban schools and for working with the full range of students: early childhood education and primary/middle education. The working group included faculty from across all three areas (early childhood, primary/middle, and special education) as well as a smaller number of colleagues from foundations (educational psychology and social/historical/philosophical foundations). Specific work on the special education postbaccalaureate program occurred within that department; progress was communicated to the larger group as a regular part of our joint work. At the time this chapter was completed, the new special education program had accepted its first cohort; the primary/middle program is moving through the first steps of the approval process with the intention of enrolling the first cohort of students in fall 1997; and the new early childhood program will begin in the following year, the fall of 1998.

The core values and knowledge serve as a single, unifying conceptual basis for the new early childhood, primary/middle, and the special education programs. In this chapter we describe in some detail the primary/middle program as an example of how we are operationalizing the core values we all share. Figure 9.1 illustrates this framework and the basic design features that will guide implementation of the programs. All design features characterize each of the three new programs: Early Childhood, Primary/Middle, and Special Education. (The only exception is that the liberal arts focus does not apply to special education and that only an institute option is offered in this postbaccalaureate program.)

Over the years, efforts had been made to reduce program fragmentation through the use of methods blocks and by linking field experiences to bridge the gap between knowledge and practice and to counter the prevailing notion that only the culminating student teaching experience was of consequence. In our new program design we sought to strengthen the block structure so interdisciplinary coursework and teaching experience could be linked integrally both within each semester and across the entire program.

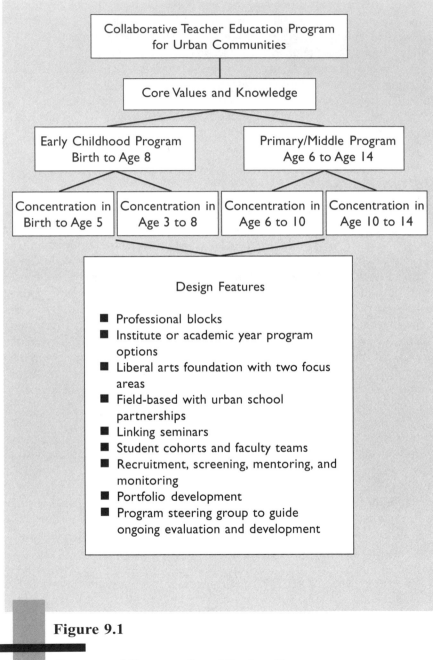

Figure 9.1

Conceptual Framework and Design Features

Following approximately 2 years of liberal arts and sciences courses, the Primary/Middle Program itself is divided into four professional blocks. A working draft of the program is presented in Figure 9.2. In these blocks, we drew upon Schwab's (1978) four "commonplaces" to guide our thinking about how to frame the interrelationships between the child, teacher, content, and context. In each block one or more of the commonplaces are brought to the foreground to provide focus and continuity to the program's organization. And, rather than prepare a student generically for grades 1–6 (which is how elementary certification is organized in the state of Wisconsin), two of the professional blocks are focused on either primary or middle years, with students selecting which area they wish to specialize in during the final block. Students will continue to graduate with certification for grades 1–6, but they now will have the specialized emphasis that helps them define their work in a more developmental sequence.

Professional Blocks

The professional program begins with the Schooling and Urban Community Block, which students take prior to formal admission to the School of Education. This block consists of a combined course and introductory field experience taken during the freshman or sophomore year, when students gain insights into teaching and learning in the urban setting. Presently, most of our prospective teacher education students come from cultural and geographical backgrounds that differ from those of the urban students they will teach. These prospective teachers bring firmly held beliefs about teaching in an urban context, beliefs that are diverse and often misinformed (Tiezzi & Cross, in press). Thus, we have stressed the importance of early, well articulated, and educative learning experiences at the university and in the urban schools and communities. The Schooling and Urban Community Block is revisited during the final semester of the program when students have a better, firsthand understanding of how schools work and can be more reflective about their roles as urban educators.

Given the commonplaces as an organizing principle and the specialized emphasis on primary and middle years, the blocks for the 2 years of the Primary/Middle Program are organized as follows:

Block I: *Child* at the Center
Block II: Interrelationships Between *Content, Context,* Child, and Teacher: The Primary Years
Block III: Interrelationships Between *Content, Context,* Child, and Teacher: The Middle Years
Block IV: *Teacher*—Defining Roles and Expanding Knowledge

Block I focuses on the learner so that prospective teachers understand how students learn and develop, see students as individuals with the full range of abilities (including students with disabilities), and understand the roles of families and communities in supporting students' learning and well-being. We place

Block I: Child at the Center	**Block II: The Primary Years—Interrelationships Between Content, Context, Child, & Teacher**
Teaching Experiences I & Linking Seminar	**Teaching Experience II & Linking Seminar**

Block I: Child at the Center

Teaching Experiences I & Linking Seminar
- Time commitment: Once per week
- Context: School; also see child outside of school—in home, community
- Age group/Format: Any age; dyads
- Role: 1:1 relationship as observer, support person; with child who differs from self

Professional Urban Linking Seminar I

Developing Learner/Diverse Learners
- Individual growth and development—methods to promote student learning; methods to promote student development; methods to promote student motivation
- Influences on child development—environmental; biological
- Multiculturalism
- Disability—challenging the deficit model; understanding learners with disabilities
- Supplementing experience with theory-based & data-confirmed approaches
- Cognitive & language development (foundations for beginning literacy & numeracy)
- Physical development

Social, Emotional, & Affective: Responsive Educational Contexts
- Issues of classroom management
- Essentials of responsive education; decision-making schema for responsive & effective classroom environments; urban contexts & educational change
- Social-emotional needs & strengths of children at-risk academically; emotionally vulnerable; culturally diverse
- Effects of urban realities & pressures on students' behavior
- Strategies for ongoing conceptual & practical analysis [follow-up course in Block IV]

Health Issues in Schools

Technology II

Focus Area Courses (6 credits)

Block II: The Primary Years—Interrelationships Between Content, Context, Child, & Teacher

Teaching Experience II & Linking Seminar
- Time commitment: 2–3 days/week—half days
- Context: School—Primary grades
- Age group/Format: Grades 1–4; 2–3 person teams
- Role: Teaching individuals & small groups

Professional Urban Linking Seminar II

Literacy: Primary

Reading & Writing in Primary Grades
- Reading & writing processes—development patterns, interactive/transactional model
- Identifying who students are as readers, writers, & thinkers
- Children as strategic readers & writers for decoding, vocabulary, comprehension, & composition
- Key instructional strategies; directed reading, thinking activity, responsive interactive teaching (coaching), conducting conferences, creating student portfolios
- Developing lifelong readers & writers
- Reading & writing technology links

Literature and Language Arts in the Primary Grades
- Characteristics of genres used at primary level
- Applying evaluation criteria to unfamiliar books for book selection
- Analyzing children's interests to match them with books
- Using children's books as a basis for speaking & listening activities
- Planning experiences to engage children in speaking & listening
- Developing integrated language arts/literature units

Mathematics: Primary
- How children develop mathematical knowledge
- Important mathematical ideas that should be learned—primary grades
- Why the teaching of mathematics has changed
- Teaching and assessing for understanding
- Organizing a hands-on, minds-on learning environment for all children

Science
- Building on minors
- Helping children become scientifically literate
- Developing children's thinking skills through science
- Learning to manage a hands-on science approach using a variety of instructional approaches

Creative & Expressive Arts
- Building on minors
- Visual arts
- Drama & movement
- Music

Technology III (continued)

Figure 9.2

A Working Draft of the Primary/Middle Program

Figure 9.2 continued

Block III: The Middle Years—Interrelationships Between Content, Context, Child, & Teacher

Teaching Experience III & Linking Seminar
- Time commitment: 3 days/week—half days
- Context: School—Middle grades
- Age group/Format: Grades 4–8; 2–3 person teams
- Role: Small groups & whole class

Professional Urban Linking Seminar III

Literacy: Middle Years

Reading & Writing in the Middle Grades/Reading in the Content Areas
- Reading and writing processes for middle-level students
- Identifying who students are as readers, writers, & thinkers
- Children as strategic readers and writers for decoding, vocabulary, comprehension, & composition
- Key instructional strategies for reading in the content areas
- Developing lifelong readers & writers; critical & creative thinkers
- Organizing for instruction—readers & writers workshops

Literature & Language Arts in the Middle Grades
- Planning ways to engage in critical & creative response to literature
- Characteristics of various genres used at middle levels
- Developing literature/language arts experiences across the curriculum
- Studying children's authors' writing processes

Mathematics: Middle Years
- Important mathematical ideas that should be learned—middle school
- Promoting mathematic discourse to engage all students
- Emphasizing connections within mathematics, to other disciplines & real world
- Criteria for selecting worthwhile mathematical tasks
- Facilitating learning with tools such as manipulatives, calculators, & computers

Social Studies
- Building on minors—social sciences contribution to social studies curriculum
- Status of social studies in the school curriculum & reforms
- Organizing an effective social studies program
- Fundamental & advanced approaches for teaching social studies
- Organizing and teaching history & geography in elementary grades
- Role of values teaching in social studies; growing as a professional
- An interdisciplinary approach

Assessment I
- Building assessment connections with content areas
- Examining assessment tools that go across content areas
- Developing a student-centered philosophy of assessment
- Historical perspective on assessment

Creative and Expressive Arts

Technology IV

Block IV: Teacher—Defining Role & Expanding Knowledge

Teaching Experience IV & Linking Seminar: Primary or Middle
- Time commitment: full-time—16 weeks
- Context: School
- Age group/Format: student selects focus with faculty advisement—primary or middle; single-person placement

Professional Urban Linking Seminar IV

Collaborative Teaching & Accommodating Students with Disabilities
- Learning about the students with disabilities in your class—multiple perspectives
- Strategies for accommodating learners with disabilities
- Defining your role & that of the special educator, teaching assistant, & others who support students with IEPs
- Manageable strategies for planning & teaching as a team
- Ongoing communication strategies with students, families, & other professionals

Social/Emotional/Affective
- Issues of classroom management/addressing conflict
- Revisiting strategies/topics from Block I
- Case analysis

Assessment II
- Role & impact of standardized testing on the classroom
- Grading and evaluation process
- Impact on evaluation practices on social, emotional, & affective dimensions
- Effectively communicating assessment information to various audiences such as parents & students

Creative and Expressive Arts

particular emphasis on moving from a deficit model to an asset model for all students. In Blocks II and III we guide prospective teachers in deciding and organizing content, or what to teach, and in understanding and shaping the contexts in which instruction occurs. Block IV focuses on defining the role of teacher so prospective teachers will become reflective practitioners and develop a well grounded and personalized approach to curriculum. In this block students begin to give serious consideration to collaboration as a means of gaining support for students. During this final block, program participants are expected to acquire a further understanding of their teaching roles and expand their knowledge base in developing areas of expertise.

The blocks are based on a career development perspective in that students are expected to identify areas of special interest and expertise as they enter and move through each block. Unlike the block structure of the past—in which each block was seen as a new and, in many ways, an "introductory" experience, a conscious effort has been made to ensure that our students have increasingly intensive experiences that build on one another deliberately and sequentially. Also, unlike the past, when students somehow had the impression that most of their professional development was completed when the 4-year program ended, most now understand their beginning teacher status and view teaching as a continuous development process.

Institute or Academic-Year Program Options

We recognize that many individuals who are working already in urban schools wish to become teachers in these urban schools. Thus, we have designed the program to be delivered in two configurations: an academic-year program for those who can participate in daytime classes, and an institute program for those who work and will require intensive coursework during the summer and less intensive coursework during the academic year. The institute structure will provide a healthy substitute for the part-time experience that too often is characterized by weariness, fragmentation, and little sense of program affiliation.

We are particularly interested in the institute structure because it enables us to work with paraprofessionals and emergency licensed teachers in the Milwaukee Public Schools. As we developed the new program, we drew on two externally funded projects that have supported the recruitment of underrepresented populations. The first, EXCEL, was a federally funded project to support students who intended to work in the field of early childhood (Hains & Maxwell, 1995). The second, the Milwaukee Pathways to Teaching Careers Program, is funded by the DeWitt Wallace-Reader's Digest Foundation and supports paraprofessionals and emergency licensed teachers in the Milwaukee Public Schools as they move through any teacher education program at UWM (Alverno College and the University of Wisconsin, Milwaukee, 1993).

For the institute option to be most successful, we hope to enact interinstitutional agreements with schools that are willing to redefine the duties of a paraprofessional so he or she can fulfill the requirements of a particular teaching experience. Our desire is to formalize and expand this strategy so the UWM and the school district can make a joint commitment to recruiting teacher candidates from the paraprofessional pool and enroll them simultaneously in the Institute Program, which would allow them to continue their employment while completing their education.

Liberal Arts Foundation with Two Focus Areas

Collaborative Teacher Education Program for Urban Communities emphasizes the role of academic content as foundational knowledge for good teaching and especially for good interdisciplinary teaching. Students begin their university career by fulfilling a 24-credit "liberal arts core" (in fine arts, humanities, natural sciences, mathematics, and social sciences). Through an early and ongoing advisement process, students work with faculty advisors to construct two liberal-arts focus areas: one in Mathematics or Science and the other in Social Studies or Humanities and the Arts.

Each focus area consists of 18 credits and is intended to build on the liberal arts core by gaining more indepth knowledge in two disciplines of interest to the student. Our traditional single-focus area, or minor, used to consist of 22 credits in a single area; most elementary teacher education students elected social studies. Now, with a forced choice in mathematics or sciences, we hope to increase the number of teachers who are confident teaching in these areas. Students also will be encouraged to draw upon these focus areas during their methods courses and in collaborative team structures where they are called upon to share their unique strengths, backgrounds, and interest areas.

Field-Based with Urban School Partnerships

Each block has a teaching experience in a school or agency setting that is selected and matched carefully with the goals of the block. For example, in Block I, where the emphasis is placed on observing and understanding the developing learner, the teaching experience involves a commitment to a child beyond the school setting—spending time with his or her family, at the community center, or at home. Also, increasingly, we are asking the cooperating teachers in these settings to see their roles as "field instructors"—to become more active partners in promoting the development of future urban educators.

Many of our students in the Early Childhood and Primary/Middle programs are placed in classrooms that are practicing inclusive education. Many schools in Milwaukee have taken a leadership role in inclusive education, and we are fortunate to be able to draw on these many examples for field placements. Students must conduct their field experiences with great attention to who they are teaching and how pupils are being included.

Collaborative Teacher Education Program for Urban Communities will require us to expand our ongoing partnerships with professional development schools as well as other urban schools. The title of the program underscores the belief that preparing teachers for urban schools is qualitatively different from preparing teachers for any school. If new urban teachers are to be well prepared, they—and the faculty that teaches them—will have to work collaboratively, drawing on the expertise and support of the other professionals, of family members, and of community people. The need to build educational practices that draw upon indepth horizontal connections among interagency and interdisciplinary personnel seems to be greatest in urban settings, where the complexities of childhood experiences are particularly challenging.

Professional Urban Linking Seminars

In each block, students attend a linking seminar to facilitate inquiry, reflection, and integration of learning experiences in keeping with the core values of the program and the overarching goals of the block. The linking seminars also help students make connections between the present experience (including fieldwork, readings, projects) and those from previous semesters.

This aspect of our new program is critical as a means of counteracting the prevailing belief that our students will develop sensible relationships between their professional experiences independently. In the past, we, like many others, have counted on the students to do this kind of linking when most have had little, if any, practice in doing so. Although certainly some of our students have made these connections well without guidance, others more often have not done so. The linking seminar is an institutionalized, yet flexible response to this dilemma and enables us to draw out these important linkages purposefully on a semester-by-semester basis.

Student Cohorts and Faculty Teams

Cohorts of 20–25 students will be admitted into the program and will experience much of their program together as colleagues. They are taught and mentored by an interdisciplinary team of faculty members who will work together to coordinate a block (draw connections among courses, share expertise, coordinate syllabi and projects), support and guide cohorts, and model collaborative relationships. In the past we called upon many talented teachers, parents, and community members to teach courses as ad hoc instructors. Our goal with the new program is to involve these instructors in more substantial and integrative ways. One proposal is to create a teacher-in-residence program (perhaps with combined funds from the university, districts, and private foundations), in which select individuals will be given a leave-of-absence from their jobs to join a faculty team for a 2- to 3-year period (S. Lilly, personal communication, July 27, 1994). They may use this also as an opportunity to pursue advanced graduate study.

Recruitment, Screening, Mentoring, and Monitoring

The purpose of this design feature is to help us pay close attention to who we are working with and how these individuals are developing. Although we consistently have more applications to the teacher education program than can be accommodated, we still are challenged to attract students who are well matched to our stated urban mission. We continue to affirm our intention to serve underrepresented students (students from minority groups, students who are economically disadvantaged, students with bilingual skills, students with disabilities, male students). Yet, our admissions and graduation reveal a great need for improvement.

In addition, we know that many of our graduates still have difficulty with the urban context and some never intend to teach in the urban setting. Recruiting and retaining underrepresented students and students who are committed to teaching in urban settings is thus one of our biggest challenges, which is also a concern nationally (Wald, 1996). In our program reform, we are addressing these challenges by (a) restructuring our admissions, mentoring, and monitoring process, and (b) building interinstitutional agreements. This requires that we advise our students regularly and develop feedback loops among faculty members to share views of student progress.

We are piloting a unified approach for undergraduate admissions based on an interview process, portfolio review, gradepoint average, and successful completion of prerequisite courses. Initial portfolio presentations are designed to anchor faculty-student relationships to gain familiarity with students' on an interpersonal basis, and to assess their entering views on teaching. Faculty teams will oversee a two-pronged approach to mentoring and monitoring. All students will receive ongoing guidance and support through the Linking Seminar and peer groups that are formed within this seminar. Students who are not progressing satisfactorily will be assigned an individual faculty mentor, who will work with the student to develop a Professional Development Plan that will be monitored carefully through the remaining blocks of the program.

We are continuing our efforts to strengthen recruitment of underrepresented students. In addition to our positive experiences with the EXCEL Project (Maxwell & Hains, 1996) and the Milwaukee Pathways to Teaching Careers Program (Alverno College and the University of Wisconsin, Milwaukee, 1993), one promising vehicle is through articulation agreements with the technical colleges in the area. For 10 years UWM has had a formalized relationship with the Cooperative Urban Teacher Education Program (CUTEP) at the Milwaukee Area Technical College. CUTEP has facilitated minority students from the Milwaukee Area Technical College entering the elementary education program. More recently, the faculty also has designed articulation agreements for technical college students in child development programs who wish to pursue a 4-year degree in child care, early childhood education, or early childhood special education. Students beginning their programs at technical colleges are advised to complete a series of prerequisite courses and general university requirements and transfer to UWM at the end of their sophomore year.

Portfolio Development

Ongoing evaluation of students is done through a portfolio process that evolves from a beginning portfolio, to a professional growth portfolio, and finally to a graduation portfolio. The beginning portfolio is constructed as part of the Schooling and Urban Community Block and is used during the admission process. Students expand this portfolio throughout their junior and senior years, including field experience evaluations, personal reflections, and sample "projects-in-practice." They are expected to share their portfolios with the teachers with whom they are assigned for each of the various teaching experiences. During the final months of the program, students will be guided in converting their portfolios into a graduation portfolio that can be used as a central component of job interviews.

Program Steering Group to Guide Ongoing Evaluation and Development

As we developed the new program, we operated from the belief that many important faculty contributions already were being made to prepare teachers for urban communities but that those contributions can be maximized only when they occur within a unified framework and not as isolated experiences. Throughout the planning process, we created a healthy sense of interdependence and understood that a program of this nature would be short-lived without a collective effort to monitor our ability to deliver it, to be consistently responsive to new developments in education requiring ongoing program revision, and to remain committed to high standards for our students' work and the work we ourselves do with them.

This takes grassroots leadership of the type we have been providing ourselves in the conceptualization phase and initial implementation. While the responsibility for our progress has been collective, the co-chairs of the working group have been keeping their eyes on the big picture and doing the critical job of keeping everyone on task and moving ahead. These efforts have been supported by a small UW System Undergraduate Teaching Improvement Grant that provided course buyouts for a few faculty members involved in this work.

As we move into the implementation phase, and as these course buyouts conclude, we have been planning how to carry out the leadership function. Recently we have been engaged in an effort to secure a 2- to 3-year special assignment for a faculty member who will work with an interdisciplinary steering group to guide the program through its next phase. The collective ethic of the working group is strong, and the leadership role will be critical to maintaining the expectation for this shared responsibility in relationship to the realistic need for someone to keep all the pieces in mind and link the efforts of the larger group. At the end of this 2- to 3-year period, we hope to recommend a permanent administrative structure to support the program.

Processes of Reform

Presently, a fully developed proposal for the *Collaborative Teacher Education Program for Urban Communities* is moving through the approval processes established by the university and our state education agency. How did we reach this point in the reform process? Although the answer to this question may differ depending on which "historian" tells the tale, the factors that have contributed to our progress are not unlike those identified by the Holmes Group: a collective will, a critical mass of faculty, and alliances with other stakeholders (Holmes Group, 1995).

A Collective Will

Like most faculties, the *will* to make change is ever present among many of our members. We do not have a shortage of faculty committed to continuously improving teacher education programs, and our past is marked with many initiatives undertaken as a result of this commitment. More challenging, however, is how to connect these efforts and pursue broader-based reform collectively.

At least two major factors facilitated our collective will to reform our teacher education programs. First, interdisciplinary collaboration was a key factor. Once the co-chairs were identified from the departments of Curriculum and Instruction and Exceptional Education, they encouraged members from their own respective departments and the other three departments to participate regularly in activities—especially faculty members who taught courses required in the teacher education programs. The co-chairs held countless individual and small-group meetings to pull in the major faculty players and encouraged their active participation. Private discussions that began in the hallway among colleagues within disciplinary programs evolved into public conversations and collective action by an interdisciplinary work group.

A second facilitative factor was the emphasis on open communication. Within the work group, the terminology used by different professional cultures and disciplines (e.g., family-centered intervention, integrated curriculum, interdisciplinary assessment, reflective practitioner, inclusive education) had to be explained. Even when common terms (e.g., social/emotional development) were used, multiple perceptions and values existed. Early on, our lengthy discussions and tangential digressions seemed unproductive; however, in retrospect, they were essential to establishing our common ground, shared knowledge, and collective will. We now have moved to the point where we are scheduling time consciously to have ongoing "conceptual discussions" as a sort of thematic monitoring of what we are communicating to our students.

The procedural aspects of facilitating communication included the circulation of agendas and minutes of meetings to all 85 faculty members in the school, open invitations to monthly meetings, and ongoing announcements about the work group's activities at administrative meetings between the dean and department chairs as well as at schoolwide meetings. This communication at various levels and with all faculty members regarding the status of activities was essential in ensuring interdisciplinary collaboration and in generating broad internal support of the efforts. It also provided high public visibility for our efforts.

A Critical Mass of Faculty

The Holmes Group (1995) suggests that many universities, schools, and colleges of education lack the number of participants to put change in motion and to sustain it. They identified four faculty groups:

1. Those ready and able for change.
2. Those capable of change but unwilling to change until a different sort of reward structure lends them the support they need.
3. Those interested in the change but in need of professional development.
4. Those who refuse to promote change and undermine it.

All groups of faculty exist in our situation; however, our efforts began and continue because we had a dedicated faculty work group made up of professionals who were ready and willing to change.

At least 20 faculty members have been involved intimately and regularly in developing the new program. The size of this group is, in large part, a reflection of two phases of faculty hiring, one in the mid-1980s and one in the early 1990s—both resulting in a new faculty with a strong commitment to collaborative work and urban education. Many of the searches conducted during the later phase were conducted as interdisciplinary efforts, signaling to potential new colleagues the value we placed on collaborative work. The combination of new faculty and existing faculty at both junior and senior levels with similar commitments gradually resulted in a critical mass of people poised for making substantial change. Many of us also were linked by a common commitment to an applied research agenda in urban education.

At a high point in our activity, the summer of 1995, a new dean arrived and provided active, ongoing support for our work. He has established this reform effort as a high priority for the School of Education and, thus, has given the new program legitimacy, which in turn has helped broaden the participation of faculty members.

We clearly have more challenges ahead of us in terms of a critical mass of faculty. First, our future depends on continued collaboration, change, and experimentation, all of which require time and resources. Essentially, program reform to this point is something we have done in our spare time, which means activities are accomplished—eventually. The few buyouts we were able to secure helped in leadership and pilot efforts, and we are aware that the whole process would have been expedited had the key players been able to be released regularly from our traditional three-course teaching load each semester during our planning. In sum, our regular responsibilities continued, but we persisted because of the interplay of personal commitment and the momentum of the group. Keeping this momentum alive is a high priority.

Alliances with Other Stakeholders

Support from the local community added insights and encouraged faculty in these endeavors and in the collective will to change. The faculty conducted three community forums for area teachers, parents, and administrators to provide feedback on proposed changes in the early childhood, primary/middle, and special education programs. We also met with groups of students at various points of our work to elicit their input and insights. These activities widened our view and provided reality checks while also giving us the sense that we indeed were moving in the right direction.

The high priority our new dean placed on active involvement with the community means that he has been visible in much of our interaction with our community and school stakeholders. We find that, throughout the community, people are aware of our efforts, interested in our progress, and have high expectations for the program, as we do.

Future Challenges

Reforming the programs described in this chapter poses at least three future challenges. First, we are moving from an individual approach to a collaborative approach. The new collaborative roles that interdisciplinary faculty members play are critical. As we implement program changes, we are changing the norms for faculty involvement. The success of each program is heavily dependent on faculty within each participating department being committed to the interdisciplinary preparation of teachers. Collaboration for program development and implementation is a new activity. The old plan of operation, in which a faculty member plans the course syllabus and shows up for class to teach, is gone. The new plan is for faculty teams planning and teaching within and across program blocks. This will require developing one's own expertise at the same time as developing the program. This collaborative role extends the traditional teaching responsibilities in higher education. In addition, the mentoring role for the student cohorts will be critical in achieving recruitment and advisement structures congruent with our urban mission. It means more than showing up for office hours.

The amount of time committed to program development and delivery is significant. How can we recognize and support these efforts along with our research and scholarship agendas? The Holmes Group (1995) suggests incentives and rewards for faculty, such as extra time, money, and attention. We will need to modify our old structures (e.g., staffing patterns and workload, merit pay plans, promotion and tenure criteria, criteria for graduate faculty status). In many ways, the faculty is breaking new ground. For these programs to succeed in the long run, new structures and systems undoubtedly will be necessary.

Second, we are moving from ambiguous to explicit programs. We are specifying our programs' characteristics as *to whom* (e.g., students representing the urban community), *for what* values, knowledge, and content, with a defined conceptual framework, in specific contexts (coursework, field experiences), and *by whom* (faculty from across departments). Will our focus be too broad or too narrow? With the public dissemination of information about our programs, we will be held to a new public accountability—to our students and to ourselves—in the program delivery. This creates situations of new ownership and interpersonal relationships. The conceptual conversations during our ongoing monthly meetings will provide a forum for continuing interactions and defining our programs explicitly.

Finally, resource development is a challenge for the future. Aided by federal and private foundation funding, we have been successful in increasing the diversity of our college student population. Recruitment and retention of students from underrepresented populations will require the institution's commitment of ongoing financial support. We cannot do it alone with grants. Similarly, resources for our critical mass of faculty are an issue: How can we avoid making person-dependent changes so that, as faculty leave, replacements are found? How are we to deal with faculty resources when turnover occurs and positions remain unfilled? Will a hiring plan be in place for these new programs, or will we continue to fill vacancies as they exist? Resource development is critical, especially in a time of budget reduction when attracting and serving more students with fewer faculty members is promoted.

In conclusion, our success in reform depends upon our simultaneous commitment to changing the way we prepare teachers and to improving the urban schools and community. Changes in the structure, content, and delivery of teacher education programs evolve slowly, but our transformation will impact the quality of teachers and, ultimately, the children, families, and communities they serve.

References

Alverno College and University of Wisconsin-Milwaukee. (1993). *The Milwaukee Pathways to Teaching Careers Program.* Unpublished manuscript.

Association of Teacher Educators (ATE), Division for Early Childhood (DEC), and the National Association for the Education of Young Children (NAEYC). (1995). *Personnel standards for early education and early intervention: Guidelines for licensure in early childhood special education.* Reston, VA: Council for Exceptional Children.

Bailey, D. B. (1989). Issues and directions in preparing professionals to work with young handicapped children and their families. In J. J. Gallagher, P. L. Trohanis, & R. M. Clifford (Eds.), Policy implementation and PL 99–457: *Planning for young children with special needs* (pp. 97–132). Baltimore: Paul H. Brookes.

Bredekamp, S., & Willer, B. (1992). Of ladders and lattices, cores and cones: Conceptualizing an early childhood professional development system. *Young Children, 47*(3), 47–50.

Bricker, D. B. (1989). *Early intervention for at-risk and handicapped infants, toddlers, and preschool children.* Palo Alto, CA: VORT Corp.

Bricker, D., & Widerstrom, A. (1996). *Preparing personnel to work with infants and young children and their families: A team approach.* Baltimore: Paul H. Brookes.

Carnegie Task Force on Education and the Economy. (1986). *A nation prepared: Teachers for the 21st century.* New York: Carnegie Corp.

Chan, S. (1990). Early intervention with culturally diverse families of infants and toddlers with disabilities. *Infants and Young Children, 3*(2), 78–87.

Christensen, C. M. (1992). Multicultural competencies in early intervention: Training professionals for a pluralistic society. *Infants and Young Children, 4*(3), 49–63.

Garcia, E. E., McLaughlin, B., Spodek, B., & Saracho, O. N. (1995). *Yearbook in early childhood education (Vol. 6): Meeting the challenge of linguistic and cultural diversity in early childhood education.* New York: Teachers College Press.

Hains, A. H., & Maxwell, C. B. (1995). *Final report: UWM preservice early intervention project: Respecting the full range of diversity across early childhood settings.* Submitted to Office of Special Education Programs, U.S. Department of Education. Unpublished manuscript.

Holmes Group. (1986). *Tomorrow's teachers: A report of the Holmes Group.* East Lansing, MI: Author.

Holmes Group. (1995). *A report of the Holmes Group: Tomorrow's schools of education.* East Lansing, MI: Author.

Interstate New Teacher Assessment and Support Consortium. (1992). *The model standards for beginning teacher licensing and development: A resource for state dialog.* Washington, DC: Council of Chief State School Officers.

Johnson Foundation. (1993). *An American imperative: Higher expectations for higher education.* Racine, WI: Author.

Lynch, E. W., & Hanson, M. J. (1992). *Developing cross-cultural competence: A guide for working with young children and their families.* Baltimore: Paul H. Brookes.

Maxwell, C. B., & Hains, A. H. (1996). *Promoting the diversity of early childhood intervention personnel: Preservice practices for recruitment and retention.* Manuscript submitted for publication.

McCollum, J. A., & Maude, S. P. (1994). Early childhood special educators as early interventionists: Issues and emerging practice in personnel preparation. In P. L. Safford, B. Spodek, & O. N. Saracho (Eds.), *Yearbook in early childhood education* (Vol. 5, pp. 352–371). New York: Teachers College Press.

McCollum, J. A., & Stayton, V. D. (1996). Preparing early childhood special educators. In D. Bricker & A. Widerstrom (Eds.), *Preparing personnel to work with infants and young children and their families: A team approach* (pp. 67–90). Baltimore: Paul H. Brookes.

"Milwaukee Public Schools: What Is Holding Them Back?" *Milwaukee Journal Sentinel,* Nov. 19, 1995, pp. A1, A21.

Odom, S. L., & McLean, M. E. (1996). *Early intervention/early childhood special education: Recommended practices.* Austin, TX: PRO-ED.

Pugach, M., & Pasch, S. (1994). The challenge of creating urban professional development schools. In R. Yinger & K. N. Borman (Eds.), *Restructuring education: Issues and strategies for communities, schools, and universities* (pp. 129–156). Cresskill, NJ: Hampton Press.

Schwab, J. J. (1978). The practical: Translation into curriculum. In I. Westbury & N. J. Wilkof (Eds.) *Science, curriculum, and liberal education* (pp. 365–383). Chicago: University of Chicago Press.

Tiezzi, L., & Cross, B. (1996). Utilizing research on prospective teachers' beliefs to inform urban field experiences. *The Urban Review.*

Twigg, C. A. (1995). Transforming higher education: Is it time for a new learning infrastructure? *Wingspread Journal, 17*(2), 16–18.

Wald, J. L. (1996). *Culturally and linguistically diverse professionals in special education: A demographic analysis.* Reston, VA: Council for Exceptional Children.

Wisconsin Department of Public Instruction. (1995). *Restructuring teacher education and licensure in Wisconsin: A report by the task force on teacher education and licensure to the Wisconsin state superintendent of public instruction.* Madison: Author.

Authors' Note

We would like to acknowledge the contributions of members of the work group on *Collaborative Teacher Education Program for Urban Communities.* The following faculty and staff members have collaborated in these reform efforts: Mary Jett-Simpson (Co-chair), Department of Curriculum and Instruction; Alison Ford (Co-chair), Department of Exceptional Education; Dave Edyburn, Department of Exceptional Education; Larry Enochs, Department of Curriculum and Instruction; Randy Goree, Department of Curriculum and Instruction; Dom Gullo, Department of Curriculum and Instruction; Ann Hains, Department of Exceptional Education; DeAnn Huinker, Department of Curriculum and Instruction; Lorraine Jacobs, Advising and Academic Services; Rhonda Jeffries, Department of Educational Policy and Community Studies; Ithel Jones, Department of Curriculum and Instruction; Elizabeth Kraemer, Department of Educational Psychology; Jean Madsen, Department of Administrative Leadership; Susan Masland, Department of Curriculum and Instruction; Chris Burton Maxwell, Department of Curriculum and Instruction; Larry Moburg, Department of Curriculum and Instruction; Paul Nichols, Department of Educational Psychology; Amy Otis-Wilborn, Department of Exceptional Education; Ron Podeschi, Department of Educational Policy and Community Studies; Linda Post, Department of Curriculum and Instruction; Marleen Pugach, Department of Curriculum and Instruction; Johnmarshall Reeve, Department of Educational Psychology; Kathryn St. Clair, Office of Field Experience; John Warren Stewig, Department of Curriculum and Instruction; Karen Stoiber, Department of Educational Psychology; Linda Tiezzi, Department of Curriculum and Instruction; and Judy Winn, Department of Exceptional Education.

A Voluntary Approach to Collaborative Teacher Preparation: A Dual-Major Program at Utah State University

Charles Salzberg, Ben Lignugaris/Kraft, and Jay Monson

I n writing this chapter we spent considerable time reconstructing the events that led to our cooperative dual-major program and articulating the reasons our program took its current form.[1] The phrase "voluntary approach" in the title reflects what we have come to believe was a central factor that shaped our dual-major program, and it is an organizing concept that we turn to frequently, beginning now as we describe the context in which our dual-major program was initiated.

The Prior Relationship Between Special and Elementary Education

The departments of elementary and special education are independent of one another. Prior to the dual-major program, these faculties interacted rarely. They had little reason to interact except that elementary education students took one special education course for certification and special education students took two required elementary education courses.

Philosophically, the elementary and special education faculties are far apart. These differences are evident in attitudes toward topics such as whole-language reading and language arts, direct instruction, and assessment. The governance of our university and also the College of Education are primarily decentralized. Thus, departments manage their own financial affairs based on their state budget allocations and externally gathered funds. No obvious direct financial incentive or disincentive exists to create collaborative programs, although some indirect or delayed outcomes could result from these initiations. The college administration encourages collaboration, but no administrative pressure within the college or the university, or political forces outside of the university, forces departments to restructure in the College of Education. All of the teacher education departments in the college have more students than they can reasonably accommodate in their programs; all review favorably for accreditation by the state and by NCATE; and all are respected within the university and the public school communities.

An Important Conclusion

Given the lack of external pressure or an administrative fiat to restructure, change in our situation is voluntary. Department faculties and administrators must undertake change willingly. This context has important implications. In this circumstance, change takes place only if faculty members in each department want it to, only in the specific ways they want it to, and only as fast as they want it to. This stands in contrast to involuntary change that may be mandated by state legislatures or university administrators.

Factors That Set a Climate for Change

In our situation, several factors set a positive climate for change. First, new faculty members were being hired in the elementary and the special education departments. These faculty members had not experienced collaborative failures or animosities in the past. They were informed, however, about the failure of prior informal attempts to negotiate dual-major programs. In these attempts, the faculty discussed reducing the number of courses in each department and, to do that, generated philosophical discussions about what beginning teachers needed to learn. The resulting divergence of opinion failed to produce a collaborative program.

This time we approached the task differently. We designed the program around actual students who were interested in completing the dual major. Both departments compromised and agreed to a program that these students could complete in 4 years. Thus, 186 hours (the minimum number of credit hours for graduation in our quarter system) became the maximum number of credit hours in the program. In addition, both departments wanted to find a way to initiate a dual-major program that avoided major program revisions and did not undercut the core curriculum of either program. Elementary Education waived its requirement for a content minor, and Special Education waived a collaboration class (given that these students were living examples of a collaborative culture) and 24 quarter hours in supporting courses.

Second, a timely move to a new building put the departments in proximity to each other for the first time in their history. Prior to this, the special education and the elementary education departments were housed in buildings on opposite sides of the campus.

Third, although administrative pressure to develop a collaborative program was absent, the dean publicly acknowledged and encouraged collaborative efforts of the new nontenured faculty in the two departments through memos and through verbal notice at administrative council meetings.

Fourth, an increasing number of students were enrolling in the elementary education program (the largest major on campus) and jobs in elementary education were becoming increasingly competitive. Many students saw the dual major as an edge on the competition for jobs. In addition, a majority of elementary education graduates told their student teaching coordinators that they did not feel prepared to work with at-risk and special education students.

Finally, in special education, the regular education initiative and calls for inclusive classrooms were taking center stage nationally. As a result, universities that proposed collaborative certification programs were more likely to receive funding in federal personnel preparation competitions. These grants supported joint planning by special and elementary education faculty and provided some support for implementing program changes. For example, an early goal of the dual-major program was to create an integrated student teaching experience rather than a two-quarter experience (one in elementary education and one in special education). Because students had at least six quarters of practica prior to student teaching (three in special education and three in elementary education), it was logical that, in student teaching, students should have an opportunity to practice their teaching in integrated contexts as much as possible.

With a federal grant supporting the collaborative development effort, it became possible to design and implement a one-quarter articulated student teaching experience in integrated public school classrooms or in situations in which students spent part of their time in an elementary classroom and part of their time in a special education program. In addition, the personnel preparation grant provided resources to engage in a range of collaborative outreach activities.

One example is a survey conducted by several special and elementary education faculty members (Monson, Lignugaris/Kraft, Byrnes, & Johnson, 1995) to identify factors that personnel directors use when deciding which applicants they will interview for teaching positions (faculty recommendations, student teaching reports, cooperating teacher recommendations, gradepoint average, which program they graduated from, and so on). Personnel directors indicated that the most important factors considered in initial evaluations were the cooperating teacher's and university supervisor's evaluation of student teaching, recommendations from respected colleagues, and samples of teaching and management skills. The survey was followed by a meeting with personnel directors co-sponsored by the departments of elementary and special education. During this meeting, the faculty reviewed the survey results with district personnel directors and pointed out the advantages of hiring dual-major graduates for the highly competitive general education positions.

Another example of a professional collaboration is the presentation by elementary education and special education faculty on portfolio evaluation in teacher education at a national conference and at an elementary education faculty meeting. The result of this collaboration was a continued refinement of the student teaching course structure and the creation of a uniform format for portfolios developed during student teaching.

Description of the Current Program

Students in the dual-major program graduate with a Bachelor of Science degree in Special Education and in Elementary Education. Dual-major graduates apply for state certification as special education teachers (K–12th grade) and as elementary school teachers (K–8th grade). The U.S.U. Department of Special Education and Rehabilitation offers preparation programs for teaching young children with disabilities, children with mild or moderate disabilities, and children with severe disabilities. The Department of Elementary Education offers preparation programs in elementary education, early childhood education, and middle education. It also offers an endorsement program for education of gifted and talented (K–12) children. The Utah State Office of Education readily approved the dual-major program, as changes in the core curriculum for each major were minimal.

Currently, the vast majority of students in the dual-major program are in the mild/moderate area in special education and the K–8 program in elementary education. The curriculum in the dual-major program is only partially integrated, but it is articulated carefully. Coordinating faculty in elementary education and special education agreed that the program of studies had to fit within 186 credit hours and had to preserve the core requirements of each program. Students were given the option of enrolling in either the special education orientation class or the elementary education orientation class. Elementary education dropped the requirement for a 24-credit-hour minor and special education dropped the requirement for a class in consultation. Coordinating faculty agreed to develop an integrated student teaching component that would require students to link their elementary and special education experiences and to expand practicum experiences to integrated classrooms as they became available in the local school districts.

The resulting program was taken to the elementary education and special education faculties for approval. Students in the dual major complete a 65-quarter hour general education core that includes courses in written communication, math, humanities, social sciences, life sciences, and physical sciences. In addition, students complete a 15- to 17-hour core of educational foundation classes that includes human growth and development, educational psychology for teachers, and instructional technology.

Program Strands

Eight program strands (which were initiated in elementary education) provide the conceptual and programmatic foundation for students' elementary and special education coursework (see Table 10.1). Notably, though faculties in both departments generally agree on the importance of the eight strands for teacher development, they have broad differences in what they emphasize within each strand and how that is translated into classroom practice. Content from the eight program strands is woven through 44 quarter hours of coursework and practica provided by elementary education and 42 quarter hours of coursework and practica provided by special education faculty. This is followed by an integrated student teaching experience of 15 to 21 quarter hours in which students develop portfolios that include teaching and management skill demonstrations and personal approaches to each of the eight strands. Careful course scheduling and early advisement permit students to complete both certification programs and their bachelor of science degree within 4 years.

Dual majors typically complete their general education requirements and initial elementary education courses during their freshman and sophomore years. In these courses, students complete a practicum in an elementary classroom and are introduced to the major strands in the program. They usually take coursework in special education during the junior year and upper-division elementary education coursework and student teaching during the senior year. Thus, special education coursework occurs between the elementary education coursework. Although there is little direct course integration, students are encouraged to recognize similarities and reconcile differences in content emphasis and faculty attitudes as they move from one program to the other and back again.

Table 10.2 presents the number of on-campus B.S. graduates in elementary and special education programs and in the dual-major program for the past 3 years and the current year. Initially, few students enrolled in the dual major. The table shows, though, that the number of special-elementary education dual majors has grown each year. In 1996, most graduates of the mild/moderate special education program were dual majors. This growth probably has resulted from two factors:

Table 10.1

Program Strands

Strand	Conceptual Overview
Classroom Management	Teachers who are effective classroom managers create positive learning environments. Students in these environments are confident learners who accept responsibility and progress academically and emotionally.
Assessment	Assessment is the part of teaching that addresses what a student knows and how much learning has been accomplished. Appropriately developed assessment tools guide learning and provide feedback about instructional effectiveness. High-quality assessment answers the questions: How are we doing? How can we do better?
Curriculum	The purpose of school curriculum is to educate and to promote student growth. The challenge to the teacher is to provide a student-centered curriculum based on learners' needs and interests so as to maximize cognitive and affective growth.
Diversity	Public school teachers today are confronted by a broad array of students with various cultural, ethnic, and learning backgrounds. The teacher's responsibility is to recognize and respect diversity and to teach all students in their classrooms effectively.
Learner	The teacher's role is to engage and support learning of all students as individuals. The teacher is responsible for observing and interpreting individual student behavior and adjusting planning and teaching to accommodate a student's diverse needs.
Parent/ Community Involvement	Parents are children's first teachers and need to maintain involvement in their child's education. Teachers must learn how to work effectively with parents, how to develop and maintain relationships with parents, and how to involve parents in and out of school.
Professional Development	At the completion of their preparation programs, new teachers must have the foundation skills that will enable them to be lifelong learners. They should have a firm grasp of their subject area, be able to analyze the needs of their students, know the standards of practice of their profession, and implement those standards with intellectual honesty and practical foresight.
Effective Teaching	Teachers must provide a range of teaching activities and utilize various instructional pedagogies to meet the needs of all students in their classrooms. Teachers complete a preparation program with only a foundation instructional repertoire. Then the teacher is responsible for continually developing new instructional strategies and learning new instructional models to benefit the students in their classrooms.

1. The word has spread among elementary education majors that the dual-major program provides extraordinary preparation for a teaching career.
2. Dual majors have more job opportunities.

Table 10.2 clearly indicates the large number of elementary education students relative to those in special education. In special education the proportion of dual majors to single majors in the mild/moderate program has increased each year and likely will increase even further. Given the disproportionate number of elementary education majors relative to special education majors, however, most elementary education majors cannot become dual majors without a substantial increase in the special education faculty, which is not likely to be forthcoming in the immediate future.

Philosophical Perspectives

Ideally, perhaps, faculty members in both departments would come together in a series of discussions and arrive at a common philosophy that, in turn, would lead to an integrated curriculum. That is not how this dual-major program originated, however. Rather, a few key people in each department planned the dual-major program. The department heads, two faculty members in the mild/moderate program in special education, and the student teaching coordinator and advisors in elementary education actively advocated and planned the elementary-special education dual-major program. The faculties never met as a totality to discuss philosophies, visions or, for that matter, curriculum. Actually, obliging them to do that might have presented a serious obstacle to establishing a dual-major program.

Table 10.2

Graduates of Elementary and Special Education Programs

	Number of Graduates			
	1993	1994	1995	1996
Elementary Education	204	231	220	242
Special Education (mild/moderate)	23	29	24	43
Special-Elementary Education Dual Major	4	5	9	15

On previous occasions, informal discussions about philosophy between the two faculties were not productive and did not produce cooperative programming. Moreover, we had a more efficient strategy available. Faculty and advisors were receiving several requests each year from excellent students to certify in both areas. Thus, a pragmatic, action-oriented strategy emerged that was supported by the administrators and core personnel in each department. Advisors and faculty members examined students' transcripts and designed a dual-major program of studies that would meet those students' needs. The general structure for these dual-major programs then was presented for approval to the faculty in each department and to the Utah State Office of Education.

In summary, it made most sense for us to forge ahead, design a dual-major program around the needs of actual students, and begin to build faculty relationships based on our students' programmatic needs. We believed that if we were to establish the program right away, time would become available later to bring faculty together to refine the program and increase program integration based on student performance data and feedback. In the meantime, a growing, enthusiastic dual-major student body would provide a context for the faculty to interact, to learn more about how each approaches teacher education, and to share credit for a successful, innovative program. As this process is now unfolding, we perceive that a new and more positive context is emerging for philosophical discussion between faculty members and now, in contrast to previous times, these philosophical discussions can be conditioned to the realities of an ongoing program in which both departments have a stake.

Through this pragmatic approach, we learned quickly that elementary and special education faculties have major points of agreement about education and curriculum.

1. Faculty members in both departments have a profound concern for students' education. As several dual-major graduates told us, "The teacher's job is to find the best way to meet students' needs and [the faculty in] the two programs have different approaches for doing that."
2. Both faculties agree on most of the basic tenets of the effective instruction literature, although elementary and special education faculties emphasize different aspects of the literature.
3. Critically important, elementary education and special education generally agree on the eight-strand teacher development structure discussed earlier, even though the two faculties approach each strand differently and also differ in how much of their total program effort is devoted to each strand.
4. Both faculties agree that field experiences are necessary for students to understand the instructional pedagogy discussed in methods and curriculum classes.

Probably the most important perspective on the content and philosophies of the special and elementary education programs comes from the students, especially as they reflect on the program after they have graduated and assumed public school teaching positions. To get that view, we conducted a qualitative program evaluation of our most recent dual-major elementary-special education graduates using an intensive telephone interview methodology.

Program Evaluation

We interviewed eight dual-major graduates of the most recent graduating class (1995). One graduate could not be located. Of the eight graduates, four enrolled initially in the elementary education program, two in the special education program, and two concurrently in both programs.

A student currently enrolled in the dual-major program telephoned the graduates, and tape-recorded and transcribed their responses. The responses then were summarized. Each interview lasted approximately 30 minutes.

Part 1

Students were asked to describe their current positions, to state whether they had enrolled initially in elementary or in special education, and to tell their reasons for applying to the dual-major program. These responses are summarized below.

Seven graduates took teaching jobs; one did not seek a teaching position. Two graduates accepted special education positions in secondary schools, one graduate accepted a special education position in an elementary school, three graduates accepted positions as mainstream elementary teachers, and one graduate accepted a special position as a dual special education-elementary education teacher. This outcome of mixed jobs is what we had hoped for: Broadly prepared teachers are providing instruction to students with disabilities and at-risk students throughout the school system.

When asked why they applied to the dual-major program, the most common answers were, "I felt I needed more preparation than I was getting in the single elementary education major" and "so I will be more marketable for a teaching job when I graduate." Two graduates indicated that they always wanted to do both, one that she wanted to work with special needs students, and one reported that she applied upon the advice from others.

Part 2

In the second part of this survey, we asked graduates to comment about similarities and differences in content of the elementary and special education parts of their programs. This was stated initially as an open-ended, general question: "In what ways do you think the elementary education and special education programs are similar to one another? In what ways do you think they are different?" Then this question was repeated with specific reference to the classroom management, effective teaching, curriculum, assessment, and diversity program strands. The results are summarized in Tables 10.3 through 10.7.

Table 10.3 summarizes graduates' comments about the *classroom management strand*. The top section of Table 10.3 presents comments that apply to both the elementary and the special education parts of the dual-major program. The bottom section reviews the specific differences that graduates noted between the elementary and special education parts of their programs. Graduates perceived that the faculties of both departments are concerned with classroom management. They reported, however, that elementary education classes focus on philosophy and whole-class management issues. In contrast, special education classes emphasize specific management procedures and applying classroom management procedures in practica.

Table 10.4 summarizes graduates' comments about the *effective teaching strand* in the elementary and special education parts of their dual-major programs. Graduates indicated a sharp contrast between elementary and special education in this strand. Generally, graduates said that special education classes focus intensively on direct-instruction methodologies, data-based decision making, and programming for lower-performing students. In contrast, elementary education classes focus on creative teaching activities, whole-language approaches, large-group or whole-class teaching, and on average and higher performing students. Some graduates reported that some professors in elementary education criticized certain instructional methods widely advocated in special education classes (e.g., direct instruction).

One might expect that this dissonance would be confusing for students. Indeed, some students tell us that early in their program the conceptual differences are difficult to reconcile. In these cases, the faculty advise students that their "job" at this point in the program is to become proficient with the teaching practices required in their field work. In essence, we are asking our students to be pragmatic and, by observing the effects of various practices on children's understanding, learn which types of pedagogy are most appropriate for various instructional situations. As indicated in the responses about effective teaching, most students valued what they got from both departments and used what they learned from each department with a broad range of students.

Table 10.5 presents graduates' comments about the *curriculum strand*. In general, graduates reported that elementary education classes emphasize the Utah Core Curriculum and what should be taught at each grade level in each content area. Special education classes focus on adapting curriculum for individual students and on broadly applicable curriculum strategies. Most graduates reported

Table 10.3

Similarities and Differences in Elementary Education and Special Education Programs: Classroom Management Strand

Elementary Education	Special Education
A1. Learned models and theories for classroom management.	
B1. Not a lot of similarities.	
C1. What motivates students, what you can do to work with individual students.	
C2. Important to have both a student-directed approach to management (ELED) and an assertive, teacher-directed orientation (SPED). It depends on the kids and the situation.	
F1. Similar in that they are both trying to meet students' needs through a variety of techniques. They have different approaches for doing that.	
H1. I've applied techniques learned in SPED in ELED classrooms.	
A1. Principal focus was underlying models and philosophy; learned about whole-class motivation and things I can use in my classroom.	A1. Went into more depth on what to do with models, specific problems, and how to reach kids.
B1. Lot on philosophy; lacks practical application.	B1. Practical application; steps (e.g., praise rate, types of praise), specific things to use for a lot of people.
B2. Point of view if you are well prepared, have interesting content and real enthusiastic *you are not going to have any problems.*	B2. Point of view—If you are well prepared, have interesting content and real enthusiastic, you *are going to have a lot fewer problems.*
	B3. Focus on positives and building kids up.
C1. Group management for the classroom.	C1. Taught more strategies than ELED.
C2. More on the "liberal" side; student-controlled, student rights; not able to put into practice what I learned so harder to retain.	C2. Assertive, teacher-oriented and teacher-controlled in SPED; was able to practice the skills while I learned.
D1. ELED not much on individual reward systems, but whole class systems.	D1. Behavior series and in other classes learned about reward systems; eye contact; proximity control.
F1, G1. Learn about it in class lectures, but it is not focused on in practicums.	F1, G1. Spent more time in each class with specific classroom management techniques than in ELED. Have to practice specific techniques like scanning and praise in practicum.

Table 10.4

Similarities and Differences in Elementary Education and Special Education Programs: Effective Teaching Strand

Elementary Education	Special Education

AI. No similarities.

BI. Both teach you strategies and different things to use.

CI. SPED is big on direct instruction, but it didn't work in the junior high where I work. They did not know the formats and did not like it. When I approached instruction the way it was taught in ELED, my junior high class did fine. It depends on the kids you are working with.

DI. ELED focused on whole language and getting kids involved in different activities so they can see real life in their learning. SPED focused on direct instruction. Need to mix both in the classroom.

FI. Both agree that you find what works for different students.

GI. They complement each other. For example, in reading you can teach thematic units (learned in ELED) using direct-instruction approaches (learned in SPED) such as word attack, specific vocabulary teaching techniques, and comprehensive techniques.

HI. Complementary—If you have low performers in the general class, you can use the direct approach. If you are getting ready to transition a student back to the general class, you use the ELED techniques in the resource room to transition back.

	Elementary Education			Special Education
AI.	Not really told how to teach, but what needed to be taught at different grades.		AI.	Indepth instruction in how to teach and how to change instruction for different levels.
A2, EI.	Focused on how to teach high and middle performers.		A2.	Primary focus on how to teach low performers.
BI, GI.	Focused on activities to make it more fun for kids.		BI, GI.	More specific and focused; SPED broke it into steps; basic strategies (you can teach this content this way).
CI.	Big-group focus; don't learn methods to teach individuals.		CI.	Smaller grouping; more individual teaching.
DI.	Did not understand question; focused on methods used in college teaching.			
EI, FI, HI.	Learned different types of techniques; different ways to do lesson plans; encouraged to use a variety.		EI, FI, HI.	Learned one instructional method (direct instruction); one way to do a lesson plan; told about other ways of teaching.

Table 10.5

Similarities and Differences in Elementary Education and Special Education Programs: Curriculum Strand

Elementary Education	Special Education
B1. Both stressed the importance of covering the content that the kids need and that the state requires.	
C1. ELED approaches curriculum from what students think about something and what they are interested in. SPED is really structured. I think students need to learn some skills regardless of what they think about it.	
E1. Go to my files and there are all these things that I can apply (from elementary education) and I know how to apply them because of my special education background.	
G1. I did not get tons of instruction from either department on curriculum.	
A1, F1. Told us what needed to be taught; looked at core curriculum, curriculum guides, and went over what you needed to teach at what grade.	A1. Curriculum not in as much depth and not structured by grade level. A2. Focused on how to get pupils to learn.
B1, G1. Broken into subjects like language arts.	B1, G1. Broken into strategies and how to teach across subjects and grade level, which complemented the ELED curriculum approach.
C1, E1. Taught about core curriculum; grade-level curriculum; teaching social studies, science, history, and study skills.	C1, D1. Learned a lot about reading and math.
D2. More detail, different ways to set up curriculum; different grade levels.	D2. SPED provides an outline that I could fit into different subjects—not lots of ideas. E1. Focus was individual for each student rather than grade level.

that they view the content from the two departments in this strand as complementary.

Table 10.6 reviews graduates' comments about the *assessment strand* of their dual major programs. Generally, graduates reported that the special education program provides more extensive training on assessment than does elementary education and focuses on specific types of assessment for diagnoses, curriculum decision making and behavior management. Elementary education emphasizes more qualitative methods such as portfolio analysis and interviews. Again,

Table 10.6

Similarities and Differences in Elementary Education and Special Education Programs: Assessment Strand

	Elementary Education	Special Education
B1.	I think they both agree that you need to assess kids.	
A1, B2.	Not complementary or similar at all in practice.	
D1.	Both brought up the idea that you need to use different forms of assessment.	
E1.	ELED gave me assessments that I can use for certain projects, and SPED focused on how to give them and use them.	
A1, H1.	Not much on assessment, more talking about student work.	A1, H1. Learned about different tests and varieties of measures.
B1, F1, G1.	Portfolios, teacher-student interviews, how you feel the students are doing; less structured approaches to assessment.	B1, E1, F1, G1. Assess regularly, use a variety of ways and make sure kids are meeting mastery (did kids reach criteria before moving on?); standardized tests, curriculum-based assessment (are your measures objective driven?); class observations; learned to do it carefully and precisely.
C1.	Objectives do not have to be observable all the time; for pleasure and fun. (That's a goal and you can't measure it!)	C1. Individual and specific; observable and measurable.
D1, E1.	Steered away from formal assessment; told you to watch kids.	D1. More in SPED about teacher-designed evaluations, classroom observations, and written testing.
E2.	Focus on using chapter tests, writing essay questions; not as precise and exact as SPED.	

some graduates reported that some professors in elementary education criticized certain assessment procedures taught in special education classes.

Table 10.7 summarizes graduates' comments about the *diversity and multiculturalism* strand. Both programs addressed diversity and the need to include all children. Elementary education classes seem to provide a stronger basis in multiculturalism, especially in regard to ethnic, linguistic, and cultural diversity. Graduates reported that special education's attention to diversity concentrates on individuals with disabilities.

Table 10.7

Similarities and Differences in Elementary Education and Special Education Programs: Diversity Strand

Elementary Education	Special Education
A1, B1, DI, FI. Got a lot from both; generally the same approach; both stressed that all kids be included.	
B2. Meet the needs of multicultural students.	
E1. ELED gave me information on false beliefs, and SPED provided me an opportunity to practice in an ESL classroom.	
G1. A lot of the same ideas can be used for both multicultural kids and kids with disabilities.	
B1. Covered strategies to meet children's needs a lot better than SPED.	
C1. A lot more through literature-based approach.	C1. Not really a lot; glossed over; minutely covered.
D1. ELED talked a lot more about diversity.	D1. In one class we talked about diversity, but I can't remember that much.
F1, G1, H1. Focus on minorities, more workshops and lectures that addressed these issues.	C1, G1, H1. Focus on disabilities and diverse kids with disabilities.

Part 3

As noted earlier, most students in the dual major begin their program by taking elementary education classes. Next they complete a year of special education coursework and practica, and finally they complete elementary education requirements and proceed to student teaching. In the third part of the survey, we asked graduates about the adjustments they made in their thinking when they moved from an elementary education block of classes to a special education block of classes and then back again. In addition, graduates commented about the strengths and deficits of the dual-major program overall and whether they would recommend it to a friend.

Table 10.8 presents the graduates' comments about movement from one program to the other. Their responses capture clear differences between the elementary and the special education departments in their approaches to teacher

Table 10.8

Graduates' Comments About Movement Between Programs

From Elementary Education to Special Education	From Special Education to Elementary Education
A. I thought it would be the same. You tell me what to do and I do it. When I got to SPED, it was different. It was, "I'll tell you the underlying principle and you figure out how to do it."	More being creative and figuring out activities the whole class could use. I had to go back to thinking about working with 30 students rather than a small group.
B. This was the first quarter I actually felt like I was at a university. I got more in class than I had in my ELED classes. I felt like I had to really know what I was talking about. I couldn't just B.S. everything.	It was easy to switch back. It was a lot of fun and I did learn a great deal. It was activities and being in the classroom. Everybody was worried about writing lesson plans, but we (dual majors) had just come from a practicum where you type a lesson plan for every day and it had to be ready two days in advance! It was great because we had the classroom management skills before we came back to ELED.
C. A big adjustment. I remember thinking, I disagree with all this. After I put it into practice, I felt more comfortable and realized that it was important. The programs are at opposite ends of the spectrum, so there's a big change in the way they look at things.	It was a hard adjustment because I had had so much SPED that I had people tell me to get my mind set out of SPED and into ELED again. There's no compromise between the departments. Probably more with SPED, but ELED doesn't see the need to work with the special needs student the way we are taught to work with them.
D. From whole language, hands-on activities and getting kids involved in activities to direct instruction, testing kids to see where they're at and having a structured environment.	Moving back to a more carefree environment and setting up activities or centers for kids to move around so students do more teaching themselves.
E. From very broad to learning precisely how to get things across to children and how to break things down.	I had to move back to a broader range of ideas. In SPED they're trying to teach you to do specific things and to teach you specific points and you have to narrow down to learn those things. When you go back to ELED it opens up again to lots of different philosophies and different views.
F. Whole language and feel good activities to structured teaching and focus on student behavior.	The move back to ELED was a lot easier because now I had had both and could pick my own philosophy. I could use what I learned about managing behavior and teaching methods from SPED and apply that to what I liked in ELED.
G. From open and broad to focused and targeted.	My mind was open to evaluate various points because now I had two areas of thought (ELED and SPED).
H. SPED presented a different way to teach. I had never seen direct instruction before.	I had to change my frame of mind and let the kids start thinking a bit more.

preparation. Most graduates began their coursework in elementary education. These classes focused on a broad range of teaching activities and on managing 30 or more pupils in an elementary classroom. When the graduates moved into their special education class sequence the following year, they found an emphasis on small-group instruction, procedural specificity, and adapting instruction for low-performing, individual pupils.

The graduates' comments also reveal how they coped with the differences in how special and elementary education faculty define the knowledge base for beginning teachers. For example, graduate C had difficulty blending the approaches and attitudes taught in elementary education with those taught in special education. In contrast, graduates B and F reported that the movement between programs provided opportunities to apply new skills in different instructional situations.

In their comments on the value of their teacher preparation program as a whole (see Table 10.9), graduates' reported that the "breadth of viewpoints" and extensive practicum experience were strengths in their preparation. They identified few program deficits and indicated unanimously that they would recommend the dual-major program to others. As graduate D said, "If I look at doing one (program) or the other, I feel like I wouldn't have gotten half of what I needed to.... So, I think you need them both."

Finally, seven of eight graduates indicated that they believe the dual-major program prepared them well for their initial teaching position. Graduate B's comments summarized this as follows:

> So I think that the elementary part really prepared me for activities and ideas and the special education taught me how I can teach those things (activities and ideas) to the kids so that I'm not always having to hold hands with the kids and sit by them.... The special education [preparation] allows me to have the time to teach and the elementary education [preparation] has taught me what to teach.

The collection of these evaluation data from program graduates has provided an important and interesting perspective on our dual-major program. It also has led to the following plans.

1. We intend to replicate this study with this year's graduates. That will allow us to find out if the opinions expressed in this study will be consistent from year to year.
2. We will be presenting the information from this survey to the faculty in both departments in a joint meeting. This should provide an occasion for elementary and special education faculty to discuss points of overlap, agreement and disagreement, and, we hope, to identify areas in which instruction can be integrated or refined further through collaboration. At the least, faculty members will be clearer about each other's viewpoints on instruction.

Table 10.9

Graduates' Comments on the Value of Their Teacher Education Program

Taking the dual major as one total program, do you think there were strengths and deficits in your preparation?

Strengths	Deficits
A. I spent a great deal of time in classrooms, and some of the professors were really knowledgeable and helpful with ideas on how to reach kids.	I think that student teaching should be split into two separate 5-week blocks so you can see the whole picture of ELED and the whole picture of SPED.
B. I haven't come across anything yet where I think, "Oh, what am I going to do?"	What am I going to do on the first day of school is kind of confusing, I guess.
C. I think a strength was that I got to see two ends of the perspective. It gave me a broader overall view to draw from.	
D. A strength is being in so many different classrooms and getting a lot of different viewpoints.	The only thing I feel nervous about is doing IEPs, and that has to do with SPED.
E. Classroom management that I learned in special education.	Inconsistency in the how to teach that was taught in both areas. It would have been nice to have more consistency throughout.
F. I have a good feeling about the whole thing. I learned a lot about curriculum, behavior, and teaching styles. I haven't found anything missing yet in my preparation.	
G. Strengths in having two backgrounds and two philosophies. Right now in my teaching the study skill curriculum from SPED is helping me and the different ways to teach different subjects from ELED has helped me, too.	I think it would be good for all ELED majors to have more training in SPED types of programs and for SPED majors to have more experience with ELED programs.
H. I have a really good background and can use my experience in SPED to work with lower students in my class.	I don't have a minor or area of emphasis.

Continuing Development of the Dual-Major Program

In some respects, this dual-major program runs counter to recommendations of the Holmes Group (1986) and the Carnegie Report on Education (Carnegie Forum, 1986). We increased rather than decreased the number of credit hours of education classes that address instructional methods and pedagogy. Students also took additional practica with their coursework. Perhaps the effectiveness of this program results, at least in part, from the close linkage between practica and methods courses in both programs. That is, more may be better only when what is taught in university classrooms is linked closely with the skills that preservice teacher-trainees are required to learn in practica.

We are optimistic about future opportunities to enhance collaboration in the dual-major program. Several activities have taken place already and others are expected. For example, recently an elementary education and special education faculty member co-taught a class on parent involvement in education. These two faculty members had distinctly different, often conflicting, views about what is appropriate in early childhood education. Despite that, both faculty members reported that it was a positive experience overall, and many readings from that class were used subsequently to expand and strengthen the parent/community involvement content strand in the elementary education program.

We also had a joint luncheon between the two faculties, which resulted in positive interaction and some fruitful discussions. We now are planning a series of joint faculty meetings that will address research and program development interests of faculty members in both departments. At a minimum, these meetings should help us understand and articulate each others' views on teacher education.

In addition, a subgroup of program staff and faculty members continue to meet regularly to refine program procedures, encourage further integration of field-based training components, and solve students' problems in completing the dual major program in a timely fashion. Possibly, as a result of these meetings, the elementary and special education faculties will find common ground on which to build a more integrated curriculum that would help our dual-major students and advance our efforts to integrate public school programs.

Several additional factors coming into play could influence the continued development of our dual-major program. *First,* Utah has recently approved a new certification standard that requires far more extensive preparation for all teachers in educating students at risk and students with disabilities. Perhaps some components of the current special education curriculum in assessment, classroom management, and effective instruction will be provided to all teacher education majors. In that event, more curriculum integration will occur across the two departments for all students.

Second, our state universities soon will convert from a quarter system to a semester system. This conversion will require all departments in the university to undergo a total revision of their curriculums. This will provide a ready opportunity to design a more integrated elementary-special education dual-major program. Department heads and key faculty members and staff in both departments have expressed a desire to accomplish that.

Third, for the first time this year, students in the program to prepare teachers for pupils with severe disabilities are applying for entry into the dual-major program. This certainly will involve additional special education faculty in the dual-major program and introduce a new complexion to class discussions and, ultimately, to the dual-major curriculum.

Fourth, a new center referred to as the School of the Future is being originated in the College of Education to provide expertise on effective practices and technological innovation in education for a national audience. Inclusive practice for all students in public schools is likely to become a central concern for this center and, indirectly, an encouragement for more integrative and multidisciplinary personnel preparation.

Finally, faculty members in special and elementary education recently proposed a new leadership program that will establish an interdisciplinary doctoral program designed to produce research-oriented teacher educators prepared to promote more effective, integrated programming for all students. If this leadership program is funded, it will lead to more extensive interaction among departmental faculty and to new, innovative teacher education programming.

Conclusions

As program architects, we make choices about the foundation skills beginning teachers need. Different programs make different choices based on their teaching and learning perspectives. The elementary and special education departments constructed their dual-major program based on those choices. Regardless of philosophies or perspectives, the elementary education and special education faculties agree that we cannot teach beginning teachers everything they will need to know about teaching. Rather, we must provide beginning teachers with the foundation knowledge and skills necessary for them to be reasonably competent initially and to continue to grow as professionals thereafter.

In our program, students develop a teaching philosophy by observing how their teaching practices affect student learning. The teaching philosophies our students write to introduce their student teaching portfolios reflect this approach consistently. For example, one student began her philosophy statement as follows:

> Through my practicum experiences, I've come to realize how difficult and challenging teaching is.... That is why I believe in using a wide range of effective teaching strategies. Through this approach, I will tap into the various learning styles of my students and have more techniques with which to meet their needs.

Another student referenced her pragmatic and empirical philosophy as follows:

> Through my teaching experiences I have found two very important techniques or "keys" which I feel are also prerequisites for being an effective teacher. These techniques include implementing effective teaching techniques along with classroom management techniques.

Although the elementary and special education faculties agree readily on the purpose and general outcome of a teacher education program, they disagree about the specific philosophies and foundation skills that are most essential for beginning teachers. That debate is certainly fruitful for scholarly inquiry and for qualitative and quantitative research, but it also can be divisive and delay or obstruct the development of a successful collaborative teacher preparation program.

For example, in a recent article, Bondy, Ross, Sindelar, and Griffin (1995) report the process they underwent to develop an integrated elementary-special education teacher education program at the University of Florida. That process involved more than a year of biweekly meetings and occasional retreats with two faculty members in elementary education and two faculty members in special education to develop a proposal for an integrated program. According to these authors, that time was well spent because it resulted in strong, positive personal relationships among these four faculty members and a common understanding and commitment to prepare teachers to serve a diverse student body in an integrated environment.

Nevertheless, over 2 years passed between the time discussions began and the time the new program was initiated. In contrast, our goal was to begin a dual major program as quickly as possible.

In light of the differences between the faculty members in our elementary and special education departments and the experience reported by Bondy et al. (1995), a critical factor in establishing our dual-major program was that professors did not have to hammer out a common philosophy or change their own programs substantially, at least not initially. Fortunately, we were able to establish a dual-major program while allowing professors in elementary and special education to continue to teach their own content and advocate their own philosophies. Students receive a wide spectrum of opinions. Sometimes those opinions conflict, but they also allow students to acquire a broad range of instructional methodologies. We believe that what is critically important in the final analysis is that our graduates acquire the knowledge and skills they need to teach a diverse student body in an integrated public school program. Our students demonstrate their ability to do that during student teaching to the satisfaction of special and elementary education supervisors. That faculty reach a philosophical consensus or even espouse compatible points of view seems less important to us.

In an exploratory study, Blanton, Blanton, and Cross (1994) found that though general and special educators have much in common, they also have clear differences in how they think about teaching and in how they approach instructional decision making with students who have learning problems. These differences seem related to different knowledge structures acquired by general and special educators and to the various ecologies that define their teaching situations.

One implication that Blanton et al. (1994) note is the need for collaborative models of preservice and inservice teacher education that permit special education and general education teachers to develop a common language and shared experiences. Graduates of our dual-major program have an understanding of both elementary and special education knowledge bases and both perspectives on teaching and learning. They also are exposed to differing points of view. We believe it is important to help students reconcile, or at least cope with, this cognitive dissonance. We have entertained three ways to do this.

1. We can let students know in advance that they will be exposed to different, even sharply contrasting, viewpoints and that professional differences in opinion are normal and may provide a rich medium for professional growth.
2. We can tell our students that, in time, they may reconcile some of these differences of opinion while they may never reconcile other differences. As professionals, they have an obligation to stay abreast of the literature in the field to be sure their opinions and actions are conditioned by emerging empirical knowledge.
3. We can let them know that, as new professionals, they must be prepared, as must we, their mentors, to live with the uncertainties and ambiguities inherent in the dynamic enterprise we call the American education system.

Our graduates have told us clearly that they recognize the program decisions we have made for them. For the most part, students respect these program decisions and are willing and apparently skilled enough to reconcile (or, in some cases, ignore) the differences so their resulting exit skills are a unique blend of instructional approaches. As one student said:

> In reading you can teach thematic units (learned in ELED) using direct instruction approaches (learned in SPED) such as [preteaching] word-attack, specific vocabulary, and comprehension teaching techniques.

As the dual-major program continues to evolve, the dynamics of faculty interaction may lead to a more integrated program. Perhaps, with interaction, faculty members with discrepant viewpoints will come closer together; perhaps not. From both a pragmatic and an academic point of view, we want our graduates to be conversant with the variety of opinions reflected by elementary and special educators, especially those that conflict with one another. We hope that, with this knowledge, our graduates will be able to successfully promote appropriate, effective, integrated programs for all students in public schools.

References

Blanton, L. P., Blanton, W. E., & Cross, L. S. (1994). An exploratory study of how general and special education teachers think and make instructional decisions about students with special needs. *Teacher Education and Special Education, 17*(1), 62–74.

Bondy, E., Ross, D. D., Sindelar, P. T., & Griffin, C. (1995). Elementary and special educators learning to work together: Team building processes. *Teacher Education and Special Education, 18*(2), 91–102.

Carnegie Forum on Education and the Economy. (1986). *A nation prepared: Teachers for the 21st century.* New York: Author.

Holmes Group. (1986). Tomorrow's teachers: *A report of the Holmes Group.* East Lansing, MI: Author.

Monson, J., Lignugaris/Kraft, B., Byrnes, D. A., & Johnson, K. (1995). What those hiring new teachers consider in initial evaluation of applicants for a teaching position. *Researcher, 10*(1), 26–32.

Note

1. We also have dual-major programs between special and secondary education and between special and early childhood education. In the interest of clarity, however, this chapter refers only to the dual-major program between special and elementary education.

Creating a Collaborative University/School Partnership: Saginaw Valley State University

Ellen Curtis-Pierce, Stephen Barbus, Susie Emond,
Miriam Sweigart, and Kimberly Prime

Recently, two similar but unrelated school reform efforts were beginning only miles from one another in Bay City, Michigan. One of the sites was Saginaw Valley State University's College of Education (SVSU/COE), and the other was at a school in Bangor Township, Bangor Central Elementary (BTS/BCE.) At SVSU several individuals had been exploring new options for teacher preparation. At BCE the staff and faculty were struggling with the challenges of including students with disabilities in the classroom. The events that brought these two groups together initiated a mutually beneficial relationship focused on finding best practices related to instructional grouping, teacher preparation, professional development, and service delivery. This chapter will detail the SVSU/BCE Partnership and the Unified Elementary Pilot Program (UEPP).

Institutional Context

Saginaw Valley State University is a 4-year state-supported regional university offering bachelor's and master's degrees. It has approximately 7,300 students and 180 full-time faculty members. The College of Education houses approximately 18 percent of the undergraduate student population and has the most graduate majors (68 percent) in the university. The College of Education has 21 full-time faculty members in three departments: Teacher Education, Educational Leadership and Services, and Physical and Health Education. The college received NCATE accreditation in 1992.

The Department of Teacher Education in the College of Education has undergraduate programs in elementary and secondary school teaching and a special education teaching certification (endorsement) in emotional impairments and learning disabilities. The largest teaching program area is Elementary Education. The pilot program in the SVSU/BCE partnership described in this chapter is part of the teacher preparation program in Elementary and Special Education. An important outcome of the pilot program is that preservice students will assume new and expanded roles as elementary classroom teachers. Students who complete the pilot program will be fully certified to teach in elementary classrooms (K–5), in grades 6–8 in two of four minor areas (math, English, natural science, social science), and they will be endorsed to teach students with learning disabilities (K–8). Currently, in Michigan, credentials of this nature require the student to complete a double major—special and elementary education—and three minors.

Saginaw Valley State University's traditional teacher preparation program includes field experience in public school classrooms as a major portion of the preservice sequence. This model of teacher preparation is grounded in an understanding of teachers as decision makers (Duffy & Ball, 1986; Greenwood & Parkay, 1989; Kindsvatter, Wilen, & Ishler, 1988; Mosston & Ashworth, 1990). The faculty believes that preparation within such a model is accomplished best through the simultaneous presentation of theory and practice—a thorough conceptual understanding of the very strategies and techniques being implemented. As such, the professional preparation course sequence requires both instruction in the university classroom and extensive experience within public school classrooms. This public school classroom experience begins in the first semester at SVSU, expands each semester in terms of management, planning, and instructional responsibility, and culminates with a 16-week associate teaching assignment.

The College of Education at Saginaw Valley State University has a long history of working with Bangor Township Schools to carry out the field experience sequence of its teacher education programs. Students have been placed in classrooms throughout the district for experiences ranging from initial observations to student teaching. Bangor Central Elementary has served as a field site for many years. As the faculty and staff at BCE moved toward an inclusive model for special education service delivery, the building became the primary site for the field experience associated with the course, Mainstreaming in the Public Schools. This course is taught just prior to associate teaching and is designed to prepare new teachers for the responsibilities and challenges of diverse student abilities.

The teaching models available to students at BCE were considered particularly appealing as the faculty and staff not only were demonstrating the modification and adaptation necessary for inclusive education but they also were providing examples of co-teaching and team teaching and effective problem solving that was totally student-centered. As SVSU faculty and students became more a part of this process at BCE on a daily basis, discussions arose concerning the nature and needs of the "inclusive teacher." The mainstreaming course, and the evolving relationship between SVSU and BCE around this course, actually precipitated the dialogue that led eventually to the formal partnership.

Inclusive Education at BCE

When SVSU first approached BCE as a field experience site for the mainstreaming course in 1991, BCE already was working to include rather than exclude students. Early in 1989 a vision of shared leadership and a philosophy and practice of inclusive education was emerging at BCE. Teachers normally isolated within their own classrooms were becoming more open and flexible in working with their colleagues. Teaming between teachers began, along with high levels of creative problem solving. In addition, the BCE staff implemented schoolwide problem-solving procedures that enhanced all subsequent staff meetings.

More students with special needs were being integrated in general classroom activities. By the end of 1989, teachers also had suggested multi-age ungraded primary classrooms. Thus, many students who formerly had been separated by age, developmental levels and special needs were included now in all classrooms.

The following year the staff investigated another form of inclusion. After visiting several sites where inclusive practice was occurring, the school staff decided to eliminate the self-contained special education classroom. All students would receive services in the general education setting. For members who were interested and involved in the transition, the principal for the staff allotted considerable time to plan.

During the 3-year period from 1989 to 1992, the momentum for inclusion was growing. Inclusive thinking spread throughout the building, partially fulfilling the BCE school's shared vision that each student can perform most successfully when placed heterogeneously with age-appropriate peers and provided adequate support. Therefore, children with physical, cognitive, emotional, and learning disabilities and children at various developmental levels, kindergarten through 5th grade, were included in general education classrooms.

Reform Plans at SVSU

In the spring of 1992, two significant events took place for the College of Education at Saginaw Valley State University. First, the College of Education received word about successful initial accreditation by NCATE, and second, the dean of the College of Education announced that he was leaving. These events led the faculty to ask a number of critical questions about the future direction of the college. Some of the questions posed were:

> Where does the College of Education see itself in 5 years? 10 years?
>
> What are the characteristics of a College of Education leader who will take the college into the year 2000?
>
> What is on the forefront nationally regarding school reform issues?
>
> What should the College of Education be doing differently in teacher preparation programs to meet the needs of children in public schools more appropriately?
>
> How might a Unified Education System, being discussed at the state level, affect teacher preparation?

In the fall of 1992, a new dean of the College of Education arrived, eager to find answers to the questions raised before her arrival. At this same time, the Professional Development Schools (PDS) movement was expanding in Michigan. Together with input from a core group of like-minded faculty, the dean proposed a concept paper (Curtis-Pierce, 1993) that provided the impetus for discussion with Bangor Township Schools (and other local school districts) for establishing a SVSU Professional Development School. The proposal was well received by the Bangor Township Superintendent and Central Office Administrators and, at a later date, by the Bangor School Board members.

During that same time, the State of Michigan was affirming its support for a mandated service delivery continuum that now would contain full inclusion as an option for children and parents. The State Board of Education asked the Department of Education and its Office of Special Education to form an Inclusion Committee to determine what changes would be necessary in the current special education structure to offer the option of full inclusion to every student in the state. The report delivered to the board described a single educational system in which law, finance, certification, programming, and teacher preparation were unified.

As a result of the recommendations from the Inclusion Committee, a Special Education Task Force was formed to outline specifically and cost-analyze the proposed changes in special education for the state. An SVSU faculty member participated on the Personnel Preparation Subcommittee to the Task Force, as well as on the original committee responding to the position statement on Inclusive Education. Consistent with the Inclusion Committee, the Task Force also described a teacher preparation procedure that removed many of the existing parallel programs for general and special education teachers. Meeting the needs of expanding diversity in the classroom, it was suggested, would require a new type of classroom teacher, one who would understand differences and strategies for addressing those differences in an integrated classroom (Council of Administrators of Special Education, 1993; Grimmett & Neufeld, 1994). A natural link was formed between the Task Force recommendations, through SVSU faculty participation on the committee and discussions within the College of Education regarding the future of teacher preparation.

With these recommendations as a basis for discussion, a core group of SVSU faculty members sketched out a proposed elementary teacher preparation program that reflected the direction of the Task Forces's recommendations. A group consisting of the dean, selected College of Education faculty members, and the Bangor Central Elementary principal and staff refined and expanded on these recommendations. The group recognized the consistency that this notion of teacher preparation had with the emerging partnership and its unified clinical environment, faculty, and curriculum. It also recognized that the partnership could serve as an ideal vehicle for a reconceptualized teacher preparation program. This core group, and later others, shaped the program described below as the Unified Elementary Pilot Program.

With the new leadership in the College of Education and the state's vision of a unified public education system, the stage was set for a successful union of SVSU's College of Education and Bangor Central Elementary. SVSU students fulfilling requirements for field work or student teaching were welcomed into the BCE classrooms in greater numbers. SVSU professors began to spend time in the classrooms, observing the building culture, and getting acquainted with staff and students. Gradually, a deeper level of cooperation and collaboration developed, which was mutually beneficial to both SVSU and Bangor Central Elementary.

The Developing Partnership

The SVSU/BCE partnership is composed of College of Education faculty members and the dean; staff members and principal at BCE; Bangor Township Administrators; and BCE parents. The partnership group met several times at the end of the 1993–94 school year to develop a shared vision and mutual philosophy that, by winter 1995, began to guide the direction for full implementation of the partnership.

The vision of the partnership, based on a Unified Community School model (Curtis-Pierce, 1993), is of a unified community school where the concept of shared responsibility for the education of all children at the school, regardless of diverse cultural, language, and learning needs, will occur. It is a place dedicated to developing the fullest potential of all individuals associated with the school, including those with disabilities. By example, all members of the school are expected to model an attitude of acceptance in which diversity is valued and where everyone belongs (Hickey & Andrews, 1993).

BCE had the potential to become such a place. It provided the framework in which a community of educators could come together to shape the school learning environment, curricula, and teaching and learning processes. The professional development mission of BCE emphasizes collaborative and creative instructional innovations, problem-solving approaches, applied research, teacher preparation, leadership development, and ongoing staff development for all members of the partnership. This mission is consistent with the philosophy of Professional Development Schools (Darling-Hammond, 1994; Duffy, 1994; Pugach & Johnson, 1995; Robinson & Darling-Hammond, 1994; Yopp, Guillaume, & Savage, 1993–94), a key ingredient of which is the need for continuous, open communication.

With this vision in place, partnership members were asked by the partnership project director, a College of Education faculty member, to list key issues, generated from small group discussions, that would serve as the focus for the partnership in its initial stages. More than 25 issues were originally submitted. A survey was distributed, asking members to prioritize these issues so the partnership could direct its resources to the areas the majority thought were most appropriate and immediate. Results of the survey and follow-up discussion produced a condensed set of six issues around which issue teams were organized. The six issues, in order of priority, were the needs to:

— mesh philosophies between Bangor Central Elementary and SVSU's College of Education
— identify specific student outcomes (both BCE's and SVSU's) resulting from efforts of the partnership
— develop strategies to increase the amount of planning time for all participants in the partnership
— recruit total district support and assure that the proportion of students with special needs in the school remains at "naturally" occurring levels (statewide, that is about 11 percent of the student population)
— utilize the partnership's resources to provide quality professional development and preservice preparation opportunities
— inform parents, students, and the community about the partnership and its goals.

As Figure 11.1 illustrates, these six issues became the spoke and wheels of the evolving partnership. Members volunteered to serve on each of the issue teams, which functioned as subcommittees. Their first task was to establish goals for their issue, prioritize these goals, and then submit a tentative timeline for achieving each. Members divided the resulting tasks and submitted, to the partnership group as a whole, a list of resources they believed would be necessary to complete the tasks. These teams met separately and were largely autonomous in their efforts. As they progressed, the issue teams presented their work to the partnership project director, who then informed partnership members of their progress.

As a result of these efforts, the SVSU/BCE Partnership was beginning to unite as a team effort. Contributing to development of the partnership were (a) an attitude of acceptance by all individuals involved in the partnership, (b) a culture of trust established at the school site, (c) caring and visionary leaders, and (d) an open receptiveness to new ideas and solutions, all coupled with years of experience in problem solving and risk taking.

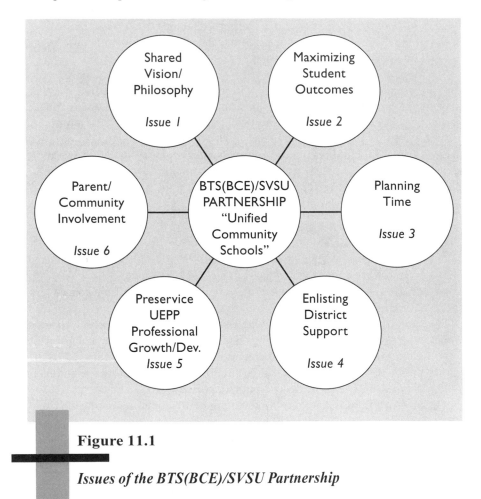

Figure 11.1

Issues of the BTS(BCE)/SVSU Partnership

Developing the Preservice Unified Elementary Pilot Program

A key component of the partnership is the commitment to explore new ways of preparing teachers for inclusive and unified settings in the schools. The College of Education dean and faculty, in conjunction with Bangor Central Elementary and Bangor Township Schools administrators, came together in 1994 to develop a reconceptualized teacher preparation program. The Unified Elementary Pilot Program (UEPP) resulted and is being piloted during the writing of this chapter. The goal of the Unified Elementary Pilot Program is to prepare classroom teachers with knowledge, skills, and attitudes for the changing K–8 classroom.

Bangor Central Elementary (BCE) serves as the primary location for field experiences in the Unified Elementary Pilot Program. A unified instructional team for the pilot program consists of SVSU faculty members from the special education and elementary teacher education programs; general classroom and special education teachers from BCE also serve on the team. All coursework, field supervision, and advising is conducted by this team. It utilizes and models co-teaching, collaborative skills, and team planning for the preservice pilot students.

UEPP, with its unified elementary and special education curricula, is designed to meet all state outcome competencies in both areas through a single course of study. This new route to existing credentials required approval from the Department of Education's (DOE) Certification Office as well as the Office of Special Education. Michigan provides for experiment, research, and deviations from approved programs through an application process that requires review by both the DOE and the Professional Standards Commission for Teachers (PSCT) and, finally, approval by the State Board of Education. The approval process requires the applicant to demonstrate how the experimental program differs from existing standards and how state-mandated teacher certification requirements are addressed. Approval for experimental programs such as the UEPP are granted for up to 2 years following board approval. The College of Education prepared and presented its application for an experimental program in the fall of 1994.

The first cohort of 23 preservice students to enter the UEPP was selected from among students who applied and were admitted to the College of Education for winter 1995. Student participants met all of the requirements for full admission to the Teacher Education Program at SVSU. In addition, the students submitted a Statement of Interest in the pilot and successfully completed an interview with the instructional team members from SVSU and BCE. During winter 1995, the preservice students all were enrolled in the first course, Teaching the Arts.

Program Description

The pilot program has been designed to consist of six categories of competencies derived from existing skills and knowledge in both the elementary and special education programs, as well as the unique competencies required of a classroom teacher in an inclusive setting (see Figure 11.2). Each of these competencies will be measured throughout the UEPP and compared with the development of skills of students in the traditional preparation program. The competencies are organized under the following categories: Theoretical Foundations; Curriculum and Instruction; Classroom Management and the Learning Environment; Evaluation and Measurement; Communication, Collaboration, and Consultation; and Instructional Systems.

Strong program features of the pilot include the focus on student cohorts and university/school teams of general and special education faculty and staff. The special education faculty is instrumental in bridging the gap between general and special education curriculums and strategies. Pilot students are taught to use a clinical model of intervention in the inclusive setting. They assess the existing skills of all students, develop lesson plans and target individual needs of students in the classroom, implement lessons by pacing activities to maximize student understanding, and then continuously monitor and evaluate student learning.

Methods instruction in the elementary preparation program, which traditionally had been taught in separate, distinct courses by subject area, is sequenced in the UEPP over several semesters, unifying those same methods courses into integrated semester-long instructional blocks around thematic units. For example, during the initial semester, Teaching Children's Literature, Teaching Language Arts, Teaching the Arts, and Special Needs in Language Arts were taught as a single 9-hour block (called the Arts Block), unifying the course objectives of the four courses around school-based themes. Two of the four classes in the Language/Arts semester were taught at the school. Thematic units and other language arts objectives taught at each grade level (K–5) for the entire semester formed the basis for a common syllabus.

Objectives for the preservice courses were coordinated with instruction in the classroom so application could immediately follow theory. For example, when the theory regarding the use of big books in Language Arts was introduced, the preservice students discussed the topic and then went to various primary-level classrooms to observe the teachers using big books with their students. The students worked cooperatively with the BCE staff and communicated effectively around issues of literacy teaching.

An instructional team of faculty from SVSU and BCE planned and implemented the instruction as a single unit over the 15-week semester. Corresponding field experiences for this Arts semester, and all of the semesters to follow, are supervised by the instructional teams at BCE. As Figure 11.3 illustrates,

I. Theoretical Foundations

Students will demonstrate an understanding of:
A. human growth and development, both typical and atypical, including affective, language, cognitive, and sensorimotor areas.
B. factors influencing development, including physiological, social, cultural, physical environment, and psychological.
C. learning and teaching theory.
D. standardized and nonstandardized assessment procedures.
E. exceptionalities and their educational implications.

II. Curriculum and Instruction

Students will demonstrate:
A. an understanding of and an ability to implement effective curriculum design and instructional strategies.
B. the ability to select, modify, and adapt curriculum content and strategies to support pupils with diverse needs.
C. the ability to develop lesson plans and adapt materials and methods of diverse needs.
D. the ability to select media and technology appropriate to instructional goals and objectives.
E. knowledge and application of principles of effective instruction.

III. Classroom Management and the Learning Environment

Students will demonstrate:
A. the ability to develop and implement individual and group behavior management procedures.
B. the effective use of resources in creating a positive learning environment.
C. an ability to apply effective instructional techniques as a proactive strategy for comprehensive classroom management.
D. competency in the processes needed to develop positive teacher-student and student-student interpersonal relationships.

(continued)

Figure 11.2

Competencies Developed in the Unified Elementary Pilot Program (UEPP)

Figure 11.2 continued

IV. Evaluation and Measurement

Students will demonstrate:
A. the ability to use appropriate assessment techniques to gather, interpret, and implement instruction.
B. the ability to use assessment data to establish goals and objectives appropriate for an individual student.
C. the ability to use a variety of collection systems to gather data that will allow analysis of effectiveness of instruction.
D. the ability to translate the results of a comprehensive evaluation into an individualized education plan.
E. the ability to determine student instructional and developmental needs through the use of curriculum-based assessment.

V. Communication, Collaboration, and Consultation

Students will demonstrate:
A. an understanding of the roles professionals and parents play in a collaborative relationship for instruction and other services.
B. an understanding of and an ability to evaluate the roles of families in helping students with special needs meet their instructional socioemotional goals.
C. knowledge of the availability of interagency collaboration to support student and family goals.
D. knowledge of the principles related to collaborative relationships with colleagues.
E. knowledge to collaborate with parents in planning and implementing instructional programs.
F. knowledge of general planning, management, and communication skills to utilize paraprofessionals and volunteers in an instructional program.

VI. Instructional Systems

Students will demonstrate:
A. knowledge of program delivery systems, including all levels of service.
B. an understanding of the roles and organizational structures of education (general and special) and the part they play in the providing service for the student.
C. knowledge of the organizational, historical, and legal factors related to instructional systems.
D. knowledge of institutional and administrative factors which facilitate the delivery of services.
E. understanding of how to identify and access interagency resources relevant to instruction and management.

Winter 1995	Summer 1995	Fall 1995	Winter 1996
▪ Children's Literature ▪ Language Arts ▪ Teaching the Arts ▪ Special Education *Assessment Curriculum Adaptation*	▪ Educating Exceptional Learners	▪ Social Studies K–8 ▪ Teaching Reading K–8 (part 1) ▪ Special Education *Curriculum design Observation & analysis Remedial techniques*	▪ Teaching Science ▪ Teaching Math ▪ Special Education *Program evaluation, team planning, adaptive techniques, consultation*
Summer 1996	**Fall 1996**	**Winter 1997**	
▪ Teaching Physical & Health Education	▪ Teaching Reading (part 2) ▪ Classroom Management ▪ Special Education— Summary	▪ Student Teaching in Elementary Education ▪ Student Teaching in Special Education *(student teaching 20 weeks)*	

Pilot Program=
Standard Course of Study (59 hours) + Exceptional Learners + Special Education Component + Classroom Management = 69 credit hours

Traditional Course of Study =
Elementary Certification (56) + LD Endorsement (32) = 88 credit hours

Note:
Special education components include: assessment, perceptual skills, program evaluation, adaptive technology, consultation, adaptation, instruction, curriculum design, and team planning as they apply to instruction.

Figure 11.3

Unified Elementary Pilot Program Course of Study

other blocks of study will include Social Studies/Content Reading (fall 1995), Math/Science (winter 1996), Reading/Classroom Management (fall 1996), and Student Teaching (winter 1997).

In the UEPP, teacher preparation curricula designed uniquely for elementary classroom teachers and elementary special education teachers is unified into a single course of study. Just as the objectives for individual methods courses are integrated into a single instructional block, the knowledge, skills, and competencies unique to special education teacher preparation are unified within the coursework and field experiences required throughout the program. As preservice teachers are learning methodology for teaching reading, language, math, or science skills, they simultaneously are developing their knowledge and skills related to learning styles, assessment, curriculum modification, and adaptation, necessary for effective instruction in those subject areas and across a more widely diverse group of children. Objectives and competencies are integrated within the semester's course block as are the Arts, Language Arts, or Children's Literature courses, for example.

Special education faculty members are full members of the instructional team, planning, co-teaching, and supervising students throughout the program. The special education component of the preparation is a strand that runs throughout the course of study. Each semester this component focuses on a competency/outcome as identified by the Michigan Department of Education, Office of Special Education. For example, in winter 1995, the focus was on assessment and curriculum adaptation as it relates to teaching the arts. Language development and classroom strategies to support language needs were emphasized.

Each competency will be measured during or following completion of the program using observation, testing, field evaluations, IEPs, and product review. Outcome measures will aid in determining if the unique aspects of the pilot program are sufficiently effective to consider them as a permanent part of the Teacher Education Program. Techniques such as integrated curriculum, onsite instruction, thematic instructional units, heterogeneous grouping, infusion of special education technique into daily planning, and team teaching all will be examined as possible innovations for the existing elementary program.

Assuming New Roles

All participants in the partnership were assuming new roles and serving as role models for our SVSU students in field placements at BCE. Faculty members from SVSU found themselves back in the classroom working directly with children, modeling instructional and intervention techniques. Professors became a part of problem-solving teams, dealing with immediate student-related issues and serving as facilitators in buildingwide discussions. The BCE staff stepped into the university classroom as adjunct faculty, aiding in the development of new courses, providing instruction, and supervising and evaluating preservice teachers during their field experiences. Lines between the special education and general education staffs from both institutions quickly blurred as instructional teaming, for the children at BCE and the SVSU students, required the faculty to give up sole ownership of courses, classrooms, and instructional responsibilities. All members of the partnership found themselves expanding their traditional roles.

The process of unification required individuals in the partnership to be open to change. Not only were partnership faculty and staff members asked to assume new roles, but new provisions for change were occurring and, subsequently, opportunities for promoting and supporting individual faculty growth and partnership growth became a critical need. A plan for monitoring the daily changes was becoming formalized.

At BCE, the general education classroom teacher's role changed considerably when children with special needs were included in the general education environment. The need to be a better classroom manager and facilitator of learning became crucial. Likewise, the ability to balance added adults in the room with children who required more assistance was a major challenge. Special education teachers now were asked to work with all children in the classrooms, teaching and assisting all those in need.

What became quite evident was that jobs were no longer clearly defined. When there was a job to be done, anyone available and capable of doing it assumed the role. The word "teacher" took on a new meaning. Chapter 1 aides, classroom aides, student teachers, noon aides, parents, and even visitors were called upon and used as "teachers." A teacher with new skills was emerging— one who is flexible and has the ability to think and adjust quickly to unanticipated daily circumstances, as well as orchestrate this complex process.

Concurrently, change required provisions for ongoing problem solving, and this now became a partnership responsibility. The Bangor Central Elementary staff had been successful in implementing problem-solving procedures within the building prior to the partnership with SVSU. Now the SVSU faculty and pilot students were an added dimension to the ongoing problem-solving model. Finding the time within the day to communicate needs and concerns became a hurdle to address in the evolving partnership.

At the university level, faculty members teaching in the Unified Pilot Program were being asked to reconceptualize their teaching of separate and discrete courses into a unified and integrated format as well as team with school-site personnel. Also, involving others in the planning and teaching of course content became a new variable to overcome. General education and special education faculty members were being asked to become both generalists and specialists within BCE classrooms. They modeled lessons in classrooms with BCE students while SVSU pilot students observed. In these settings SVSU faculty became keenly aware of the pilot students' questions, concerns, and perspectives. The special education faculty has been extremely helpful to the BCE staff in suggesting options and alternative strategies for aggressive and difficult-to-teach children at BCE. Subsequently, the SVSU faculty has become energized by the involvement in classroom teaching and learning.

The dean's role also has changed. She became visible at the school site. As a colleague, she met with the principal and teachers frequently. She was able to negotiate and trouble-shoot when necessary. She also is an active listener and sounding board. The dean helped plan and participate in professional development inservice activities at the school site. As became evident, a high priority for the College of Education dean at SVSU was promoting and supporting partnership efforts. The mutual sharing of professional talents between SVSU and BCE staff is a strength of the partnership.

Professional Development Efforts

Reform efforts in teacher education must go hand in hand with reform efforts in the schools. The Professional Development School model is a place where restructuring is occurring in both arenas (Darling-Hammond, 1994; Goodlad, 1994; North Central Regional Educational Laboratory, 1994; Swanson, 1995). Bangor Central Elementary is an excellent example of this simultaneous renewal.

As a part of the reform agenda, professional development became a key issue in the process of unification. This component was chaired by the College of Education dean. The committee, composed of staff representing both SVSU and BCE, identified needs and made plans to meet the needs of the partnership participants to build a true learning community. At the beginning of the partnership, a Professional Growth Questionnaire, adapted from the Concerns-Based Adoption Model Project (Hall, 1986; Hall & Hord, 1987), and a revised version of an open-ended Professional Growth Plan from the Bangor School District were distributed to all SVSU/BCE staff members involved in the project. Initial data were tabulated and will be used later to ascertain individual professional growth. Comments from the open-ended Professional Growth Plan also were used as a means of planning for professional development activities for the first year.

Four professional development workshops were conducted during the winter 1995 semester on topics on mutual interest. The SVSU College of Education faculty members involved in the partnership were presenters for three of the four sessions. The topics centered on integrating course content in unified/inclusive settings, such as on integrating science education and content reading across the curriculum and into inclusive settings. The partnership staff has identified some future professional development sessions for the next academic year.

One need identified is an interest in visiting other inclusive sites within the state, and this activity has been arranged.

To support these efforts, the partnership has received state funding for two separate statewide efforts. One focuses on professional development linked to preservice teacher education, and the other is tied to a regional consortium grant to establish model sites for teacher preparation in a unified education system.

Many issues related to professional development are unresolved. Two key issues at present are:

1. Time to interact with others, to plan with team members within and across grade levels, and to engage in mutual mentoring
2. Responding more appropriately and completely to the individual needs of students in a unified classroom.

Opportunities for individual and partnership growth will continue to be a high priority in this partnership.

Benchmarks and Future Plans

The response from the total faculty in the College of Education with regard to this new and innovative pilot program took three forms: the initiators, the ponderers, and the resistors. The College of Education as a unit was supportive of the preservice elementary pilot program. It is an actualization of what many consider to be best practice (Levine, 1992; O'Hair & Odell, 1995) and what is known and advocated by many COE faculty members. In addition to the faculty members in elementary and special education are the faculty members in the Educational Leadership Department of the college who are eager and committed to working in the pilot program.

In contrast, the project director, forthright in trying to solicit all of his colleagues in the Elementary Education unit of the Teacher Education Department to become a part of this new program, was able to interest only a handful of faculty members. Initially there was a great deal of fear that this pilot program would become the *only* elementary program in the College of Education. In reality, this Unified Elementary Pilot Program will be evaluated at the end of the 2-year experimental period, and it will be determined at that time exactly how the information gained through the pilot program can contribute to the existing COE's elementary education program. At present, only a small group of faculty within the Teacher Education Department has committed to play a role in the pilot program.

The ultimate measure of success of the pilot program will be the effectiveness of the cohort of 23 students. This cohort is an enthusiastic group of learners who have developed relationships with one another as well as with many of the partnership staff. The group has met frequently and informally to encourage friendships and an esprit de corps. The students are supportive of each other and are committed totally to the success of the pilot.

As in any process of change and evolution of a new innovation, the SVSU/ BCE Partnership must continue to build new bridges with people and sites and concurrently tackle obstacles that seem to block future progress. Three key areas emerge:

1. Reconfiguring and institutionalizing of the Unified Elementary Pilot Program (UEPP) within the SVSU's teacher education program.
2. Districtwide collaboration at all Bangor Township building sites.
3. Wider acceptance of a unified system focus for Bangor Township Schools.

First, reconfiguring the total preservice elementary education program and, subsequently, the possibility of institutionalizing the unified program in the COE will require ongoing evaluation throughout the 2-year program and at the conclusion of the pilot. The evaluation of the pilot project and its role in the partnership will provide the College of Education with information about the project's role in restructuring and reforming the public schools.

Next, at the school district level, bridge building must continue to focus on the relationship between SVSU/COE and Bangor Township Schools other than Bangor Central Elementary. The original intent of the partnership included districtwide collaboration. To date, little interaction has taken place between the partnership and the other three elementary buildings. Attempts were made to include the teachers in the other buildings in the professional development activities, but this did not materialize. Fortunately, some progress was made this past year with the junior high school (6th–8th grades) when the building administrators asked the project director to plan workshops with the junior high staff. Responses to the workshops were positive, and this gave impetus to efforts planned for fall 1995. A core group of general education and special education junior high teachers seem to be interested in teaming. In addition, these teachers are interested in including students in the pilot cohort in their co-teaching efforts to provide them with experience at the junior high school level.

Finally, concern has been raised about districtwide teacher consensus on a unified education system. In past years, the 6th-grade students with special needs were not receiving the same support in general education classrooms at the junior high as they had received at BCE and, consequently, these students were not progressing with the same rapidity or enthusiasm. This concern is beginning to be addressed. The staffs at both sites have listed transition issues between 5th and 6th grade as critical.

Plans for the 1995–96 school year for the SVSU/BCE partnership focused on including all district schools in activities of the partnership. The superintendent and Central Office personnel established an initial meeting in conjunction with the SVSU College of Education dean and the project director, for mid-August 1995. This meeting involved all school site administrators and the SVSU partnership staff. The outcome of the meeting was to encourage and support other building personnel to explore ways of including special needs students into their general education classrooms, thus promoting the Unified Education System. As a result, new linkages with other building sites have been initiated.

The SVSU/BCE partnership is a dynamic and evolving joint initiative built on a strong foundation of collegiality, collaboration, and mutual support. We are pleased with the progress we have made over the last few years and, most specifically, the gains after initiation of our Unified Elementary Pilot Program. The partnership echoes the initiatives of the Michigan Department of Education, Office of Special Education, and other national efforts in that it is preparing teachers for a unified education system. The SVSU faculty members involved in the partnership are passionately committed to actualizing the Unified Education System and envisioning ways to restructure preservice preparation programs.

In retrospect, we are beginning to experience the difficult process of change. Although we know change evolves over time, we still would want involvement to come more willingly. We have begun to see apprehension and skepticism about getting involved in the project turn into excitement and optimism by being actually involved in the project. We have experienced the frustration of never having enough time to meet, plan, and share ideas individually or in small groups. We have learned to celebrate the incremental accomplishments thus far and, most important, we have found that open communication, trusting relationships, and commitment to a mutual vision are paramount in establishing meaningful relationships.

References

Bayer, E. (1995). *The basics school: A community for learning.* Princeton, NJ: Carnegie Foundation.

Council of Administrators of Special Education. (1993, April). *CASE future agenda for special education: Creating a unified education system.* Albuquerque, NM: CASE, Inc.

Curtis-Pierce, E. (1993). *Focus 2000: The unified community school—A teacher education reform effort.* Saginaw Valley, MI: Saginaw Valley State University.

Darling-Hammond, L. (Ed.). (1994). *Professional development schools.* New York: Teachers College Press.

Duffy, G. (1994, April). Professional development schools and the disempowerment of teachers and professors. *Phi Delta Kappan, 75*(8), 596–600.

Duffy, G., & Ball, D. (1986). Instructional decision making and reading teacher effectiveness. In J. V. Hoffman (Ed.), *Effective teaching of reading: Research and practice* (pp. 163–180). Newark, DE: International Reading Association.

Goodlad, J. (1994). *Educational renewal: Better teachers better schools.* San Francisco: Jossey-Bass.

Greenwood, G. & Parkay, F. (1989). *Case studies for teacher decision making.* New York: Random House.

Grimmett, P., & Neufeld, J. (Eds.). (1994). *Teacher development and the struggle for authenticity.* New York: Teachers College Press.

Hall, G. (1986). *Measuring stages of concern about the innovation: Concerns-based adoption model project.* Austin, TX: Southwest Educational Development Laboratory.

Hall, G., & Hord, S. (1987). *Change in school: Facilitating the process.* New York: SUNY Press.

Hickey, D., & Andrews, D. (1993). Creating successful partnerships. *Educational record, 74*(3), 41–45.

Kindsvatter, R., Wilen, W., & Ishler, M. (1988). *Dynamics of effective teaching.* White Plains, NY: Longman.

Levine, M. (Ed.). (1992). *Professional practice schools: Living teacher education and school reform.* Washington, DC: ERIC Clearinghouse on Teacher Education.

Mosston, M., & Ashworth, S. (1990). *Spectrum of teaching styles: From command to discovery.* New York: Longman.

North Central Regional Educational Laboratory Policy Brief. (1994, Report 4). *Professional development: Changing times.* Oak Brook, IL: NCREL Publications.

O'Hair, M. J., & Odell, J. (Eds.). (1995). *Educating teachers for leadership and change: Teacher education yearbook III.* Thousand Oaks, CA: Corwin Press.

Pugach, M., & Johnson, L. (1995). *Collaborative practitioners, collaborative schools.* Denver: Love Publishing.

Robinson, S., & Darling-Hammond, L. (1994). Change for collaboration and collaboration for change: Transforming teaching through school university partnership. In L. Darling-Hammond (Ed.), *Professional development schools* (pp. 203–219). New York: Teachers College Press.

Swanson, J. (1995). Systemic reform in the professionalism of educators. *Phi Delta Kappan, 77*(1), 36–39.

Yopp, H., Guillaume, A., & Savage, T. (1993–94). Collaboration at the grass roots: Implementing the professional development school concept. *Action in Teacher Education, 15*(4), 29–35.

Framing the Progress of Collaborative Teacher Education

Cynthia C. Griffin and Marleen C. Pugach

As we reflected on the cases that comprise the chapters in this book and in particular, on the nature of the programs they describe, we developed 10 postulates of what we believe to be true about collaboration in teacher education. Each program description offers an important example of serious advancement toward collaborative programs in teacher education. Within this collective movement some programs can be placed at one end of a hypothetical continuum of development, and others at the other end. Despite these evolutionary differences, each program and each group of faculty has made significant steps toward programmatic reform.

After considering what these programs have accomplished already, we thought about how they might be improved. We asked ourselves questions such as: Have these programs gone far enough? What areas haven't they addressed? Would differences in the nature of the process used to arrive at the new program have changed the outcome in any way? As we questioned certain features of the existing programs, we also thought about programs yet to be developed. We then generated sets of questions that appear in the second half of this chapter, which we hope will serve all of our readers as they work to strengthen existing collaborative programs and promote the development of new ones.

Postulates

We begin our list of postulates by answering the perhaps obvious question of whether collaboration in teacher education is achievable. Our previous discus-

sion of the continuum of development suggests that it is. Further support for
this, and the nine additional postulates, follow.

Postulate One: Collaboration in teacher education is possible.

More than a decade ago Allen-Meares and Pugach (1982) recognized that
preparing preservice teachers in isolation from one another was a significant
barrier to collaboration across disciplines. Today, many schools and colleges of
education continue to deliver separate programs to prepare general educators,
special educators, administrators, school psychologists, and school counselors.
Although many barriers (e.g., lack of planning time, lack of knowledge about
each other's discipline) can hinder successful collaboration, the chapters presented in this text show clearly that these barriers can be overcome. It can happen across disciplines and departments, within small liberal arts colleges and
large land-grant institutions, and among faculties who have very different philosophies of education. This diverse range of possibilities is what chapters 2
through 11 represent. A summary of program characteristics appears in Table
12.1. The following example illustrates the ends of the continuum.

The collaborative teacher education program at Providence College is an
example of a program developed at a small, private, liberal arts college. As the
table shows, Providence College has 3,600 students. Eight faculty members serve
the 370 students in the Education Department. In contrast, the University of
Florida (UF) serves more than 38,000 students universitywide and 1,500 in the
College of Education. Also taking into consideration the 18 tenure-line and grant-
supported faculty members in the Department of Special Education and the 40
faculty members in the Department of Instruction and Curriculum (not to men-
tion faculty members who represent three other departments in the college) at
UF, the difference in the size of these two institutions is striking. The size and
mission of each institution involved in teacher education reform has differential
effects on the kinds of issues each one must resolve.

For example, at Providence the department had to deal with the tension that
often exists in a liberal arts institution between faculty in the liberal arts and
sciences programs and faculty in professional programs, particularly professional
programs in education. The merged elementary/special education program had
to be integrated with the liberal arts, 4-year curriculum. Discussions with the
Education Department's planning team centered on what teachers should know
and be able to do, and how to best include it within a minimum number of courses.
These discussions were "lively, exhausting and painful." At UF, the faculty had
to negotiate many meetings designed to seek official approval of the program in
the departments of I & C and SE. These meetings became challenging for the
unified faculty because "consensus was difficult to achieve."

What is evident in these, as well as the other programs described in this
text, is that even though collaboration was, and continues to be, complex, it can
occur in teacher education if all parties involved realize that (a) change is a

Table 12.1

Summary of Program Features

Institution	Size	Program	Certification	Partnerships
University of Alabama	Tuscaloosa has a population of about 50,000 people; 20,000 students at Alabama; 2,300 in the College of Education	*Multiple Abilities Program (MAP)*; institutionalized; undergraduate	Multiple Abilities, K–6, which is equivalent to holding three certificates: Early Childhood, K–2; Elementary, 1–6; Mild Learning & Behavior Disorders, K–6	Teachers helped design the MAP program; teacher mentors in MAP also serve as cooperating teachers to program students
University of Cincinnati	Cincinnati is located in an urban community; 35,000 students at UC; 2,500 in the College of Education	Institutionalized; 5-year undergraduate/graduate programs in Elementary, Secondary, and Early Childhood; 1-year graduate program (master's in Special Education)	Option A: Severe Behavior Disabilities & SLD; Option B: Developmental & Multiple Disabilities; Option C: Hearing Impairment; & Option D: Early Childhood Special Education	Professional Practice Schools created by the Cincinnati Initiative, Cincinnati Public Schools, and the Cincinnati Federation of Teachers
University of Connecticut	Located in rural Storrs; 24,000 students; 375 students preparing to be teachers in any given year	Institutionalized; 5-year undergraduate/graduate; subject-area major in the liberal arts; cohorts of about 125 students per class	State department traditional with special education certification being noncategorical PreK–12	All of students' clinical work over six semesters takes place in Professional Development Centers
University of Florida	A rural community, Gainesville has about 100,000 residents; 38,000 students at UF; 1,500 in the College of Education	*Unified Early Childhood Program*; institutionalized; 5-year undergraduate/ graduate	Birth to age 4 preschool; age 3 to grade 3 PreK/ primary; PreK Handicapped Endorsement (3–5 yr. olds with disabilities)	Professional development efforts through faculty-cooperating teacher partnerships

(continued)

Table 12.1 continued

Institution	Size	Program	Certification	Partnerships
University of Wisconsin-Milwaukee	Milwaukee is an urban community; 25,000 students at UWM; 2,500 in the School of Education	*Urban Teacher Education Program for Collaborative Communities*; institutionalized; 4-year program with an optional 5th year in Special Education	Early Childhood, ages birth–8; Primary/Middle, ages 6–14; Special Education certification in 5th year postbaccalaureate option	Urban Professional Development Schools at the elementary level; courses taught at many school sites
California State University, San Marcos	Located in north San Diego county; 3,000 students total; 300 in College of Education	*Concurrent Credential Program*; institutionalized; 4-year program	Concurrent Multiple Subjects (Elementary); Bilingual/Cross Cultural Language and Academic Development; Special Ed in Learning Handicapped (K–12)	College students take program courses taught at local schools; development of consortia with school districts
Providence College	Providence is located in an urban community; 4-year, undergraduate college of liberal arts and sciences; 3,600 students; 317 in the Department of Education	*Merged Elementary/Special Education Program*; institutionalized; 4-year program	Elementary Education; Special Education (mild/moderate disabilities)	Professional Development Partnerships with two urban elementary schools
Saginaw Valley State University	Located in Bay City, Michigan; 4-year state institution; 7,300 students at the University; 1,300 of those in Education	*Unified Elementary Pilot Program in Elementary and Special Education*; pilot; 4-year undergraduate program	Elementary (K–5); two areas in Math, Science, English or Soc. Studies (6–8); Learning Disabilities (K–8)	SVSU/BCE partnership composed of faculty, school staff, and parents
Syracuse University	Syracuse, New York, is an urban community; undergraduate/graduate private institution; 14,000 students; 240 in the collaborative program	*Inclusive Elementary and Special Education Program*; institutionalized; 4-year undergraduate program	Elementary (PreK–6); Special Education (K–12)	Professional Development Schools engage Syracuse-area public schools and the community in the teacher education process
Utah State University	Located in Logan, Utah; undergraduate/graduate public institution; 20,000 students; 3,000 in Education	*Dual-Major Program in Elementary and Special Education*; institutionalized; 4-year undergraduate program	Elementary (K–8); Special Education (K–12 in mild/moderate)	Programmatic foundation in parent/community involvement

process, not an event (collaboration takes time); (b) anxiety, difficulties, and uncertainty are intrinsic to all successful change; and (c) reform must focus on the culture of the institution, as well as the structure, policy, and regulations inherent to the institution (Fullan & Miles, 1992).

Postulate Two: Collaborative programs can be initiated from many departure points.

In the 10 programs described in this book, the stimuli for reform came from many sources and situations. At Utah State University, for example, development of the Dual-Major Program was precipitated by new faculty hires, a move to a new building that placed the two departments in closer proximity to one another, and concerns expressed by some general education graduates who did not feel prepared adequately to teach students with learning and behavior problems. The University of Alabama had to contend with a loss of nearly "half a million dollars in permanent funds." This loss was the college's gain because it required that faculty reassess the nature of its work and reorganize teacher education in the college.

At Florida, external funding was a catalyst. These various stimuli often intersected with philosophical allegiances that moved reform ahead, often occurring simultaneously with new waves of faculty members. "Armed with the belief that it is our legal and moral obligation to educate all of our nation's youth," the faculty at Connecticut were poised to undertake "a radical reconceptualization about how teachers can best be prepared." At San Marcos, the opportunity to build a teacher education program from the ground up, without the "baggage" of a traditional institutional culture, meant that the faculty could forge ahead quickly.

In most of these cases, the communication, good will, and common ground necessary to develop collaborative teacher education programs took place across departments without changing the departmental structure. Within the traditional framework of separate departments, serious collaborative planning and programming have taken place. At the University of Wisconsin-Milwaukee, an explicit decision was made to turn away from changing the departmental structure as a goal in favor of more immediate programmatic reform. Although we cannot be certain whether progress might have been more efficient had departments been integrated, or whether departmental integration might be a logical, eventual outcome of collaborative programs, restructuring of departments was not the jumping-off point for reform.

Postulate Three: Collaboration requires real time for communication.

When we think about collaboration in teacher education, we must explore the role of communication simultaneously. Good communication is essential for good collaboration. The importance of preservice teachers' acquiring good communication and relationship skills has been strongly supported in the literature (Friend, 1984; Friend & Cook, 1996; Pugach & Johnson, 1995) but has not been modeled well in institutions of higher learning that, by nature, are competitive and individualistic. Teacher educators can start to develop communication skills and strategies that will assist them in developing and sustaining collaborative relationships. In the programs described here, this often began by engaging in philosophical discussions leading to a careful articulation of the philosophy and goals of the program.

At Syracuse University, for example, during informal discussions about what is now called the Inclusive Elementary and Special Education Program, the faculty drafted formative versions of a unified statement of purpose, an ongoing activity that it found helpful in articulating "shared values, principles, and practices that were a guiding force later as the program was implemented." Among the shared values identified were inclusion and equity, teacher as decision maker, multiculturalism in education, innovations in education, and field-based emphasis. The University of Connecticut decided to express its program philosophy and goals in another way—through programmatic themes (Barnes, 1987; Howey & Zimpher, 1989; Katz & Raths, 1992; Kennedy, 1990; Pugach, 1992). The themes of reflection and inquiry, and diversity, were agreed upon and embedded into early discussions centered on program development, resulting eventually in co-authored articles and a co-authored book on reflective practice.

Having a clearly stated philosophical commitment and goals for the collaborative program were critical to the successful development and implementation of these two programs and were characteristic of other programs described in this text as well. Where such prior discussions did not take place—for example, at Utah State University—a byproduct of the dual-major program is that faculty members now are beginning to have these discussions across departments, after the fact.

Discussions that centered on program philosophy and programmatic themes served to gather faculty members around the table—many of whom had not engaged in such shared dialogue before. These discussions were designed to help faculty members trust that their commitments to certain principles would be represented in the shared beliefs they developed. In addition, these initial discussions about philosophy helped the faculty establish a climate of trust, explore alternative perspectives, define problems and issues, resolve conflicts, and use specific strategies that facilitate further communication (Friend, 1984). As trying as these conversations were, they formed the foundation for future work. At the University of Wisconsin-Milwaukee, the formal codification of a set of shared, core values was preceded by a period of informal collaborative conversations and interactions that made the eventual decisions somewhat smoother.

During the early stages of collaboration, the University of Cincinnati faculty asked an important question about communication within its own department: After years of maintaining separate programs of study in special education, how do faculty members begin a dialogue about core beliefs?

Despite considerable barriers to communication (e.g., heavy instructional responsibilities, strong feelings of ownership to aspects of the old program), faculty members were able to begin discussions and learn how to talk with one another by building consensus around a set of shared principles.

Other techniques included sharing one-page interpretations, or response papers, to assist the faculty in thinking about a concept or idea (e.g., diversity, inclusion) between meetings. In addition, the entire college engaged in discussions about reform through cross-departmental committees that facilitated collegewide communication. Faculty representatives from one department attended meetings in another department with the mission of infusing issues and ideas important to their discipline into the conversation. For example, Special Education faculty members attended meetings in Elementary Education to bring up the idea that concepts related to special education should be infused into programs rather than presented in add-on courses taught by Special Education.

In general, communication takes time, and having time together is essential to collaboration and team building (Bondy, Ross, Sindelar, & Griffin, 1995) and to developing "a foundation of shared concern and a shared sense of purpose" (Rudduck, 1991, p. 97). It also involves a wide variety of constituents, or stakeholders, both internally and externally, including faculty, university students, deans, school teachers, school administrators, parents, and community members.

The "journey" at Cincinnati spanned a number of years, not days or weeks. Over time, the faculty attended many meetings. Some meetings were called to gather together small groups of like-minded people. Larger, more diverse groups were formed for other meetings, depending on the topic of discussion. Minutes were kept at meetings to provide a record of commitments and accomplishments. And proposals were drafted and circulated across colleges and schools for feedback and revisions.

Communicating with stakeholders external to institutions of higher education themselves was another source of ideas and was used to build support for change. At CSU San Marcos and Alabama, for example, teachers and administrators in the local area districts had major input into how the new programs would be conceptualized. Community forums at the University of Wisconsin-Milwaukee were places to share progress on program development with local constituencies. In many cases, external stakeholders came into play more in relationship to the field-based component of the programs (see Postulate Five).

The amount of time needed to accomplish shared communication and a shared set of values, goals, and expectations is extraordinary. Further, the time necessary for communication does not end once the program is initiated. At Milwaukee, for example, ongoing "conceptual discussions" are being woven into new, normative faculty practices in terms of program monitoring. At the same time, the challenge of finding the time seems to have been tempered by the stimulating character of the dialogue itself, the belief that this is a new and unique set of conversations, and the real progress resulting from the time invested.

Postulate Four: Supportive leadership is essential.

Before many of the reform efforts described in this book began, influential local leaders supported and promoted the concept of collaboration in teacher education. At Utah State University, the dean "publicly acknowledged and encouraged the collaborative efforts...in the two departments through memos and through verbal notice at administrative council meetings." The dean at the University of Alabama created a task force charged with making "recommendations regarding preparation programs that...assist prospective teachers to develop appropriate attitudes and expertise in instructional strategies that (a) meet the needs of a wide range of students, (b) are child-centered rather than label-centered or program-centered, and (c) are collaborative in nature."

Change efforts require resources in addition to supportive leadership. Consequently, supportive leaders first must believe that collaboration creates benefits that offset added costs (Whetten, 1981), then work to provide professional development, new materials, and space, and above all, additional time. The need for more time requires leaders to reconfigure schedules and workloads creatively, and to find alternative sources of funding (Fullan & Miles, 1992).

Although supportive, visionary leaders are important to help begin and sustain change efforts, several collaborative programs represented in this volume began with a core group of faculty, not administrators, who were committed to developing a collaborative program. Sometimes that core consisted only of two or three faculty members, as in Florida, Providence, Syracuse, and Connecticut. At others, such as Milwaukee, a larger group constituted the core. In all cases, faculty members were familiar with the calls from professional organizations and in the literature for unification and reform in teacher education, and they felt compelled to respond. The resourcefulness of deans and department chairs throughout the development continued to be critical, but in these cases the impetus for change came from visionary faculty members themselves.

Postulate Five: New programs occur in conjunction with strong school partnerships.

The 250 teacher preparation programs that are members of the Holmes Group are working to improve education in a number of ways. One significant way is through the creation of Professional Development Schools (PDSs) that foster partnerships between universities and public schools (Holmes Group, 1986, 1990). For many of these programs, the involvement in PDSs provides an opportunity for the simultaneous renewal of schools and teacher education. In her collection of seven case studies of newly emerging professional development schools, Darling-Hammond (1994) tells of both the successes (e.g., preparation and professional development of teachers) and challenges (e.g., lack of expansion of the

PDS model into the rest of the school) facing these partnerships. Increased, intensive, field-based experiences are characteristic of most of the programs described here. Many have integrated their collaborative efforts directly with school partnerships, some designated as PDSs and others not designated formally.

The University of Cincinnati's and Syracuse's memberships in the Holmes Group served as a catalyst for development of a system of PDSs in the Cincinnati and the Syracuse area public schools. These schools have become learning communities where adults (teachers, teacher educators, and administrators) and children learn continually (Holmes Group, 1990) and where all of these groups "are present and work together at the school site regularly" (Pugach & Johnson, 1995, p. 202).

At the University of Cincinnati, special education faculty and school faculty members collaborate for a variety of reasons. They are "to gain insight into the process of educating all children, to assist the schools in educational change activities, to encourage school faculties to become more inclusive in their practices, to engage in professional development activities, to model teaching practices, and to learn from faculty members who are implementing theory and providing daily guidance to the student interns."

At Syracuse, students in their junior year become part of a Professional Development School cadre that remains together through the student teaching semester and graduation. Each cadre consists of 12 preservice teachers and 12 to 15 cooperating teachers (both general and special educators) from two or more schools, at least one urban and one suburban.

The Saginaw Valley State University (SVSU)/Bangor Central Elementary (BCE) School Partnership includes College of Education faculty, the college dean, staff and administrators from the school and the district, and school parents. A key purpose of the partnership is to explore new ways of preparing teachers for inclusive and unified settings. Through this partnership the Unified Elementary Pilot Program was created. Program participants develop knowledge and skills in both special and elementary education, including competencies required of a classroom teacher in an inclusive setting. These students learn to practice inclusive education at BCE, where both university and school faculty model teaching and collaborative problem solving.

Another important outcome of the partnership between SVSU and BCE has been the development of professional development workshops for all parties involved. As expectations for professional collaboration grew, the need for professional development increased as well (Lieberman & Miller, 1991). For example, participants found themselves assuming new roles in the program, and at that point the need for staff development became, and continues to be, critical. Participants agreed upon a first set of workshops focusing on the topic of integrating course content (science education and content-area reading) in unified/inclusive settings.

Although the program at Alabama does not describe formalized relationships with specific schools, the intense nature of the field-based component is evident both in amount and structure. Teacher mentors are key to developing MAP students' skills, and MAP also has integrated a unique parent mentor component, specifically in relationship to the special education goals of the MAP program.

Dynamic relationships with area schools also characterize the Concurrent Program at CSU San Marcos. The new College of Education was developed specifically with strong school partnerships as a basic, underlying value, and a strong field-based component is integrated throughout the program. The notion of partnerships is enacted further through the Distinguished Teacher in Residence program, which institutionalizes the partnerships for the long term.

The partner schools that work with the University of Connecticut include 32 schools in parts of nine school districts, representing rural, suburban, and urban settings. These Professional Development Schools are places where colleagues from the schools and the university, with their respective students, come together to prepare future teachers and renew the teaching profession (including university teaching), and where there is shared dedication to the improvement of schools. At Connecticut, faculties from all departments in the School of Education, not just those in general and special education, are working in PDSs.

Where strong relationships with schools are not a part of the initial efforts, the need to develop such sites becomes apparent quickly. In the Unified program at Florida, the stark reality that few places existed where students in this program could play out the approaches they had learned, or view programs representing the unified early childhood philosophy, led to a subsequent emphasis on developing strong partnerships in the future.

Postulate Six: It is possible to work with State Departments of Education.

More often than not, state departments of education lead the way in deciding course requirements for certification. And these certification policies typically determine whether teacher education programs in special education are categorical or noncategorical (Lilly, 1992; McLaughlin, Valdivieso, Spence, & Fuller, 1988). Despite the influence state departments of education seem to have on the design of teacher education programs, a number of programs described in this text were designed first and then taken to their respective state departments for review.

The University of Alabama submitted a proposal to its State Department of Education describing the Multiple Abilities Program (MAP). Subsequently it received a new certification area, Multiple Abilities Certification, K–6. The Multiple Abilities Certification wraps three certificates (Early Childhood, K–2; Elementary, 1–6; and Mild Learning and Behavior Disorders, K–6) into one.

The faculty at CSU San Marcos anticipated difficulties working with the

California Commission on Teacher Credentialing (CTC) because of the "traditional separatist approach to certification in general and special education." Yet it proceeded with a presentation of its proposal for a new program. The faculty was surprised to receive "accolades for the forward-thinking approach to the program design" from the CTC. Students completing the collaborative program (the Concurrent Credential Program) at CSU receive full credentials in elementary education, special education (learning handicapped), and bilingual, cross-cultural education.

At SVSU, there was a reciprocal relationship between working on reform at the statewide level and local reform of the program. Faculty members who were involved directly in program reform also served on a state task force explicitly designed to address inclusive education. A natural link was formed between the task force recommendations, through SVSU faculty participation on the committee, and discussions within the College of Education regarding the future of teacher preparation.

In other cases, the teacher education programs had to side-step problems associated with state department requirements. For example, the titles of courses included in the merged program at Providence College reflect only what the state accreditation agency requires in the program coursework, but do not represent the nature of the content included in those courses. What is important to note is that the incompatible certification structure at the state level does not seem to present an insurmountable obstacle. Program faculty may push for new credentialing structures or may re-create programs under existing course titles. In either case, the goal of reform seems within reach.

Postulate Seven: Even if some people do not buy into the changes, progress can be made.

The University of Connecticut claims to have two special education departments! One consists of faculty members who have bought into the integrated teacher preparation program, and the other consists of a small group whose members believe their role is to serve as a graduate research faculty or provide categorical programs of study for special education teachers. This second group of faculty has refused to support the new teacher education program. Despite this bifurcation, significant progress toward program development and implementation has occurred. One might ask how this could happen.

Fullan (1991) may respond that not all people, or even most people, should be expected to change. Change involves such a complex interplay of forces that reforming a large social institution such as a school or college of education may seem almost impossible. Despite this, progress does occur, and it occurs in steps that serve to increase the number of people who are affected. For example, the success of the MAP effort conducted by a handful of faculty members at Alabama led to a larger conversation regarding the structure of other programs. Instead of being discouraged by naysayers, Fullan suggests that reformers concentrate on their accomplishments. Faced with resistance, the core reform faculty in many of the 10 institutions included in this book propelled themselves forward by celebrating their achievements and continuing the communication despite apparent or real resistance.

Postulate Eight: Evaluation is an important component of program development.

Determining the success of collaborative programs requires, at a minimum, an examination of (a) outcomes and (b) the satisfaction program participants feel before and after graduation (Friend & Cook, 1996). Many of the collaborative programs include an evaluation component, particularly in the area of participant, or consumer, satisfaction. The University of Connecticut has a system of program evaluation consisting of surveys, interviews, focus groups, observations, focused discussions, and field notes, among other methods. Evaluation has been conducted for accreditation purposes, programmatic review, and modification of program elements. Master's- and doctoral-level research have focused on program evaluation, and the findings have served to change or alter elements of the program and have been disseminated widely.

Through the use of telephone interviews, Utah State University asked the first graduating class of dual-major program graduates what motivated them to enroll in the program, what they saw as similarities and differences across the elementary and special education programs, how they dealt with the differing perspectives offered in each of the programs, and how well prepared they thought they were for their first year of teaching. Of the eight graduates surveyed, three were elementary teachers, three were special education teachers, one was teaching both elementary and special education, and one was not teaching.

The University of Cincinnati takes a four-pronged approach to evaluation. Students evaluate courses, a cohort group of school and university-based faculty members evaluate course syllabi, student teachers and PDS faculty evaluate the relationship between courses and the demands of the internship, and graduates of the program are surveyed each year. In addition, a system of feedback is structured around discussions that lead to shared problem solving.

The data collected across collaborative programs reflect many positive comments from graduates and from the constituent groups that have worked with and employed these graduates. Selected comments suggest that districts seek these graduates; they are confident first-year teachers; they are committed to the principle that all children can learn; they are aware of the multifaceted needs of children and youth; and they are mastering the practices of collaboration and individualization.

Postulate Nine: Collaborative programs can be responsive to the community surrounding the university/college.

Teacher education programs traditionally have sustained a separation of spheres between school and home/community. Consequently, no clear model or established tradition of learning in community exists (de Acosta, 1996, p. 13). As de Costa relates, teacher education programs have not responded well to issues of community, or to the impact the community has on children's learning. She recommends community placement for preservice teachers to help them develop "relationships that support caring and trust," understand "what social and cultural capital is available," and learn how to select and use "family involvement models and practices" (p. 13).

In a few cases, the importance of community is made explicit in the nature of the coursework and the design of the experiences students receive in the collaborative program. Both Syracuse University and the University of Connecticut place students in PDSs located in urban, suburban, and rural settings. The focus on urban field placements for students in the Collaborative Teacher Education Program for Urban Communities drives the work at the University of Wisconsin-Milwaukee. The emphasis on multicultural communities is evident in the coursework leading to the Bilingual Cross Cultural Language and Academic Development credential that is part of the certification package offered at CSU San Marcos, as well as the Multicultural Issues course that is a part of the Unified Early Childhood program at the University of Florida.

Postulate Ten: Collaboration forces a confrontation with new or alternative conceptions of teaching and learning.

Whether faculty members engage in *a priori* philosophical discussions of their beliefs about teaching and learning, or whether the conversations emerge during the implementation phase of collaborative programs, their proximity and interaction set the stage for a confrontation with different ideas and practices about teaching and learning. This simply does not occur in isolation. Today, for example, terms such as constructivism, apprenticeship learning, learning communities, meaningful activities, authentic assessment, classroom dialogue, responsive instruction, and socially shared cognition (Leinhardt, 1992) represent concepts that teacher educators in general education value and are quite familiar with.

For example, with few exceptions (e.g., Englert, 1992; Montague, 1992; Palincsar & Klenk, 1992), special education has been slower to embrace a social constructivist perspective in which teaching and learning are viewed as highly complex. This approach requires a teacher to operate in an ever changing context of decision making that goes beyond narrow assumptions of teaching and learning as the transmission of information (Merseth, 1992). For special education, collaborative efforts to prepare teachers have brought faculty members into close contact with their general education colleagues and forced a meeting with these alternative conceptions. In this way, it becomes more difficult to reject such approaches outright as inappropriate for children and youth with disabilities and pushes faculties to reconsider the predominantly behaviorist tradition in special education. Likewise, it should promote a real consideration of which specific aspects of behavioral practice might be useful to all teachers.

In a number of the programs described in this book, themes, activities, and assignments typify new conceptions of teaching and learning. For example, at the University of Florida, Unified Early Childhood students reflect on their interactions with young children by conducting semester-long action research projects. These projects allow pairs of students to explore, in more depth, questions that surfaced during their student internships. At CSU San Marcos, the "deemphasis on overt error correction and discrete skills instruction and the emphasis on meaning...and cooperative and flexible groupings," as well as the development of risk-free environments for children, are infused throughout the coursework. Use of the ecological case study in the Concurrent program also provides students with the opportunity to observe, interview, and report on a child.

The emphasis on reflective teaching, facilitative learning, and authentic assessment and instruction in the MAP Program at the University of Alabama provides yet another example of how conceptions of teaching and learning have changed as new collaborative programs are developed. A "reflective mindset" is fostered in MAP students through weekly journal entries that reflect students' philosophies and assumptions about teaching and learning. The MAP faculty responds to students' entries in an attempt to help them examine their past and current experiences in ways that respect diversity and are empowering to children.

Syracuse's emphasis on the role of the teacher as reflective practitioner in the program goal areas is another example. Within this role, the teacher is viewed as a learner, an inquirer, and a problem solver. In the program goal area of curriculum, faculty members model a thematic approach that is both inquiry-based and community-based. And at the University of Wisconsin-Milwaukee, the Professional Urban Linking Seminar is designed to promote a holistic understanding of the programmatic values, themes, and practices in the challenging context of urban schools. Left isolated, many teacher education programs in special education might not consider the importance of linking the components of a program.

These teaching and learning activities it represents are not the last new developments to come along and challenge the practice of teaching and teacher education. For example, some things about social constructivism may outlast its faddish nature, just as things about behaviorism should be taken seriously. The point is that when teacher educators do their work together regularly, they no longer can retreat handily into their prior practices. Public conversation and the public practice of teacher education seem to result in richer conceptions of teaching and learning and a much faster integration of more complex, more contemporary modes of education in schools and colleges of education. This, ultimately, is one of the most important developments in collaborative teacher education.

From Postulates to Critical Questions

Let us say unequivocally that the 10 programs described in this book indicate the depth of change possible when a faculty decides to address the question of who it is we expect all teachers to teach. Faculties in these programs have managed, through hard work, will, and strong intellectual commitment, to begin to bridge the gulfs that in many ways are institutionalized in higher education. This is no small feat, and as teacher educators, we all need to acknowledge the strides these programs illustrate in breaking down the longstanding barriers that have mitigated interdependence in teacher education for so long. More important, faculties have come together to define what they believe to be a shared base of knowledge for all teachers. Although this is not a new goal (Reynolds began calling for the same thing as early as 1980), this is, to our knowledge, the first time such productive conversations have taken place between special and general education on a more than incidental scale—dispersed widely geographically and among different kinds of institutions of higher education.

The processes and programs described here exemplify many of the benefits gained when teacher educators, administrators, the school faculty and staff, parents, and communities work together toward the goal of nurturing and teaching all children and youth. Despite the magnitude of progress to date, as we analyze the gains made, we also have identified four issues that are unresolved yet crucial to the eventual success of teacher education that is committed to preparing its graduates to work more effectively with all students. The progress achieved thus far has opened a window onto a deeper set of questions, questions that stretch beyond the commitment to the common framework these teacher education programs have achieved already. How is special education defined? How are special education and diversity related? What is the role of faculty development in reforming and supporting the development of teacher education? What is the role of program evaluation? We turn now to an analysis of these unresolved issues. We hope these questions will push those who already are collaborating and those who are interested in establishing new collaborative teacher education even further in their thinking about some of the most challenging issues regarding what it means to prepare teachers to work with and meet the needs of all children and youth.

How Will We Define Special Education?

In most of the programs reported here, the impetus for collaboration was finding the commonalties between special and general education. To achieve collaboration, one of the first things the faculties in these programs did was to find their points of convergence. Placing the child at the center of the deliberations, many faculty members were able to transcend longheld assumptions about what special or general educators believe, how narrow or broadminded they may be, or whether they really are diehard behaviorists or rampant humanists. Indeed, some degree of compatibility was found to exist. Some began from ground zero, and others used existing programs as departure points.

At one end of the continuum, Alabama and SVSU began with existing competencies and placed them in a more unified structure. At the other end, at Connecticut and Milwaukee, debate regarding commonalties drove programmatic change. At Cincinnati, uncovering the commonalties among special education faculty members themselves was considered to be a critical first step in defining its contribution to the preparation of general educators. In the program at Utah State, questions of commonality among faculty members are only beginning to emerge after substantial experience with a dual-certification program that explicitly rejected this task initially as unproductive.

In reaching agreement at varying levels, the roles of special and general educators in these programs often are described as interchangeable, overlapping, or unified. This terminology suggests a common commitment to children on the part of all teachers and the common ownership of all students—a situation that differs markedly from traditional educational practice in the schools and in institutions of higher education. Whether they are prepared in a unified program at Syracuse, an experimental program at Alabama or SVSU, or a dual-certification program at Providence or Utah, preservice teachers who complete them are prepared explicitly for a commitment to accepting all children as full members in their classrooms. In this way, the goal of access—of who belongs in general education classes, of having teachers who are not willing simply to reject or marginalize students—is well served by each of these 10 programs. Even so, are access and interchangeable teacher roles in and of themselves sufficient goals for collaborative programs of teacher education, or is more at issue here?

Those who are wary of bringing special and general education together and engaging in collaborative teaching or teacher education often begin by posing the question, "What's special about special education?" (e.g., Zigmond, 1995). They begin by seeking to identify the *differences* between special and general education. The history of the relationship between special and general education has presented problems, however, precisely because we have failed, time and time again, to find our common ground. We have allowed difference to dominate and have looked at education as an "either-or" proposition: Either we operate from a large-group perspective or we provide for individual instruction, but one system can't seem to include both. We have not been able to conduct our work from a conceptual framework that makes a place for both classwide community building and learning—the hallmarks of general education—and effective models of intensive instruction—the purpose of special (and much of remedial) education (Pugach, 1995; Pugach & Seidl, 1996).

By first asking the question "How are we alike?" the professionals in these teacher education programs have been successful in beginning to establish that common framework. In the case of Florida, the commitment to developmentally appropriate practice is what formed the unifying framework and enabled the early childhood faculty to go beyond the traditional behaviorist/humanist split. In the case of CSU San Marcos, it is the capacity to provide strong general education experiences to children who are excluded inappropriately for a variety of reasons, including language or disability. At Milwaukee, the press of the urban environment frames common values. Empowerment underlies the MAP work at Alabama. At Providence College, collaboration itself provides the framework. Even in the absence of unifying themes, the student at Utah State who begins to grasp that direct instruction has a place within a whole-language approach is moving toward a larger, more complex unifying framework.

These are monumental changes. And they begin to address one of the most problematic aspects of special education: how to move teachers beyond the practice of overlabeling students and passing off responsibility for them to special education teachers alone. But few of these programs then have taken what we see to be a complementary step—that is, to identify what a special cadre of teachers might provide in schools. For example, many students need intensive instruction in the area of literacy, and special education's traditional approach of decontextualized basic skills instruction has not been successful. How will such intensive instruction be defined and carried out, and by whom?

These kinds of questions challenge us to consider whether we are really comfortable with teacher roles that are completely interchangeable and see this as an endpoint for collaborative teacher education, or whether special (or other named) educators should be expected to provide specific things that general educators—however well prepared and however willing they may be to work with children with disabilities—should not be expected to provide. One of the greatest challenges we see to the success of collaborative teacher education is being able to define and then integrate what various teachers have in common *as well as what they do not have in common* in redesigning teacher education.

This is not a simple challenge, because what we do not have in common—that is, what constitutes special education—has to be completely redefined in relationship to the common framework these programs have established. It is not just a matter of adding what special educators always have done onto the monumental agreements these programs have achieved. That is not progress. Instead, program faculties have to engage in substantive dialogue about the differences in much the same way they have engaged in dialogue about the similarities. From the array of programs here, this corollary activity seems to have occurred infrequently. This piece of the collaborative teacher education puzzle demands that special and general education faculties alike question their own prior beliefs and assumptions and keep at the forefront of the conversation the balance between what can be achieved in the best of classrooms with the most inclusive of teachers, and what reasonably will have to be carried out as intensive instructional support in those same, exemplary classrooms.

From a political perspective, to suggest an upfront consideration of differ-ence is risky when in so many institutions of higher education what is common in the preparation of teachers has yet to be explored. In the current climate of often hostile debates about inclusion, it would be easy to draw up sides with people lining up along traditional inclusion/anti-inclusion lines in a discussion of differ-ence. What the programs described here have demonstrated so well is that this kind of rancorous interaction can be overcome—with deliberate and ongoing opportunities for serious dialogue about what is best for all children in schools.

How Appropriate Is the Diversity Umbrella?

Almost without exception, one of the strongest stimuli for creating these, and many other, collaborative teacher education programs is to meet the increasing diversity of the school-going population. Diversity spans disability, class, race, and gender for MAP students at Alabama. At Florida, students are to prepare curriculum "for all children, including children with disabilities and diverse cultural backgrounds." The new teacher in Michigan is to meet the needs of "expanding diversity" (SVSU). Nearly every program we included situated its collaborative efforts in a larger context of diversity.

Students with disabilities are part of the fabric of our diverse student populations. Special educators are particularly sensitive to issues of access and participation, and rightfully so. By linking diversity and disability, special educators bring their concerns about equity and access under a broader and well established umbrella in education as we move into the next millennium. Diver-sity is posed as a point of commonality, and diversity and disability are linked readily throughout the descriptions of these programs.

As argued elsewhere (Artiles & Trent, 1994; Ball & Harry, 1993), however, diversity and disability do not constitute an exact parallel. Diversity, as repre-sented in the multicultural literature, is grounded in a sociocultural view of school-ing, teaching, and learning. These sociocultural phenomena operate whether a child does or does not have a disability. If we are to understand disability in relationship to diversity, we have to be able to understand children through this sociocultural screen (Pugach & Seidl, 1996).

Collaborative teacher education programs based on a desire to pair diver-sity and disability have to incorporate a strong, carefully grounded, high-level multicultural component. Otherwise this complex relationship between diver-sity and disability is likely to go unexplored. In the worst-case scenario, pro-gram graduates might talk about disability as another aspect of diversity, yet not be able to talk wisely about or understand why, for example, the overrepresentation of black males continues in special education. On the whole, special educators have not been forthcoming in discussing issues of diversity in their literature (Gottlieb, Alter, Gottlieb, & Wishner, 1994; Pugach, 1995; Pugach & Seidl, 1996). Although teacher educators in general education also are struggling with how to address diversity most effectively, the issue there is part of a much more public agenda.

The point is that just because collaborative programs are described as meeting the diverse needs of all learners, we cannot take for granted that its graduates, or its faculty, have a clear understanding of diversity in all of its cultural, linguistic, racial, ethnic, and socioeconomic complexity—in addition to considerations of disability. Some of the programs in this book include strong multicultural components. Others do not. Yet the latter often ground their work in the language of diversity. Early on, the faculty at Providence understood that dealing with diversity from a typical special education perspective—namely, "through the accommodation of individual differences"—did not adequately address issues of cultural, racial, and linguistic diversity and sought a new, more appropriate, and complex understanding of disability and diversity.

If the trend toward collaborative teacher education is to move us beyond our longstanding conceptions of who does and does not belong in general education, our understanding of diversity itself has to move beyond appending disability concerns to a perhaps narrow idea of what diversity is all about. Developing collaborative teacher education programs represents a limitless opportunity to bring together faculties across special and general education to grapple with, and begin to come to terms with this difficult and challenging issue.

What is the Role of Faculty Development?

The critical need for professional development becomes apparent rather quickly as faculty are absorbed in activities such as team-teaching and developing new content in a redesigned program. In the programs described here, professional development is fostered in significant ways, through the: (a) Professional Development Schools that have been cultivated at Cincinnati, Connecticut, and Syracuse; (b) lengthy and frequent conversations many faculty members have had about their programs; and (c) collaborative inservice presentations and co-authored publications and grants developed at Connecticut and Florida. Despite these efforts, few programs have addressed professional development directly or concretely. We believe teacher educators, particularly teacher educators working in collaborative programs where professional growth is crucial, must articulate a conscious commitment to on-going professional development for faculty. Teachers must become, in Fullan's (1991) words, "simultaneously and seamlessly inquiry oriented, skilled, reflective, and collaborative professionals," and if they don't, "educational reform will never amount to anything" (p. 326). This established link between continuous professional development and programmatic and institutional improvement suggests that teacher educators must continue to learn, or collaborative teacher education never will become a reality.

Achieving the aim of continuous learning as a valued and integral part of the college culture is not easy, but it is necessary if we hope to answer critical questions asked by teacher educators involved in the redesign of their programs. Questions such as, "How do we come to agreement on what we believe?" and "What do we mean by terms like 'diversity,' 'disability,' and 'special education'?" cannot be answered well if we approach professional development sporadically, without the benefit of follow-up or the attention to individual needs and concerns and site-specific issues (Hall & Hord, 1987). We must create a long-term plan for our own professional development efforts, and these efforts should be incorporated into as many activities as possible. Our goal is to create new habits and structures, as opposed to isolated policies and practices.

How Important Is Program Evaluation?

Traditionally, teacher educators have conducted program evaluations with follow-up studies of recent graduates and of their supervisors (Raths, 1987) and outcome studies of graduates' teaching competencies (Galluzzo & Craig, 1990). These established practices, however, have been criticized primarily for not providing data needed for meaningful program renewal (Katz, Raths, Mohanty, Kurachi, & Irving, 1981). Findings from follow-up studies tend to be too generic, and outcome studies do not draw on the graduates' perspectives, only the judgments others have of their performance. Most of the programs described here did not evaluate their programs in ways that went beyond traditional practices.

Current evaluation efforts must be ongoing, interactive, both short- and long-term, and employ multiple methods. Only then will we be able to address questions such as, "How will growth in attitudes, beliefs, values, knowledge, and skill, as well as graduates' socialization into the profession, be documented?" and "How do teacher educators assess these indicators in ways that assist them in improving their programs?" In short, the value of a comprehensive model of program evaluation cannot be disputed.

Concluding Comments, or Cautious Optimism for Collaborative Teacher Education

The 10 programs presented here attest to the reality that we can make real progress in teacher education and not hide behind old ways. We applaud the collaborative programs and the people working in them for their vision, determination, and skill. With sincere respect for their efforts, we conclude with one more question, one we hope will invite one last reflection.

Reform in teacher education has to be real, not cosmetic. To be authentic, conversations must take place in great depth, accompanied by serious joint reflection on the practice of teacher education. An important question to consider is whether we have been using the term "collaboration" too glibly. If the conversation between teacher educators in special and general education is not directed to the most difficult issues—for example, issues of equity, or fundamental shifts in curriculum and instruction—collaborative efforts will be surface-level and short-term. To be enduring, the most pressing needs of children and youth must drive our efforts. The cases presented here reflect a strong sense of commitment, convincing us that the hard dynamics that collaboration requires will continue to occur and that their example will encourage others to work as earnestly.

References

Allen-Meares, P., & Pugach, M. (1982). Facilitating interdisciplinary collaboration on behalf of handicapped children and youth. *Teacher Education and Special Education, 5,* 30–36.

Artiles, A. J., & Trent, S. C. (1994). Overrepresentation of minority students in special education: A continuing debate. *Journal of Special Education, 27,* 410–437.

Ball, F. W., & Harry, B. (1993). Multicultural education and special education: Parallels, divergences, and intersections. *Educational Forum, 57,* 430–436.

Barnes, H. L. (1987). The conceptual basis for thematic teacher education programs. *Journal of Teacher Education, 5*(4), 56–60.

Bondy, E., Ross, D. D., Sindelar, P. T., & Griffin, C. (1995). Elementary and special educators learning to work together: Team building processes. *Teacher Education and Special Education, 18*(2), 91–102.

Darling-Hammond, L. (1994). *Professional development schools: Schools for developing a profession.* New York: Teacher College Press.

de Acosta, M. (1996). A foundational approach to preparing teachers for family and community involvement in children's education. *Journal of Teacher Education, 47*(1), 9–15.

Englert, C. S. (1992). Writing instruction from a sociocultural perspective: The holistic, dialogic, and social enterprise. *Journal of Learning Disabilities, 25*(3), 153–172.

Friend, M. (1984). Consultation skills for resource teachers. *Learning Disability Quarterly, 7,* 246–250.

Friend, M., & Cook, L. (1996). *Interactions: Collaboration skills for school professionals* (2d ed.). White Plains, NY: Longman.

Fullan, M. G. (1991). *The new meaning of educational change* (2d ed.). New York: Teachers College Press.

Fullan, M. G., & Miles, M. B. (1992). Getting reform right: What works and what doesn't. *Phi Delta Kappan, 73*(10), 745–752.

Galluzzo, G. R., & Craig, J. R. (1990). Evaluation of preservice teacher education programs. In W. R. Houston, M. Haberman, & J. Sikula (Eds.), *Handbook of research on teacher education* (pp. 599–616). New York: Macmillan.

Gottlieb, J., Alter, M., Gottlieb, B. W., & Wishner, J. (1994). Special education in urban America: It's not justifiable for many. *Journal of Special Education, 27,* 453–465.

Hall, G. E., & Hord, S. (1987). *Change in schools: Facilitating the process.* Albany: State University of New York Press.

Holmes Group. (1986). *Tomorrow's teachers: A report of the Holmes Group.* East Lansing, MI: Author.

Holmes Group. (1990). *Tomorrow's schools: Principles for the design of professional development schools.* East Lansing, MI: Author.

Howey, K. R., & Zimpher, N. L. (1989). *Profiles of preservice teacher education: Inquiry into the nature of programs.* Albany, NY: State University of New York Press.

Katz, L. G., & Raths, J. (1992). Six dilemmas in teacher education. *Journal of Teacher Education, 43,* 376–385.

Katz, L., Raths, J., Mohanty, C., Kurachi, A., & Irving, J. (1981). Follow-up studies: Are they really worth the trouble? *Journal of Teacher Education, 32*(2), 18–24.

Kennedy, M. M. (1990). Choosing a goal for professional education. In W. R. Houston (Ed.), *Handbook for research on teacher education* (pp. 813–825). New York: Macmillan.

Leinhardt, G. (1992). What research on learning tells us about teaching. *Educational Leadership, 49*(7), 20–25.

Lieberman, A., & Miller, L. (Eds.). (1991). *Staff development for education in the '90s* (2d ed.). New York: Teachers College Press.

Lilly, M. S. (1992). Research on teacher licensure and state approval of teacher education programs. *Teacher Education and Special Education, 15*(2), 148–160.

McLaughlin, M. J., Valdivieso, C. H., Spence, K. L., & Fuller, B. C. (1988). Special education teacher preparation: A synthesis of four research studies. *Exceptional Children, 55,* 215–221.

Merseth, K. K. (1992). Cases for decision making in teacher education. In J. H. Shulman (Ed.), *Case methods in teacher education* (pp. 50–63). New York: Teachers College Press.

Montague, M. (1992). The effects of cognitive and metacognitive strategy instruction on the mathematical problem solving of middle school students with learning disabilities. *Journal of Learning Disabilities, 25*(4), 230–248.

Palincsar, A. S., & Klenk, L. (1992) Fostering literacy learning in supportive contexts. *Journal of Learning Disabilities, 25*(4), 211–225.

Pugach, M. C. (1992). Unifying the preservice preparation of teachers. In W. Stainback & S. Stainback (Eds.), *Controversial issues confronting special education: Divergent perspectives* (pp. 255–270). Needham Heights, MA: Allyn & Bacon.

Pugach, M. C. (1995). Twice victims: The struggle to educate children in urban schools and the reform of special education and Chapter 1. In M. C. Wang & M. C. Reynolds (Eds.), *Making a difference for students at risk: Trends and alternatives* (pp. 27–60). Thousand Oaks, CA: Corwin Press.

Pugach, M. C., & Johnson, L. J. (1995). *Collaborative practitioners, collaborative schools.* Denver: Love Publishing.

Pugach, M. C., & Seidl, B. L. (1996). Deconstructing the diversity-disability connection. *Contemporary Education, 68*(1).

Raths, J. D. (1987). An alternative view of the evaluation of teacher education programs. In M. Haberman & J. M. Backus (Eds.), *Advances in teacher education* (Vol. 3, pp. 202–217). Norwood, NJ: Ablex.

Reynolds, M. P. (1980, April). *A common body of practice for teachers: The challenge of Public Law 94–142 to teacher education.* Washington, DC: National Support Systems Project, University of Minnesota, and American Association of Colleges for Teacher Education.

Rudduck, J. (1991). *Innovation and change.* Bristol, PA: Open University Press.

Whetten, D. (1981). International relations: A review of the field. *Journal of Higher Education, 5*(1), 1–28.

Zigmond, N. (1995). An exploration of the meaning and practice of special education in the context of full inclusion of students with learning disabilities. *Journal of Special Education, 29,* 109–115.

Index